THE TWILIGHT OF THE U.S. CAVALRY

Lucian K. Truscott, Jr., 1931

THE TWILIGHT OF THE U.S. CAVALRY

LIFE IN THE OLD ARMY, 1917–1942

GENERAL LUCIAN K. TRUSCOTT, JR.

Edited and with a Preface by
COLONEL LUCIAN K. TRUSCOTT III
Foreword by
EDWARD M. COFFMAN

UNIVERSITY PRESS OF KANSAS

Modern War Studies

Published by the University Press of Kansas (Lawrence, Kansas 66049), which was organized by the Kansas Board of Regents and is operated and funded by Emporia State University, Fort Hays State University, Kansas State University, Pittsburg State University, the University of Kansas, and Wichita State University

Library of Congress Cataloging-in-Publication Data

Truscott, Lucian King, 1895–1965.
The twilight of the U.S. Cavalry : life in the old army, 1917–1942 / General Lucian K. Truscott, Jr. ; edited and with a preface by Colonel Lucian K. Truscott, III ; foreword by Edward M. Coffman.
p. cm. — (Modern war studies)
Includes index.
ISBN 0-7006-0403-0 (alk. paper) ISBN 0-7006-0932-6 (pbk.)
1. United States. Army. Cavalry—History—20th century.
2. Truscott, Lucian King, 1895–1965. I. Truscott, Lucian K., 1921– II. Title. III. Series.
UA30.T78 1989
357'.0973—dc19 88-27152
CIP

British Library Cataloguing-in-Publication Data is available.

Printed in Canada
10 9 8 7 6 5 4 3 2

The paper used in this publication meets the minimum requirements of the American National Standard for Permanence of Paper for Printed Library Materials Z39.48-1984.

CONTENTS

FOREWORD

When General Eisenhower evaluated his key subordinates in February, 1945, he ranked Lucian K. Truscott, Jr., behind only Patton among his seven army commanders and crisply characterized him: "Experienced, balanced fighter, energetic, inspires confidence." Since the landing in North Africa in the fall of 1942, this tough, hard-driving general had achieved outstanding success as a battlefield commander, in succession, of a regimental combat team, a division, a corps, and a field army. His handling of the Third Division in Sicily, his saving the day in the Anzio beachhead, and his Sixth Corps's awesome sweep through southern France were brilliant examples of his great talent. A few months before, in its October 2, 1944, issue, *Life* magazine had celebrated him with a cover photo and a lengthy biographical profile. Handsome, jaunty, with his scarf and leather jacket, cavalry breeches, and boots, he pushed his men to the limits of their capabilities. He certainly had more than enough of that steel in the soul that good generals require. Balancing that attribute, and this could well be what Eisenhower meant when he called Truscott a "balanced fighter," he had a keen analytical mind and the ability to learn the right lessons from combat. Again and again, Eisenhower called upon him for difficult missions, and Truscott always met the challenge. There were ample rewards in the decorations, the eventual promotion to full general, and, most of all, the high regard of his peers and the historians who have studied the war in Europe.

In 1954, eleven years before his death at the age of seventy, Truscott published his memoir of the war years—*Command Missions: A Personal Story.* This book is one of the best (some might argue the very best) of the American generals' memoirs to come out of World War II. A largely self-educated and obviously well-read man, Truscott was a good writer. His prose is clear and concise, and he could turn a fine phrase without being pretentious. In telling his story, he also demonstrated that he had an eye for the appropriate detail needed to give the reader the sense of the man or the event. Finally, there was his objectivity in describing and analyzing not only his actions but also those of other commanders. At the time, reviewers commented on how informative and fair-minded he was in this memoir.

Although he won his fame as an infantry commander during his three years in Europe, he had spent almost twenty-five years in the cavalry and, indeed, was a cavalry regimental commander when the war began. There is an inherent fascination about cavalry. For one who loves horses, that is reason enough to be interested. For others, it is the past glory of medieval knights, the dashing Civil War generals, and the Indian fighters. Then there are the thrills of the mounted sports—jumping, hunting, and polo. If any branch of the Old Army evoked romance, it was the pageantry of cavalry, with the military horsemen in full panoply, the chattering bugles, and the snapping red and white guidons. The cavalry might be glamorous, but it was also tough and physically demanding. The recruiting sergeant who told a volunteer in 1930 that the cavalry was the toughest branch was right. Cavalrymen not only had to master their horses the army way; they also had to spend long hours caring for them. And there certainly was a lot of riding. General Omar Bradley, an infantryman, attributed the comparatively long lives of his cavalry contemporaries to the healthful benefits of all that riding.

Lucian Truscott loved the cavalry. He had come to it at the age of twenty-two after completing one of the hardest apprenticeships imaginable—that of teaching in rural one-room schools for six years. That experience taught him, at an early age, the necessity and value of discipline and how to maintain it. Most of the cavalry remained on the Mexican border during World War I, and so did Lieutenant Truscott. During the twenties and thirties, he commanded troops for almost eight years and spent some twelve years as a student and instructor at the Cavalry School and the Command and General Staff School. Riding was naturally a dominant part of life in a cavalry regiment and at the branch school. Even at Fort Leavenworth, where picked officers studied the command and staff duties of large units, the horse was much in evidence. During this stage of his career, Truscott became known as a topnotch officer, who studied seriously his profession, and as one of the best polo players in the army.

The army was changing dramatically during this interwar period. To be sure, as in the past, it remained relatively small and tightly bound by budget restrictions. With a strength of under 150,000 throughout almost all of those two decades, it ranked eighteenth in size among the world's armies, lower than that of Belgium, among others, in 1935. To be sure, at the tiny garrisons, one day seemed much like the one before and the year before that, as officers and men went about their daily rounds in units that were usually at half strength or less. Indeed, a cavalry veteran of the Indian Wars of the late nineteenth century would have soon felt at home in one of the Texas or Arizona posts in the 1920s and 1930s. But cavalry was coming under fire. The experience of the Western Front seemed to hold out little hope for any future for mounted units. While the conversion to mechanization was slow, in great part because of the lack of money, some of the best cavalry officers were beginning to think in terms of machines rather than horses, and by 1940, these men had made the change in allegiance. The other change was the great emphasis on schools. The small budget virtually eliminated the possibilities of practical field training with large units. This meant that the army had to depend upon the schools to give professional polish to young officers and to teach the rudiments of wartime command and staff work to the older ones. When World War II came and peacetime captains and majors found themselves wearing stars and commanding larger numbers of men than they had ever even seen before, the schools bore their fruit in the successes of those officers.

Peacetime, understandably, does not evoke as many military memoirs as does war. Why should it? The high stakes and drama of battle are obvious bases for accounts that attract a large audience. Routine is merely routine, and it becomes so deeply ingrained in those who practice it that it is difficult for them to consider it of particular interest to anyone else. Of course, there is the specialized interest of students of military history, who would want to understand the environment in which the American military leaders of World War II developed. Drastic and sudden change, as in the case of the disappearance of cavalry in World War II, however, does provoke more general interest. For those who knew the horse cavalry, there might well be a strong sense of nostalgia. For those who did not and for their children, who could never know firsthand what it was like to live on a cavalry post, it seems strange, even exotic.

During the last years of his life, Lucian Truscott set about the task of describing the way of life that had captivated him. He used the subtitle *A Personal Story* for his World War II memoir, and it is that. In this book, in contrast to most memoirists, he tells the reader virtually nothing about himself. His son's introductory essay, however, fills this gap as he provides the reader with a vivid sense of his father's personality. What General Truscott does is to give the reader a well-written, meticulously detailed portrait of cavalry life as it neared extinction. He describes the physical appearance of each post on which he served, and he details the routine of training. With carefully chosen words, he evokes the sights, the sounds, and even the smells of those days. Here one finds descriptions of the system of making formal calls, the parties, and the ingenious way in which officers procured liquor in the days of prohibition, as well as the means of recreation for the women and children that shared the garrison life. The fact that he does not intrude himself into the story except as the ever-present observer does not mean that there are no personalities. He brings to life in a few words many of the cavalry officers of his acquaintance. And what better comment on the problems of a peacetime army than his description of the turmoil created by a general—a World War I corps commander and later chief of staff—who was furious about the oil stains left by parked cars on the streets of his post. While Truscott's heart was with the cavalry, he was too much of a professional to ignore the schools where he spent so much of his time. The reader learns all about the organization, the curricula, the routine, and the problems of those schools when Truscott was there. The story moves to the national level when he gives an excellent description of the military side of the Bonus March incident. He commanded one of the troops that drove marchers out of Washington. As war approaches, his story again shifts to events on the national scene, as he serves briefly in one of the mechanized units and then on a corps staff with Dwight Eisenhower. Near the end of the book, Truscott gives a beautiful description of a large review of mounted troops. They were, in fact, passing into history.

This is an incomparable introduction not only to the cavalry but also to the Old Army by one of its most distinguished veterans, who also happened to be a very talented writer.

Edward M. Coffman
University of Wisconsin–Madison

EDITOR'S PREFACE

My father belonged to that generation of remarkable military leaders such as Dwight D. Eisenhower, George C. Marshall, Douglas MacArthur, Henry H. Arnold, and Omar N. Bradley who emerged from the small peacetime army to play vital roles in the defeat of the Axis powers during World War II. Like Marshall (a graduate of the Virginia Military Institute), my father did not attend West Point. Instead, he was commissioned from the First Officers' Training Camp (the original "Ninety Day Wonders") in August, 1917. Then he received a Regular Army commission in the cavalry in October of that year.

In 1920, he was fortunate enough to be promoted to captain and thus did not have to serve as a lieutenant for the fifteen years before his next promotion—as many did in those days in the army. He had normal cavalry assignments during the first two decades of his career: the Seventeenth Cavalry on the Texas border and in Hawaii; back to the Texas border with the First Cavalry Regiment; the Cavalry School at Fort Riley, Kansas, both as a student and as an instructor; troop duty with the Third Cavalry at Fort Myer, Virginia; and the Command and General Staff School at Fort Leavenworth, Kansas, both as a student and as an instructor.

From August, 1940, when the country started preparing for World War II, he had brief assignments at Fort Knox, Kentucky, at Fort Lewis, Washington, and at Fort Bliss, Texas, before he was assigned to head a Combined Operations Headquarters in London in the spring of 1942. That fall he participated in the invasion of North Africa as the commander of a combat team of the Ninth Infantry Division. Although he was a brigadier general at the time, he commanded a reinforced infantry regiment (a regimental combat team) in the fighting for Port Lyautey. And during the remainder of the war he commanded the Third Infantry Division in Sicily and Italy; the Sixth Corps on Anzio and in the invasion of southern France; and the Fifth Army in northern Italy from the fall of 1944 until the end of the war. Later he was assigned to relieve Gen. George S. Patton in command of the Third Army in the occupation. I know of no other American officer who has successively commanded a regiment—although technically his command was a regimental combat team in North Africa—a division, a corps, and an army in the same war.

After the war, a senior officer, who had served under my father during much of it, told me that those were some of the roughest years of his life. He explained that he was not only talking about the war but also about what a stern disciplinarian and perfectionist my father was. My reply to him was something like this: "Hell, Sir, you only had to serve under him for three years; I had to serve under him for eighteen!"

He was a handsome man, attractive to women, but not big, being perhaps five feet-ten and about one hundred and eighty pounds when he was in good physical condition. But he *seemed* like a big man. He had large eyes, a prominent nose, large but not protruding ears, broad shoulders, a big chest, and huge hands, with big, square fingers. When I was young he would tell me proudly that "they're working man's hands." And they were, and those of a craftsman. He had amazing talent at designing (with my mother's help) and making beautiful furniture by hand, *never* with a power tool; he made his own polo mallets; and he could repair anything with those hands. But he always kept them immaculate—originally at my mother's insistence, I'm sure. I remember watching him clean and trim his nails with his razor-sharp pocketknife, thinking that he did it because well-cared-for hands were the mark of a gentleman. And they were. And he wanted to show that he was a gentleman. And he was. A rough one, but still a gentleman.

He was a stern, always demanding, and frequently ruthless disciplinarian; he was physically strong; and when my sister and I were small, he was unhesitating in the use of physical punishment in the form of a razor strop to ensure that his rules were strictly adhered to. As children we were expected to adhere unquestioningly to the rules, and when we got too old for spankings, confinement to our room was the standard punishment. I remember coming in late one night—two minutes later than the ten o'clock deadline he had prescribed—and even though my watch said I had a minute left, his said I was two minutes late. I spent a week in my room every afternoon after school, as well as the entire weekend. But I was permitted to get a horse from the stables and ride, by myself, every day. We had two or three dogs over the years, and they were always perfectly behaved and capable of performing numerous tricks. But they weren't "loved." Like horses, they were animals to be disciplined, used, and kept in their places.

He had great patience and was a good teacher, of both small boys and of men. I recall his frequently taking time out from his carpentry to teach me how to use all of his tools. "No, don't push it so hard, Son," as I would bend a saw double, trying to force it through a piece of wood. "That's why they put all those teeth in there and why I sharpen them all the time. Let the saw do the work, not your arm." Or, "Look at what you're hammering, Son, not the hammer or your finger. Just as sure as you look at your finger instead of the head of the nail, you'll hammer your finger." And he taught me how to play polo by insisting that I spend months on the wooden horse in a padded pen with sloping floors, so that one could hit a polo ball time after time and have it roll back so that he could hit it again. "When you get out on that horse I want you hitting the ball and not his legs or ankles." He taught me teamwork on the polo field by letting me play on his team for many games. Then he taught me the rough part of the game by making me play on the opposite team for what seemed like forever. Innumerable times he rode me completely over the sideboard from the middle of the field, with his knee in front of mine, his shoulder in my ribs, laughing all the way, both of us at a full gallop and me powerless to do anything about it. The first time I successfully rode him off the ball and completely took it away from him, he said something like, "You know, goddammit! I might make a polo player out of you yet!" Later, my quickness and his aging allowed us to play on almost equal terms!

His bark was worse than his bite. Shortly after the war, my wife and I were visiting home after our return from a tour of duty in Japan, and one evening after dinner with several family members and friends we were having coffee at the dining-room table. I sat on his left, where I had sat at the same table for three meals every day of my life at home. He took a cigarette from the silver box by his right hand. As he did so, I took my lighter from my shirt pocket, snapped it, and held it to light his cigarette. He turned to me and said: "Son, something you've got to learn is that one of the first things I always taught my damned aides was that I can light my own cigarette."

"Dad," I said without thinking, "something you've got to learn is that I'm not one of your damned aides."

There was a dead silence at the table. The lighter burned on. He looked at me for what seemed an eternity, then he took my wrist in that huge hand, gently pulled it toward his face, and lit his cigarette. I think he'd finally realized that I was a man. And I realized that this grey-haired man beside me, who had commanded hundreds of thousands of men in World War II, was someone besides that domineering father image of my youth.

Although I doubt he would have admitted it, he was an emotional man, and very sentimental. I saw him cry when his mother died. On several occasions over the years I noticed his eyes get misty when he sang with his friends. (Singing was very important to the young officers when they were growing up in the cavalry. Invariably when a group of them got together, they would sing before the night was over, and it seemed another of those elusive things that bound them together—like the horse, polo, and pride in their regiment.) One night on his small farm in northern Virginia after the war, we stood leaning on an old fence in the moonlight, and I asked him about the war—about the death and destruction and fear and about what it was like to be an infantryman in combat and whether he still thought about it. (I was an infantryman about to leave for the Korean War in July, 1950, and as I look back on it now, I think I was sort of frantically trying to find out what I was really getting into.) In a brief conversation he told me about it, particularly about Anzio, apparently the worst of all his experiences. Tears came to his eyes when he described the innumerable dead, on both sides, and how he would never forget how young they all were. Even then I think he was overwhelmed by the sheer numbers of the dead. He added that there would always be something of him on that damned beachhead. And tears came to his eyes again when I left for Korea a few days later in July, 1950.

Polo was a big part of his life when he was growing up in the cavalry, and he was one of the best players in the army. He was absolutely fearless, which gave him an advantage over many opponents who would eventually back off a little when he pushed them too far. And he played to win. For sport and exercise, too, but mainly to *win*. As Gen. Douglas MacArthur once wrote about athletics at West Point: "On the fields of friendly strife are sown the seeds which, in other days and other ways, will bear the fruits of victory."

I doubt that my father had ever heard the quote during his polo-playing days in the twenties and thirties, but victory was *his* purpose when he played. (He reminded me of this little story years later, when we were discussing what makes a good combat commander.) When I was about fourteen, he was playing on the underdog team in a tournament, and it had managed to reach the finals in an elimination that had been played over two or three days. His team was leading by a goal in the final minutes of the game when he fouled an opponent who had a clear shot at the goal posts. After a *long* conference among the officials, which even included two men from the grandstand, the player was awarded a close-in penalty shot, which he missed, and the game ended, my father's team the victors. After the game, though, instead of the players gathering on the sideboard to drink hot tea and replay the game with words, which they *always* did after *every* polo game, all of the players on both teams turned in their horses and walked toward the grandstands to rejoin their families. My father and I sat alone on the sideboard, and I remember feeling so sorry for him that I almost cried. But he dismissed my sorrow with a few well chosen words, spoken without emotion in that sort of raspy voice of his that many men, in addition to the small boy sitting beside him, would learn to pay strict attention to.

"Listen, Son, goddamit. Let me tell you something, and don't ever forget it. You play games to *win*, not lose. And you fight wars to win! That's spelled W-I-N! And every good player in a game and every good commander in a war, and I mean really *good* player or *good* commander, every damn one of them has to have some sonofabitch in him. If he doesn't, he isn't a good player or commander. And he never *will* be a good commander. Polo games and wars aren't won by gentlemen. They're won by men who can be first-class sonsofbitches when they have to be. It's as simple as that. No sonofabitch, no commander." (I learned later from the stable sergeant—and I have *no* idea how true it is—that the conference of the officials had included the commanding general from the stands, and its purpose was to decide on whether my father would be put out of the game. The general had ended the "conference" with the comment, "No officer and gentleman would intentionally foul another player like that.")

It was either that summer or the next in 1936, when I was fifteen, that my father and his close friend then Captain E. M. Daniels from the border and Riley days (and later World War II) took me with them on a visit back to Fort Riley. For three days they relived their days as both students and instructors by taking me as their new "student" on every wild ride they had ever been on in those earlier years: in and out of all the canyons; down all of the slides; fording and then swimming the Republican River, in the water holding on to the horse's tail and being pulled along behind him; over every type of jump known to man; galloping wildly through the mounted pistol course, the saber course, and the course that was a combination of the two; dashing through a modified stakes course; and finally a two-hour night ride rather than the six or eight of their earlier years. When it was all over they informed me that I was the only man to graduate from the Advanced Equitation Course in three days, but only because of the high quality of the instructors, not the ability of the student.

The biographical data prepared for my father after the war indicated that he had "moved to Oklahoma in 1901, attended public schools, including Teachers Institutes, and taught in public schools." Since his formal education had stopped with the normal school that he attended to get his teacher's certificate, he spent a lot of time over the years educating himself. He and my mother taught themselves French, and while at Fort Leavenworth, he translated the *French Cavalry Journal* for the library of the Command and General Staff School. And he and I discussed algebra and geometry problems when he was studying the subjects along with me when I was in high school.

I've mentioned my mother once or twice. This is a sentence from what my father said to her on the flyleaf of his World War II memoirs, *Command Missions*, published in 1954. "You were a far better soldier than I was over all these years." To which I would say: "Well, yes and no, Dad. Yes and no!" Regardless, her influence on him was immeasurable. She was a true southern gentlewoman, even more so than those who peopled the pages of *Gone with the Wind*—except maybe Scarlett. In an earlier generation my mother could have *been* a Scarlett. She was a fourth-generation granddaughter of Thomas Jefferson, and she had the fire, the determination, the will, and the ambition to convince my father that he could succeed in anything he attempted. She did. And he did.

She knew all of the social amenities, and she taught them to him over the years: the silverware, the linen, the beautiful furniture, perfect manners, neatness, orderliness, only the best in clothes and food and wine, and as I mentioned earlier, *always* three meals a day formally at the dining-room table. She had three interests in life: her husband, her house, with its beautiful furnishings, and her children; and without disparaging her priorities, I think her interests were in that order. She helped him become the gentleman who in later years would feel perfectly at ease with both infantry privates in foxholes and royalty in palaces. To this day I can see her sitting quietly at the crowded dining-room table, watching him become more and more boisterous and then saying quietly during a pause in the conversation, "Lucian, you're *not* being very attractive." Everyone would chuckle, the conversation would resume, and invariably he would be more subdued than before.

She was a loving person to whom touching us was as important as a vocal expression of affection. But not to him. Physical contact between him and us children was rare, as was any other expression of love. Yet, later, I think he was much more inclined to consider the feelings of others, to be more sensitive. I don't think he was a "politician" type. But there were times when he would seem to hesitate for fear of hurting someone's feelings. Maybe it was because he was getting older. At any rate, my wife reminds me, he was certainly a pushover for his grandchildren in the few years immediately before he died. It was with great nostalgia that I would hear the same words again: "Look at what you're hammering, Son, . . ."

As I went over these pages again and again during the past few months, I relived much of *my* life because I was born in chapter 2, "Hawaiian Interlude," and I left home in chapter 7, when the family moved to Fort Knox. There were many times I wanted to say, "Dad, what did you mean by this?" Or, "Why not add a little more detail here." Or, "Why not tell the story about. . . ." But I couldn't. I had no recourse to any of his references or sources—especially the primary one: his mind. So I left things pretty much as he wrote them, and I'm sure *someone* will tell me what a clacksmith is!

Finally, please remember that this is *his* book. Although I am listed as editor, my work has consisted primarily of correcting grammar, spelling, and punctuation (and not much of that) and eliminating occasional repetition. But the writing is my father's; it's his story. As he says, it is a "faithful portrayal . . . of cavalry *life* as one cavalry officer and his family lived it and loved it."

I would add that I think it is a delightful little piece of American history which I will always be grateful to the University Press of Kansas for publishing.

Lucian K. Truscott III
Colonel, United States Army, Retired
Albuquerque, New Mexico
August, 1988

AUTHOR'S PREFACE

Come all who are able, go down to the stable,
  And water your horses, and give them some corn;
For if you don't do it, the Colonel will know it,
  And then you will rue it, as sure as you're born!

The lilting strains of Stable Call are heard no more on our military posts where for so many years it reminded the cavalryman that he had an added responsibility which no dismounted branch of the service had and which set him apart from them.

In these days, vast numbers of American men and women have served in the armed forces in peace and war. Our people are well informed of military life by experience, personal knowledge, and association and by the press, radio, and television. Enormous military budgets consume the major portions of our national expenditures and constitute a tax burden on every American citizen. Military services are provided with an abundance of modern military equipment, adequate living accommodations and rates of pay, training aids and facilities, varied technical support, and all of the material requirements of military training, life, and progress.

It was not always so. It certainly was not so during the quarter of a century between World War I and World War II, when the United States Cavalry was one of the important branches of the United States Army. The cavalry branch was ever an elite one, though a small one in an army that was itself small. Much of the cavalryman's service was on small posts and in small garrisons. Yet this period was one of the most productive periods in our entire military history for the development of military training, of tactical doctrine, and of military thought. In all of these areas the cavalry made important and essential contributions. Cavalry life was interesting and instructive during this period between the wars.

The mounted man was an intimate part of American life throughout practically all of our history, and cavalry played a vital role in the development of our country. But the cavalry horse and the cavalryman he carried have passed into history so far as our own armed forces and the armed forces of most of the Western nations are concerned.

The United States Cavalry became a part of history as a mounted combatant arm of the United States Army with the passage of the National Defense Act of 1947. Actually, it had ceased to be a mounted branch to all intents and purposes when the last two cavalry divisions left their horses behind and shipped out for overseas theaters of war during 1943. The First Cavalry Division was to write a brilliant page in military history as a dismounted division in the Pacific Theater of War. The Second Cavalry Division was to arrive in North Africa in the spring of 1943 only in time to be transformed into labor and service units.

There is something more than nostalgia in regret that young men of today can never know the experience of life that cavalrymen knew and loved. For cavalry service during the last twenty-five years of its existence was not only gay and pleasant; it was also interesting and fruitful, a wonderful training ground for fighting men and for fighting combat leaders. There are all too few left who ever responded to Stable Call or to Boots and Saddles; too few who knew the warmth and glow of a cavalry stable at feed time, who knew the thrill of mounted drill or the exaltation of a thundering cavalry charge; too few who ever witnessed the magnificent spectacle of a cavalry review; too few who delighted in the association with other cavalrymen. There are all too few who knew the warmth of cavalry life. And our young men today can never know it.

This volume is in no sense the biography of an individual. Nor is it the history of the cavalry during its last years. Such a history would require many more pages and much more detailed research than is here attempted, even if such were desirable. This volume is a faithful portrayal in outline of cavalry *life* as one cavalry officer and his family lived and loved it in the stations and on the posts in which he served. There were many other cavalry posts, not mentioned in these pages, where cavalrymen and their families also lived and loved cavalry life: Fort Ethan Allen, Vermont; Fort Oglethorpe, Georgia; Fort Brown, Fort Clark, and Fort Ringgold, Texas; Fort Huachuca, Arizona; Fort Des Moines, Iowa; Fort Sheridan, Illinois; Fort D. A. Russell (later Fort Francis E. Warren), Wyoming;

Fort Stotsenberg, Philippine Islands. They were all cavalry posts. All of these and many camps of more or less temporary nature knew the hoof prints of cavalry horses.

And there were many other stations for cavalrymen, stations where cavalry officers and men served and contributed to cavalry life of the period. Cavalrymen were assigned to duties as instructors with organizations of the National Guard and the Organized Reserves. Many others were professors of military science and tactics in the Reserve Officers Training Corps in the colleges and universities; more were instructors in the Junior Reserve Training Corps in the high schools across the nation. The War Department General Staff and the staffs of every important headquarters and the faculties of the service schools—all numbered cavalry officers among their members.

All of these cavalrymen also served in purely cavalry stations. All of them lived the "life of Riley." A large proportion of them attended the Command and General Staff School at Fort Leavenworth, Kansas. All of them experienced the cavalry typical of that described in these pages. And all of them will recall their service with nostalgia. This volume is an appreciation of and a testimonial to that period of cavalry life from which all cavalry officers drew so much satisfaction and inspiration.

This volume is dedicated to cavalry officers and cavalrymen.

L. K. Truscott, Jr.
Cavalryman

A GAY YOUNG CAVALRYMAN

I'm a gay young Cavalryman
And I ride (drink, hunt, play) whenever I can,
And when I've had my fill—
I can always ride (drink, hunt, play) just a little more still,
For I'm a gay young Cavalryman.

I'm the wife of a Cavalryman,
And I dance (play, etc.) whenever I can,
And when I've had my fill—
I can always dance (play, etc.) just a little more still,
For I'm the wife of a Cavalryman.

1. ARIZONA DAYS

If you want to have a good time, jine the Cavalry.—
From a favorite song of Gen. J. E. B. Stuart

Douglas, Arizona, in the summer of 1917 was permeated by two odors. Each was characteristic of an important segment of the economy which made the city a flourishing metropolis on the Mexican border at the southern end of Sulphur Spring Valley in Cochise County. One was the acrid smell of sulfuric smoke from the towering stacks of the two great copper smelters just west of the city. The other was the pungent and perhaps more characteristic odor of twenty thousand or so horses and mules and the bubbling of dozens of troop kitchen incinerators in Camp Harry J. Jones on the eastern edge of the city. Copper and horses were two vital elements in the national effort then under way in the mobilization for the First World War. The smell of sulfuric smoke is still in the air and familiar to those who live near copper smelters. But the smell of stables, horses, and leather was to be familiar to cavalrymen and the army for only a few more years. It would then fade into history along with the saber and the saddle—and the horse, the reason for it all. This is one man's account of those last few years.

THE CAMP

Camp Harry J. Jones was established during the border troubles which began with the Mexican Revolution in 1911 and ended with the Punitive Expedition under General Pershing in February of 1916. It was a semipermanent camp, according to the Field Service Regulation, 1914. This was a formal manner of saying that troops were housed in tents stretched over floored wooden frames. There were some buildings of temporary construction, a few of lumber, and others of adobe brick found in the border areas. These housed kitchens, mess halls, storerooms, latrines, as well as headquarters offices and a few quarters for officers. But predominately it was a sea of canvas which housed the First and Seventeenth Cavalry Regiments, the Tenth and Eleventh Field Artillery Regiments, a camp hospital, several mule-drawn ambulance companies and wagon trains, signal companies, pack trains, and other assorted mounted units. The camp sprawled out from the eastern edge of Douglas for about two miles, parallel to the high barbed-wire fence that marked the international boundary less than a mile to the south. The road from town led through the length of the camp and continued on generally parallel to the border, a distance of eighteen or so miles to Slaughter's Ranch. The flat mesa between the camp and the fence was a drill area for the First Cavalry, where desert winds raised spiraling clouds of dust when drilling troops did not. There was a similar area, dust included, north of camp for the Seventeenth Cavalry.

The road to Slaughter's was really a wagon trail. It led from the camp and was parallel to the international boundary, a little more than a mile from it in most places. There was no habitation along it, few cattle or any other signs of life, just barren, craggy hills with a few stunted trees along deep canyons.

The ranch itself had been a part of cavalry life along the border for many years. Lying in the San Bernardino Valley astride the international boundary, it had been a frequent station for cavalry detachments during the long period of unrest. During 1917 and 1918, it was still a favorite objective for practice marches for troops, squadrons, and regiments in their field training. More than half the ranch lay in Mexico, but there was no traffic or communication across the border in those days. The international boundary across the San Bernardino Valley was marked only by the boundary monuments placed about every half mile, and in places these were well concealed by the dense thickets of mesquite and greasewood. This could and did lead to trouble, as we will see later.

The layout of the Seventeenth Cavalry area was typical of the times. Facing the border was a row of five or six small adobe houses, the Field Officers' Line, where the regimental commander and several of his senior officers lived. Immediately in rear of this line but facing in the other direction was the regimental headquarters. It was a long, low, tin-roofed building of adobe divided into three rooms each about 24 feet square. The regimental commander and adjutant divided one end room. The central room housed the regimental sergeant-major and his four or five clerks. The regimental supply officer, the supply sergeant, and two or three clerks occupied the other room.

Close by the regimental headquarters building was another tin-roofed adobe building, in one end of which were the officers' showers and on the other end an open pavilion or porch, where officers assembled at Officers' Call to receive the orders of the day. The headquarters building was located in the center of the end of the regimental area, with the Troop Officers' Line of small wall tents and a few adobe huts on one side and the row of kitchens and mess halls, which stood at the head of each troop street, on the other. By the kitchen doors, cord-wood fires kept the incinerators boiling away the liquid swill while the fire itself consumed any kitchen waste which could not be converted into steam. This was a major part of the characteristic odor of the camp, and our adobe haciendas were rather aromatic when the wind was blowing in the wrong (our) direction.

Each of the fifteen troop streets consisted of seventeen or eighteen tents. At the far end of each were the storerooms, bathhouses, and latrines. The stables occupied the space across the street from the latrines, running the length of the regimental area. In each long, open stable, about a hundred horses stood in pairs in double stalls facing inward across a center aisle down which the stable crew passed with feed carts to fill the mangers with fragrant hay and to measure out the rations of grain into feedboxes of galvanized iron. There were usually two or three box stalls for the accommodation of such special animals as the horses of the captain, first sergeant, and stable sergeant or for sick horses requiring special care. Each stable had tack rooms for the storage of the riding equipment of each platoon, and a separate building furnished space for feed storage and the horseshoers and saddlers. On one side of each stable was a picket line, a cable of rope or wire, for tying out the animals for grooming and saddling. Each stable and picket line were surrounded by a corral with board fences, where the horses were turned loose during some part of the day. The entire regimental area occupied a rectangular space of somewhat more than a half mile in length and over a quarter mile in width. This is where we lived and learned to be cavalrymen.

THE MAKING OF A CAVALRY LIEUTENANT

The National Defense Act of 1916, was the result of both the troubles along the border, culminating in the Pancho Villa raid on Columbus, New

Mexico, in March of that year, and the uncertainties caused by the war in Europe. It expanded the Regular Army, increasing the number of cavalry regiments from fifteen to twenty-five. There had only been about five thousand officers in the entire army prior to the passage of the act. More were needed. One source was the offering of provisional commissions to candidates who could qualify by passing examinations and tests. If their service proved satisfactory during a period of two years, the provisional commissions would be made permanent. Many of the provisional officers received their basic training in camps at Fort Leavenworth, Kansas, during 1916 and 1917. The first group of officers from the First Training Camp joined the Seventeenth Cavalry in Camp Jones in August of 1917. Even after our training, our military background was sparse, to say the least. Most of us were completely ignorant of things military. One or two had briefly attended military schools. Several had attended land-grant colleges which had some military drill. But the rest of us had had no previous military training whatsoever and had never seen an organized unit of the army or a Regular Army officer until admission to the training camp.

Military education at the training camp had been austere and elementary. It had been conducted for the most part by instructors who seemed to know little more than the candidates. But most of us were eager and looked forward with anticipation to joining Regular Army units where we would learn from professionals. And learn we did!

At Camp Jones the bugler of the guard regulated all of our day's activities. He ruled our lives with the clear notes which penetrated every corner of the camp. During those war days, Reveille sounded at half past five in the winter months, so our days began well before dawn. Troop officers took turn standing Reveille with their troops and, after roll call, reported to the officer of the day midway down the regimental street. Such reports were made again at Retreat in the evening and again at Taps at eleven o'clock at night after a bed check by the noncommissioned officer in charge of quarters. The bugle blew on numerous other occasions during the day at prescribed intervals: Mess, Police, Sick, and Drill calls early in the day; and later, Recall, Stable, Officers', and First Sergeants' calls. No bells, PA systems, telephone calls, or radio messages. Just the bugle. And we followed its orders.

Morning drill was usually of three hours' duration, consisting of equitation, squad, platoon, and troop drill at the walk, trot, and gallop; exercises in fighting on foot, which the cavalry had to be prepared to do in war; and other varied and complex cavalry movements. On certain days each week the squadron, regimental, and, in some cases, troop commanders, all practiced formations, drills, parades, reviews, or other mounted ceremonies. Two thousand maneuvering horses stirred up great clouds of choking dust that coated men, horses, and equipment with a fine powder.

Officers' Call sounded at 11:45 A.M. daily except Sundays and holidays. After passing along routine orders and directives for the day, the adjutant usually announced the regimental commander, who then commented in detail and with some degree of displeasure on errors noted in his rounds of the camp area and drill field that day. At the same time, the first sergeants were receiving instructions and details for the troops from the regimental sergeant major. During these early months of the war there were typewriters in each troop and regimental office but no telephones. Routine business was transacted orally or by handwritten or typed memoranda. As a rule, only official correspondence to higher headquarters, especially that dealing with financial and property accountability, was prepared in more than a single copy.

The regimental staff was small, no more than four or five officers besides the commanding officer, and about the same number of noncommissioned officers and clerks. Great stress was placed on form in military correspondence and communications, and the use of the third person and the passive voice were habitual. Files were not extensive. A small portable field desk, about thirty inches on each side, held all troop records, property accounts, the complete file of correspondence, and necessary regulations and manuals. Typewriters were coming into more general use, and the regimental commander required each new second lieutenant to type a report in person to show that if need be, he could type a letter in the proper format.

The Regimental Personnel Section had its origin during this period. The assistant adjutant became the personnel adjutant. Correspondence and records were increasing, because of the war, in the form of such things as allotments to dependents, the purchase of war bonds, and war-risk insurance. Mimeograph machines were soon to follow, along with file cabinets. And the clerical staffs would grow as a result. Administratively at least, things would never be as simple again.

The schooling of the junior officers in the Seventeenth Cavalry was typical of both the place and the times: simple and direct. Immediately after our arrival, Lt. Daniel A. Connor, the adjutant of the Seventeenth Cavalry, took our group of a dozen provisional officers for a ride on horseback to familiarize us with the area and to introduce us to the mounted service. Most had ridden before, having come from towns, farms, and ranches of the Southwest. Few of us, though, had any experience with military equipment or with military riding. After two or three quiet, gentle rides with Lieutenant Connor, instruction in equitation began in earnest under one of the senior hard-bitten officers of the regiment, Lt. Edwin N. ("Pink") Hardy, a graduate of the Military Academy, class of 1911. He was a man of rugged appearance, even more rugged character, and a fine horseman. Hour after hour of his suppling exercises at a slow trot without stirrups certainly went a long way toward developing our cavalry seats!

We attended drills and other formations with the troop to which we were assigned. There, under the wing of an experienced noncommissioned officer, each of us gradually acquired the rudiments of the technique of command and learned to apply them in putting our platoons through equitation: "The School of the Trooper Mounted," and the other complexities of mounted and dismounted drill formations by voice command, signal, and whistle. The noncommissioned officers who guided us during these days of our early careers almost invariably remained close friends during the many long years of service which followed.

The instructional content and methods of training in the regiment differed little from that in the officers' training camps. Texts were few in number. Each of us had a copy of the basic manuals: "Cavalry Drill Regulations, 1916"; "Field Service Regulations, 1914"; "Rules of Land Warfare"; the "Manual of Interior Guard Duty"; and the "Engineer Field Manual." In the troop orderly rooms we had access to a copy of the "Army Regulations, 1913"; "War Department General Orders and Bulletins"; the "Manual of Physical Training"; the "Manual for Stable Sergeants"; and the "Army Cook's Manual." Perhaps more important than any of these, though, we also had access to the advice and counsel of an experienced first sergeant.

Typical of our instructors was Capt. Roy W. Holderness, a graduate of the West Point class of 1904, a real "old timer" in our eyes. He was a colorful personality, genial and attractive, and full of endless stories of life in the "Old Army." His instruction usually consisted of assembling our group of a dozen or so young officers in an open-air dance pavilion, which afforded shade from the blazing afternoon sun and some degree of shelter from the desert winds. Then he would read from the manual the lesson assignment for the day. There were no charts, no diagrams, no photographs, no illustrations, no training aids of any sort. No practical work for the students; no question period. He read. We listened. Then, the day's reading done, he would regale us with tales and anecdotes of colorful cavalry personalities and past cavalry history. Most of us doubtless learned more from these sessions than we did from the reading of the dry, styleless military manuals, for Captain Holderness was a storyteller of rare ability.

We young officers received practical instruction in our troop areas. In the orderly rooms, the first sergeants and the troop clerks introduced us to the mysteries of morning reports, sick reports, duty rosters, council books, and the details of troop administration and correspondence. Mess sergeants explained how the rations were managed so that the men were fed adequately on thirty or forty cents a day. We inventoried property with the supply sergeants and inspected feeding and horseshoeing with the stable sergeants. We made road sketches and practiced signaling, for semaphore and wig-wag flags were standard communications equipment.

One of the most interesting afternoon schools was that of Pack Transportation. The pack train itself consisted of a pack master, a stevedor, a clacksmith, a cook, and ten packers. There were one bell mare, fourteen riding mules, and fifty pack mules. These last carried loads of two hundred pounds or more, divided into top and side loads lashed to a pack saddle of Moorish-Spanish origin called an *aparejo.* A sling rope balanced the loads on each side of the aparejo. The top load was placed on top of the saddle and then lashed in place by means of the "diamond hitch," an intricate but most effective way of securing the load to the aparejo by means of a long lash rope. The packers worked in pairs, and it was from them that we learned something of the terminology and the techniques of the art of packing. They were civilians, men of long service on the western frontier, all colorful characters with a language all their own. Pack trains had provided most of the transportation through the roadless west, especially in the mountainous areas. Their tales found ready listeners. A pair of these men could lair [layer?] up loads, saddle the mule, place the load, and lash it with incredible speed, all with the exchange of just five words: cinch, rope, go, tie, and rope. The pack train on the march was a sight none of us would ever forget: the loose pack mules trailing along behind the bell mare; the packers astride their riding mules along the flanks or in the rear; the swaying loads; and the amazing distances disappearing under the rapid, swinging pace of the animals in a single day.

THE MEN WHO MADE US CAVALRYMEN

Most of us new officers thumbed with interest a relatively new, small clothbound red book entitled "Officers' Manual," usually referred to as "Moss's

Manual" from the name of the author. In his prefatory remarks, Colonel Moss said: "This manual is a compilation of 'Customs of the Service' and other matters of a practical, worth-knowing nature, things of value and assistance to the inexperienced, most of which cannot be found in print, but must be learned by experience, often by doing that which we should not do or failing to do that which we should do." The last phrase is a good description of how we learned and also of the manner in which the commanders and senior officers of the regiment seemed to view their responsibility of teaching us.

If Captain Holderness was an old-timer in our eyes, Lt. Col. James J. Hornbrook, who commanded the Seventeenth Cavalry during these days, was practically a page out of history, having graduated from West Point in 1890, before any of us were born. His nickname, "Sunny Jim," was not at all descriptive of the personality he exhibited to young officers. He was, in fact, a martinet of the old school, with an eye for minute detail. A ruthless disciplinarian, he was strict, abrupt, and treated words as though they were drops of water in a canteen in the desert. His day began long before daylight when, mounted on his big bay horse, and trailed by the commanding officer's orderly—the soldier selected at guard mount the previous day in competition with all others of the guard detail—he rode the length of the regimental street while the troops were standing Reveille. He then retraced the route, examining in detail the condition of the kitchen and mess-hall areas. Woe betide the troop commander at Officers' Call whose area at Reveille was in an improper state of police or whose incinerator fires were not blazing away with the swill pans bubbling. "Sunny Jim" was always present for mounted drill, where his high-pitched voice was often heard correcting some faltering young lieutenant. And any young officer who started to explain some movement to his platoon, beginning with the words: "Now, boys, . . ." was certain to bring forth a piercing scream which cut cleanly through all of the drill-field noise, "Mister Truscott, they're men, goddamit! They're men! Every one of them! They're men! Men! MEN!"

Colonel Hornbrook believed that the way to instruct young officers was to assign them a task and then let them work out their own solution. The provisional officers had only been in the regiment a few days when we were directed by the adjutant to report to the commanding officer. One after the other we went into his small office, reported, and received our instructions. (It took us several days to figure out that the same thing had happened to each one of us!) When we entered the office, the colonel's stoutish figure was motionless, his face absolutely expressionless, hands folded on the plain table before him, and his blue eyes were fixed coldly on the uncertain young officer standing before him at rigid attention. He spoke with his high, nasal twang: "Lieutenant, I am going to have a Russian ride next Sunday morning. All officers of the regiment will attend. Do you understand, Lieutenant? There will be twenty-four jumps, Lieutenant, and you are going to build two of them. You will build them at the locations shown on this sketch and to the exact specifications indicated thereon. You will build one sand-bag jump sixty feet long and three feet high and one brush jump sixty feet long and three and one-half feet high. They will be ready for the Russian ride Sunday morning. Do you understand, Lieutenant?" No lieutenant dared to say "No, sir."

So each of us received his instructions for two jumps: either sand-bag, brush, post-and-rail, ditch, chicken-coop, or another variety. Each understood the colonel's words perfectly. But the depressing fact was that none of us had ever heard of a Russian ride, had ever seen such jumps, or had any idea of the details of construction of them in spite of the colonel's sketch. Only three days were available for the work. However, the time-honored mentors of second lieutenants, the first sergeants, came to the rescue. They provided us with the necessary advice, materials, and details of men—and construction! (Later, some of us were even brash enough to wonder about collusion between the colonel, the sergeant major, and the first sergeants!) Some of the jumps were of a form probably never seen before or since, but all seemed to pass muster, for the colonel led all officers of the regiment over the twenty-four jumps, spread out over the three-mile course of his Russian ride on Sunday morning.

Col. George H. Morgan was another commander of the regiment during this period, for the last year before his compulsory retirement at the statutory age of sixty-four years in January of 1919. He was one of the select band of heroes who wear the Medal of Honor, having won it in one of the campaigns against the Indians in the year 1882, just two years after his graduation from West Point. He was a man of distinguished appearance, tall, slender, and erect, always dressed with meticulous care, and he had a light, springy step that belied his grey hair and neatly trimmed grey moustache. He had a ready wit and was always entertaining us with tales of the frontier and the "Old Army." However, he amazed us young officers by maintaining that the War Department had made a great mistake when it had abandoned the old single-shot Springfield for the Model 1903, caliber .30, then standard in the army. He insisted that the repeating rifles and machine guns wasted ammunition and encouraged soldiers in careless habits, while the old single-shot rifle caused the soldier to exercise due care to make every shot count. Considering that the machine gun was dominating the battlefields of Europe at the time, Colonel Morgan's views provided us junior officers with a great amount of conversational material and did little toward increasing our confidence in some of our superiors.

However, the old gentleman should not be subjected to too much criticism, for cavalry life had romantic associations with the western frontier. After the Civil War the requirements of Indian warfare dominated cavalry life and thought, prescribing its missions, its deployment in the various stations in the West, and in general posing the problems that controlled cavalry organization and tactics. After the campaigns against the Indians, the last of which occurred in the last decade of the nineteenth century, there was a flurry of cavalry activity during the Spanish-American War and the Philippine Insurrection, and the same activity had been continuous along the border from the time the Mexican Revolution endangered the border region of the Southwest. However, there was no great threat to the national security during these years; no threat to stimulate broad military thought and give purpose to the modernization of military organization and training. No threat until the raid of Pancho Villa on Columbus, New Mexico, on March 9, 1916. The inadequacies of the Punitive Expedition against Villa and the growing danger of entanglement in the European war underscored the lack of military preparedness.

Cavalry units had been scattered about the country in small garrisons, with little association with the other branches of the service or with civilian communities. Because army appropriations were usually on the most austere basis, the units were always understrength, pay was extremely low, and equipment was scarce. Experience in our own Civil War dominated ideas of tactical employment, but the Indian Wars provided the basis for some change, and the European views on organization and training and equipment were beginning to have some modern influence. Riding and the care of animals constituted the principal items of instruction in the mounted-service schools. Garrison training was for the most part routine. Drill, form, ceremony, customs, traditions, protocol, and dress were the vital elements in garrison life. These factors may explain why some of the senior officers seemed so out of date to us.

A NONCOMMISSIONED VIGNETTE

In those days of 1917, military life in Camp Harry J. Jones was a succession of hectic changes, as it usually is when a nation gathers its military, economic, and political strength for war. General Pershing was in Europe, beginning the build-up of the American Expeditionary Force. The two artillery regiments departed the camp, as did signal, ordnance, and quartermaster units, all destined for overseas duty. Most of the Regular Army officers in the regiments received temporary promotions and departed for other assignments. Nearly all of the senior noncommissioned officers were commissioned and, along with the more experienced enlisted men, were transferred from the regiments for assignment to the divisions in the national army then being formed. Troops were left in command of recently commissioned reserve and provisional officers, and the ranks were filled with volunteer and drafted recruits. Many of them came from the cities of the East and were having their first experience with horses, with military life, and with the desert country of the border between Arizona and Mexico.

The Fifteenth Cavalry arrived from recent station in the Philippine Islands. Two thousand or more remounts were shipped in to mount the regiment and provide remounts for the First and Seventeenth Cavalry Regiments. No sooner did the Fifteenth receive the horses than it was ordered to turn them in again. Shortly thereafter it departed for overseas because, according to rumor, General Pershing had once served in the regiment and personally requested it. Eventually, only the First and Seventeenth Cavalry Regiments remained in the camp. They, together with the Tenth Cavalry at Fort Huachuca, Arizona, constituted the First Cavalry Brigade of the Ninth Cavalry Division, recently organized with headquarters at Fort Bliss, Texas, near El Paso.

The fact that officers and men came and went continually did not have a completely adverse effect on the regiment. Sufficient "old-timers" among the senior sergeants remained to keep things running smoothly. The loyalty, resourcefulness, and initiative of these noncommissioned officers are reflected in the following incident, which took place at Slaughter's Ranch, previously mentioned as being some twenty miles east of Camp Jones on the border.

The valley at Slaughter's was well watered by several immense artesian wells which in other days had provided irrigation for the fields along San Bernardino Creek south of the border. The main ranch buildings were some distance north of this group of wells. Another group of ranch buildings, less than a mile south of the international boundary, was in use during this period by *rurales*, or Mexican police, and by Mexican customs officials. In this area the valley was covered by thickets of greasewood, through which ditches carried the water that had been used for irrigation. The area was a favorite hunting ground for officers and men; quail, doves, water fowl, and small game abounded. Few weeks passed when some detachment, troop, squadron, or other unit did not make the march to Slaughter's for training and hunting.

The lack of a border fence and the fact that some of the boundary monuments were concealed in the brush led to an international incident of unusual nature, one that caused no small amount of concern in the headquarters of the regiment, the camp, the Southern Department, and, in fact, the War and State departments. And this in the midst of the great war in Europe!

Troop B of the Seventeenth Cavalry, then commanded by First Lt. David H. Blakelock, a member of one of the provisional classes of 1917, pitched camp at Slaughter's during the latter part of one afternoon. Blakelock, accompanied by another officer, a noncommissioned officer, and Blakelock's orderly, set out into the greasewood for an hour or so of quail hunting while the camp was quiet and the cooks were preparing the evening meal. Intent upon their quest, the little party may well have wandered across the international boundary. At any rate, they suddenly found themselves surrounded and staring into the muzzles of a half dozen Winchesters, held in the hands of as many Mexican *rurales*. Caught by surprise, the party, except for Blakelock's orderly, had no option but to surrender. The orderly, trailing the party by some distance, had dived into the underbrush when he saw the Mexicans. Remaining in observation, he saw his troop commander and companions led away to the small group of buildings a half mile south of the border. Then he sped back to camp and reported the incident to the first sergeant. It was now dusk. But the first sergeant rapidly assembled the troop, issued ammunition, gave the necessary terse orders, and set out to rescue his troop commander and his comrades. His tactics were perfect. Dispatching one platoon to proceed under cover to a position south of the group of buildings, where they could prevent escape by the Mexicans, and holding one platoon in reserve for an emergency, he closed stealthily in with the other one. Surprise was complete. He not only recaptured his troop commander and party; he also captured all the Mexicans.

Lieutenant Blakelock immediately struck camp and returned to the regiment, arriving in the early hours of the morning. There he confined the half dozen Mexicans in the regimental guardhouse and reported to the regimental commander. Then the telegraph wires began to crackle. There were inspector generals from Fort Bliss, from Fort Sam Houston in San Antonio, and from Washington. Weeks passed. The Mexicans worked like any other prisoners in the guardhouse; no one knew what to do with them. Blakelock and his first sergeant were on pins and needles. There was no contact whatever across the border between American customs and immigration officials in Douglas and their Mexican counterparts in Agua Prieta. And Washington maintained an ominous silence. Eventually, however, the matter was settled, for the prisoners were taken to the customs house on the border and released to Mexican authorities. No more was heard of the incident. We never forgot the prompt and decisive action of the first sergeant.

SOCIAL LIFE—SUCH AS IT WAS!

There was considerable rejoicing among military personnel when the Congress in 1917 authorized an increase in pay. Officers received a flat increase of fifty dollars a month. Pay of privates was increased from thirteen to thirty dollars a month, privates first class from fifteen to thirty-five, and pay of noncommissioned officers proportionately. This all seemed enormously generous. However, pressure was soon applied to compel men to make allotments for dependents, for war-risk insurance, and for the purchase of war bonds. Since deductions were always made for laundry, post-exchange coupons, lost equipment, and other such items, soldiers were soon leaving the pay table with the same or less personal spending money than they had before the seemingly generous raises.

Douglas was a thriving city of about fifteen thousand during this period, with the cultural and recreational facilities to be expected of a city of that size and at that time. There were churches of various denominations, a YMCA, schools, and a small country club that had tennis courts and a nine-hole golf course, with oiled sand for greens instead of grass. In the principal business district along G Avenue and Tenth Street there were several popular drugstores, restaurants and cafés, billiard and pool parlors, hotels, and some excellent stores. Hotel Gadsden was a first-class modern establishment with an excellent dining room, popular among the officers. In Pirtlesville and other outlying areas there were numerous neighborhood stores, chili parlors, and "soft drink" emporiums, always popular with soldiers. In these areas there were many adobe cottages occupied by Mexican laboring folk, and among these areas the usual array of camp followers was to be found.

Arizona was "dry." It had adopted prohibition when it entered the Union in 1912. There was plenty of liquor in the Mexican village of Agua Prieta, just across the international boundary, but the border was closed to all traffic. There was no official intercourse between the two cities or between the two countries. There was some smuggling of the potent Mexican beverages such as tequila, mescal, and sotol across the border; however, wartime restrictions prohibited alcoholic liquors within eighteen miles of any military camp. The camp authorities supplemented the customs and immigration patrols with mounted patrols east and west along the international-boundary fence during the hours of darkness.

New Mexico was still "wet" at this time, and the town of Rodeo, just inside the Arizona–New Mexico state line some fifty miles to the northeast of Douglas, did a thriving business. Rodeo was a typical western cow town, with more saloons and gambling houses than all other establishments combined. Bootleggers made the trip to and from Rodeo almost nightly. One energetic Cochise County deputy sheriff made himself quite a reputation as a law-enforcement officer by his success in apprehending "rum-runners" along the Rodeo to Douglas road. He also acquired a large measure of unpopularity among officers and men of the camp by these industrious activities.

A streetcar line ran from Douglas along Tenth Street to the camp; another followed G Avenue from the customs house north to the village of Pirtlesville on the northern edge of the city. There were few automobiles, but there was a stage line utilizing Winston touring cars that ran between Douglas and Bisbee, located in the Mule Mountains about twenty-five miles to the west. A two-lane concrete road connected these two cities. A graveled road led from Bisbee over "The Divide," Mule Pass, to Tombstone, the county seat of Cochise County, another twenty-five miles to the northwest. South of Bisbee about ten miles was the town of Naco. The international boundary separated it from the Mexican town of the same name. One troop of cavalry was stationed in Naco for patrolling the border to the east and west.

Recreation facilities in Camp Harry J. Jones consisted of one large recreation hall, operated by the Red Cross, and dance pavilions in each regimental area, where dances were held occasionally when girls could be brought from Douglas and Bisbee under chaperon. There was some baseball during the spring and summer, but never on any well-organized basis. Occasionally, regiments would conduct track-and-field meets for competition among the troops, and there would be occasional field days, which would feature such mounted events as gymkhana, races, and tug of war.

A few of the younger officers were married and had brought their wives to Douglas. No quarters were provided for them, however. They rented and lived in adobe cottages in the neighborhood of the camp, but there was no social life in the camp itself for families—no dinners, bridge, or tea parties. Most social activity among the officers was limited to regular dances at the Douglas Country Club, for those who maintained the associate membership that the club extended to officers, and to the occasional dinner dances and entertainments of that nature which the regiments might sponsor there.

For officers and men both, a principal social pursuit was gambling. Poker and dice games were of almost nightly occurrence in some officer's tent or adobe shack. They were continuous in the troop areas around payday, so long as men had money. There was some clandestine drinking, and there was always the "postman's holiday"—riding. In general, however, occasional meals in town, the movie theater downtown, ice cream and soft drinks at the drugstores, and pool and billiards helped bachelor officers and soldiers alike pass such time off as they might have. There were occasional forays on weekends to Rodeo and Bisbee, but these were rather limited in scope because of expense and transportation difficulties.

During these months practically all of the military personnel, both officers and men, were fresh from civilian life. Young officers were impressed with the concept that it was the responsibility of every officer to enforce all orders and to maintain the customs and traditions of the service. Some young officers seemed to regard this as almost a recreational activity on the streets of Douglas, which were always crowded with soldiers on their time off from duty. Woe betide the hapless recruit who passed one of the "ninety day wonders" without rendering the appropriate honors or with blouse unbuttoned or uniform otherwise awry. "Well, soldier, where do you think you're going?" "Down town." "Don't you know you're supposed to say 'Sir' to an officer?" "Yessir." "Well, let's see you salute properly." Then repeated salutes and corrections until the officer was satisfied. "Now, what's your name and organization, soldier?" The business of writing the name and organization and another exchange of salutes with probably another correction took more time, and then the soldier would go on his way, his evening ruined. Then the young officer would seek another diversion. No doubt such incidents were repeated in every town adjacent to military camps. It is not surprising that so many men ended the war with a hatred of things military, for which they blamed the Regular Army.

Then there was the colonel's French school. No one in the regiment knew any French, so the colonel arranged for a French priest from the Catholic Church in Douglas as instructor. There were no texts, but regimental headquarters had received a few copies of the *Oxford English and French Conversation Book for Army and Navy Men*. This was a small cloth-bound phrase book, printed by Oxford-Print, Boston, Massachusetts, which the War Department was beginning to distribute. Classes were held in the evening. Officers of the regiment crowded into a small room, took seats on folding chairs, and the class began. No one except the padre, the regimental commander and the adjutant had copies of the text, but the padre began with pronunciation of the French alphabet—ah, bay, say, day, etc.—and the officers repeated after him. He explained accents and some of the peculiarities of the French language. Then he started with useful phrases and sentences. These periods were two-hours long, and the padre's English was difficult to understand. Officers of the regiment were relieved when the classes were discontinued after about ten days. No one acquired a French accent!

SONGS

Soldiers sang during the First World War. They sang by order. The War Department and all intermediate headquarters saw to it. Some one, perhaps "Tin Pan Alley," had convinced the authorities that singing was an indication of high morale. Perhaps it was, for occasional songs were floating back from overseas. We didn't sing the romantic songs of the past, such as "Just before the Battle Mother," or "Bluebell, My Heart Is Breaking," or even "There'll Be a Hot Time in the Old Town Tonight." Tin Pan Alley was turning out songs almost daily to fire up the war effort. And these songs were brought to the camp by a succession of special chorus masters. Singing was a military formation. Troops were marched to it by regiment, columns of fours winding along the dusty roads and into the great recreation hall, a huge barnlike structure sheathed in galvanized iron, with a floor space where ten or fifteen thousand men could stand. They were packed in dense formation about a central platform. On this platform, the chorus master, megaphone in hand (the loudspeaker of the day), sang the selections for the day: "Katy," "Over There," "Tipperary," "Smiles,"

"A Long, Long Trail," "Keep Your Head Down, Fritzy Boy," or whatever other songs he selected. He repeated each song in four directions, like an Indian Chief propitiating the Great Spirits in the four directions with puffs of smoke from a peace pipe. Then he would have the soldiers join in, uncertainly at first but continuing until the iron sides of the huge ramshackle building rattled, echoed, and reverberated with the chorus of thousands of voices. One or more new songs were added each session, each of which was about two hours and repeated two or more times a week.

And there were singing contests. Solos, duets, quartets, choral groups of various sizes. There were contests between troops, squadrons, and regiments. The only regimental trophy which adorned the regimental commander's office in those months was a silver first-prize cup won in the Inter-regimental Singing Contest. For us young officers, cavalry songs were to come later and far more informally.

AND MACHINE GUNS

Cavalry weapons in 1917 were the rifle, pistol, and saber, but there were a half-dozen machine guns in the newly organized Machine Gun Troop. The existing British Vickers machine guns were to be replaced later on by the American Browning. There were no weapons schools in the camp; all training was limited to that conducted in the troops and by the troops. Then, in preparation for overseas service, schools were established at Fort Bliss to train instructors for conducting training in the various weapons. These schools included machine guns, the bayonet, both hand and rifle grenades, and trench warfare. Initially, the principal instructors in these schools were British officers and a few French officers who could speak English well. They were all officers with much combat experience in the type of warfare that had then been in progress for three years or more. Officers from all regiments along the border were detailed to attend these courses, which were extremely rough and rugged and made so purposely. Instruction was thorough, and the officers who attended these schools considered themselves to be extremely fortunate.

Officers who qualified as instructors in the schools at Fort Bliss were detailed to organize brigade schools to spread the gospel more widely. The Machine Gun School that the authorities ordered organized at Fort Huachuca was typical of these brigade schools, and the signing of the armistice was not allowed to interrupt the planned course. Fifty officers from the First, Tenth, and Seventeenth Cavalry Regiments and the Twenty-fifth Infantry were detailed as students. All were either provisional or reserve officers, including the instructors, who were recent graduates of the Division Machine Gun School at Fort Bliss.

Fort Huachuca was a permanent cavalry post, dating from the days of the Indian Wars. It was situated in a beautiful wooded valley in the eastern edge of the Huachuca Mountains, surrounded by towering forested peaks, and looking out eastward on the San Pedro Valley. This valley, some ten or fifteen miles in width, lay between the Huachucas on the west and the Mule Mountains and the Dragoons on the east. It was supposed to have been the route followed northward by Coronado in his search for the Seven Cities of Cibola during the sixteenth century, the first exploration of this western region by Europeans. The town of Tombstone lay directly across the valley from Fort Huachuca. Permanent buildings on the post were of stone or brick, but there were some temporary buildings of wartime construction.

The Machine Gun School utilized the barracks of the Tenth Cavalry's Machine Gun Troop, which was temporarily quartered with other elements of the regiment. The school also utilized the training areas and the weapons and equipment of the troop, which also constituted the "school detachment" during the eight-week course. The barracks of the troop housed the entire school, except for instructors, and provided the academic buildings, administrative offices, student officers' dormitory, and student officers' mess. The mess sergeant and cooks of the troop operated the mess, but the student officers, of course, footed the bills.

The faculty of the school consisted of Capt. Francis H. Boucher, Seventeenth Cavalry, the senior instructor, and Capt. J. H. B. Bogman, Tenth Cavalry, the assistant instructor. Both were recent graduates of the Division Machine Gun School at Fort Bliss. Captain Bogman was also the commanding officer of the Tenth Cavalry's Machine Gun Troop.

Students were about evenly divided among the four regiments. Two majors, both reserve officers from the Twenty-fifth Infantry in Nogales, were the senior officers in the class. They acted as platoon leaders of the two platoons into which the class was divided, each platoon having three squads. The entire class occupied the squad rooms on the second floor of the barracks, where, in addition to the iron cots and wall lockers for each student officer, mess tables had been provided for study, letter writing, and card playing. Officers used the troop showers in the basement and the troop dining room. The mess was reasonably good, but it turned out to be quite expensive, as was usually the case unless supervision was close and adequate.

The troop day room, cleared of its usual paraphernalia of pool tables, writing tables, and chairs, was the classroom. The six squads of officers each gathered about a mess table, each officer sitting on a mess stool. Two machine guns were available for each squad, one Vickers and one Browning. A small podium at one side held the instructor's notebooks. The assistant instructor and selected noncommissioned officers from the Machine Gun Troop, Tenth Cavalry, assisted and demonstrated as necessary. There were no textbooks of any kind. No manuals. And no charts. The instructor read from his own notes, compiled during his course at the Machine Gun School at Fort Bliss. Assistant instructors demonstrated, and the class copied furiously in their own notebooks which had been prescribed for them.

Over and over again the students practiced and repeated the instruction. Over and over again. Nomenclature. Stripping and assembling. Immediate action. Tactics and technique. Blindfolded and not. Until every student was letter perfect. Every Saturday there was inspection of men and equipment, tests and inspection of notebooks.

Officers were "encouraged" to rent typewriters for the keeping of notebooks, and "fortunately," rental typewriters were available at the sum of three dollars a month. Rental of typewriters was not "compulsory," but student officers were told that legibility and neatness of notes counted heavily in marks for the course. There were none who failed to rent typewriters!

So the course proceeded. Indoors and outdoors eight hours every day during Arizona winter days and nights, for there were frequent night drills and night exercises. There was range practice first on the "thousand inch" range, where errors of an inch on a target represented errors of a yard on the range at one thousand yards. And there were frequent examinations.

The course was not without its scandals. Both Captains Boucher and Bogman, the instructors, were provisional officers. Captain Bogman, as mentioned, was also commander of the Machine Gun Troop, a colored unit responsible for the administration of the school. He was a fine officer, a man of outstanding appearance, and a very pleasant personality off duty. On duty, however, he was a martinet, and imitated some of the hard-boiled characters of the "Old Army." He was often rough and sarcastic in speech, and impatient with suggestions relative to improvement of the student officers' mess or other aspects of school administration.

He was often rather condescending in his attitude toward student officers. In consequence he was not particularly popular with the class, most of whom were also provisional officers. And his attitude brought him into conflict with the two majors, the two student platoon leaders, both of whom were former enlisted men of long service. They still had something of the old first-sergeant's attitude so far as young, inexperienced officers were concerned.

Captain Bogman's mess sergeant and cooks were operating the student officers' mess. When the students received a mess bill for the exorbitant sum of six dollars a day, the two majors, as spokesmen for the class, complained to Captain Bogman. He brushed the complaints aside and was extremely brusque with the majors. They then hailed him up before the post commander forthwith for disrespect to senior officers.

Just when this incident was attaining scandalous proportions, a student captain in the class was caught "cribbing," or cheating, on an examination. Then the school was truly in an uproar. There were investigations by the instructors, by the post commander, and by the inspector general from higher headquarters. The course ended in a very-much-subdued atmosphere, since the cheating captain resigned his commission rather than face a general court-martial, which otherwise would have been his fate. And Captain Bogman made his peace with the refractory majors.

Boucher and Bogman may have had organizational and administrative faults in their conduct of the school. But the officers who completed the course of instruction never forgot the details of nomenclature, stripping and assembling, immediate action, and all the other techniques concerned with machine guns. Years later they recognized the wording of their own notes in newly published manuals.

AND SADDLES

There was another incident during this period which was typical of bureaucracy and army methods of the day. In 1858, the War Department adopted a saddle designed by George B. McClellan, later the major general of Civil War fame. He had made a careful study of saddle equipment used by foreign armies, and the saddle he designed had been adopted and used by all of the mounted services since that time. The McClellan saddle was small and light in weight. Seats came in two sizes, twelve and fourteen inch. A roll on the high pommel in front contained a grain bag, with feed for the horse, a feed bag, and the trooper's slicker. A roll on the high cantle in the rear contained shelter half, tent pole, and pins, and the saddle bags right and left carried mess kit, rations, horseshoes, nails, and cleaning materials. Stirrups were of wood, hooded with heavy leather for protection both against riding through brush and cold weather. The rifle was carried in a boot under the trooper's left leg, and the saber was attached to the pommel on the right side, to correspond with the rifle on the left. The rider fitted snugly between the high pommel in front and the cantle in rear, especially when the saddle was fully packed for field service.

Complaints against the McClellan saddle were its small size, the discomfort of the seat, the method of carrying the rifle. It was also considered unsuitable for equitation, jumping, and cross-country riding because of the pommel and stirrups and, again, its size. Many efforts had been made to improve the saddle and to produce a more comfortable and efficient saddle for the cavalry. These efforts culminated in the development of the Riding Equipment Model 1912.

The design of the saddle, Model 1912, had been influenced by the types of saddles in use in European armies. It was a very comfortable saddle for riding, with a long seat, comparatively low pommel and cantle, and steel stirrups of excellent design. The pommel and cantle rolls and saddle bags were on the same order as those of the McClellan saddle equipment, but allowed the rider more room and comfort. The rifle was carried in a leather bucket, or boot, which was attached to the saddle in rear of the trooper's left leg. The butt of the rifle was inserted into this bucket, with the muzzle pointing upward through a wide ring which was strongly affixed to the trooper's cartridge belt. The rifle was attached to the trooper's belt by a leather strap with a quick-release device, which was snapped into the trigger guard of the rifle. Thus, when the trooper dismounted, he lifted the rifle from the boot, and it was attached to his person by the strap on his belt. His hands were thus left free until he had dismounted, grasped the rifle, and released the quick-release device from the trigger guard. The bucket was designed to tilt so that the rifle would fall free if the trooper was thrown or if his mount fell. The saber was carried on the right side, in rear of the trooper's leg, in a frog attached to the saddle. The "old timers" in the cavalry complained about the equipment. They were concerned with the manner of carrying the rifle and the fact that the numerous straps and buckles made adjustment of field equipment complicated. Most soldiers who had been brought up with the McClellan saddle considered it to be more satisfactory for cavalry service.

There had been innumerable tests before the Model 1912 equipment was adopted even for experiment. And the equipment had been used in the Punitive Expedition in Mexico in 1916. Nevertheless, the controversy continued even as the war in Europe progressed. Finally, Troops L and M of the Third Squadron, Seventeenth Cavalry, under the command of Maj. E. N. Hardy, were directed to make a final test. A designated board would make a final determination. One troop was equipped with the new Model 1912 equipment; the other, with the McClellan saddle. The two troops marched from Douglas to Globe, Arizona, and returned, a distance of about four hundred miles, in a period of about two weeks. As a result of the recommendation of the board following this test, the Model 1912 equipment was abandoned, and the mounted services returned to the use of the historic McClellan saddle.

From the experience of this "saddle controversy," we young officers drew one important lesson which would stand us in good stead. There is always resistance to change in established habits, to traditional customs, and to familiar equipment. And this resistance is always extremely difficult to overcome.

THE WAR ENDS—A JOURNEY BEGINS

Although Armistice Day was a joyous occasion throughout the country for signaling the victory of the Allied powers, it deflated the hopes for service in France for many adventurous souls. Most officers and men who were in for the duration were eager for release and return to civilian pursuits, and the professional soldiers wondered what was to come next. Senior officers who had received temporary promotions were for the most part returned promptly to their permanent ranks. Among the professional soldiers were the group of provisional officers who hoped for a permanent career and also enlisted men who had received temporary commissions. This latter group naturally wanted to retain the advantage of commissioned status as long as possible, and some of them hoped for an opportunity for permanent status.

The Seventeenth Cavalry was to make a sea voyage, but it was not to be in the direction of France. Special Orders Number 74, Headquarters Southern Department, March 20, 1919, contained this paragraph:

> 14. The 17th Regiment of Cavalry, Douglas, Arizona, having been designated by the War Department for station in the Hawaiian Islands,

will, in accordance with instructions contained in telegram from the War Department, dated March 12th, 1919, proceed to San Francisco, California, in time to embark on Army Transport sailing from that port on or about April 5th, 1919.

Under instructions contained in indorsements from the War Department, dated February 12th, 1919, the Medical Officers assigned will accompany the regiment to Honolulu. Such enlisted men of the Medical Department as may be necessary will accompany the regiment to San Francisco, and upon completion of this duty will be directed to return to Douglas, Arizona, for assignment to duty at the Camp Hospital.

Such of the ordnance enlisted personnel as are not entitled to discharge will accompany the regiment to Honolulu.

The impedimenta accompanying the regiment will move on first section ahead of the troops to arrive in San Francisco with five officers and one hundred (100) men after midnight April 3d, 1919. The regiment should arrive in San Francisco after midnight April 4th, 1919.

The regiment will take ordnance, tentage, quartermaster supplies, ammunition, machine guns, horse covers, engineering supplies, and troop typewriters for war strength regiment, and athletic supplies. Explosives will be shipped subject to usual regulations for their shipment. Wagons and harness now in possession of the regiment will be turned over to the Camp Supply Officer, Camp Harry J. Jones, for shipment at the proper time to the Auxiliary Remount Depot, Fort Bliss, Texas.

Under authority contained in telegram from the War Department, dated March 18th, 1918, all officers' mounts will be shipped to the Superintendent Army Transport Service, Fort Mason, California, just prior to the departure of the regiment for San Francisco, all animals before being shipped from Douglas will be given the mallein test. One enlisted attendant for each five animals or fractions thereof will accompany the animals until they reach Honolulu.

The date and hour of departure of each section, and probable time of arrival, will be reported by telegram to the Commanding General, Western Department.

The quartermaster Department will furnish the necessary subsistence and transportation, and arrange all details and matters incident thereto.

The journey is necessary in public service.

The "journey" by train was slow but uneventful. Men traveled by tourist sleepers, and there was a standard Pullman for officers. In addition to baggage cars for personal baggage and impedimenta, there was another baggage car in which field ranges were installed. Here mess sergeants and cooks prepared meals which were carried by kitchen police to the various cars and served out into individual mess kits. The last section arrived at dockside early morning April fifth, where troops detrained and boarded the United States Army Transport *Sherman*. Baggage was soon stowed aboard. Such officers and noncommissioned officers as were married were reunited with families, which had preceded them.

A few hours later the good ship *Sherman* passed out through the Golden Gate and headed into the swells of the broad Pacific, loaded to the gunnels with dreams.

2. HAWAIIAN INTERLUDE

The Loveliest Fleet of Islands That Lies Anchored in Any Ocean.

> No alien land in all the world has any deep, strong charm for me but that one; no other land could so longingly and beseechingly haunt me sleeping and waking, through half a lifetime, as that one has done. Other things leave me, but it abides; other things change, but it remains the same. For me its balmy airs are always blowing, its summer seas flashing in the sun; the pulsing of its surf beat is in my ear; I can see its garlanded crags, its leaping cascades, its plumy palms drowsing by the shore; its remote summits floating like islands above the cloudrack; I can feel the spirit of its woodland solitudes; I can hear the splash of its brooks; in my nostrils still lives the breath of flowers that perished twenty years ago.
>
> —*Mark Twain*

There is a romance about voyage by sea, and this one was no exception, even though travel by troopship does have some inconveniences and disadvantages. The old United States Transport *Sherman* was loaded to capacity. In addition to more than a thousand officers and men of the Seventeenth Cavalry bound for Honolulu, there were on board army personnel, bound for the Philippine Islands, and navy, marine, and State Department personnel, enroute to various stations in Hawaii and the Far East. Junior officers were separated from their wives because of lack of cabin space, and the young wives found themselves sleeping on sofas and settees in cabins with older women and their daughters. Life on board soon settled into the normal routine of shipboard after the first wave of seasickness had passed. Those passengers then were able to join the "good sailors" in the enjoyment of good meals, fine weather, and the pleasant associations and agreeable amusements of transport life. Every afternoon there was entertainment: boxing matches, song-and-dance acts, band concerts, wrestling matches, and dramatic skits. All of it was amateur, of course, but nonetheless enjoyable. But Seventeenth Cavalry personnel on board were filled with keen anticipation when it was announced that the *Sherman* would pass Diamond Head early in the morning of the eighth day of the voyage.

There is one thrill that can come only once in a lifetime. It is the first view of Diamond Head against the blue Hawaiian sky, the entry of the ship into Honolulu Harbor . . . the gaiety and excitement on ship and shore as the ship is edged into her berth . . . Hawaiian boys diving from amazing heights in the rigging into the water for coins tossed overboard by passengers who line the rails and watch from every vantage point on shipboard . . . bands playing on shore . . . friends on shore greeting arrivals on shipboard . . . flowers and leis . . . all the confusion that accompanied the arrival of transports in Honolulu is an unforgettable memory.

Sea voyaging has a fascination, a romantic atmosphere that no other form of travel can ever equal. Even though shipboard friendships and romances may not survive the vicissitudes of separation imposed by the prosaic business of living, one can only be better for having experienced the pleasure and satisfaction of an ocean voyage.

The *Sherman* docked early, and debarking was soon completed. Staff cars awaited to transport families to the new post. Troops were soon formed and marched the few blocks to the station, where trains awaited. The Oahu Railroad was narrow gauge; the cars were small. Trains moved out in sections when loaded. The distance to Schofield Barracks, where the regiment was to be stationed, was about twenty miles. The railroad followed the flat coastal plain about half the distance, passing huge canning factories and cane fields. At Waipahu, a spur turned inland and climbed more than a thousand feet to the small Castner station at Schofield Barracks.

Schofield Barracks is situated on the Leilehua plain, near the center of the northern part of the island of Oahu, between the Koolau and Waianae mountain ranges, which, after Diamond Head, are the dominating terrain features of the islands. The post was about twenty-five miles from Honolulu by road, a two-lane concrete highway that followed the general line of the railway. When the Seventeenth Cavalry arrived, only one regiment of the Hawaiian National Guard remained under arms as the garrison of Schofield Barracks. Its early demobilization soon left the Seventeenth

Cavalry in lone splendor as the only line combat unit on the post, with only medical, quartermaster, ordnance, and service detachments for company. The regiment was to remain so for a year, until infantry and artillery units arrived to begin the formation of the Hawaiian Division. There were several Coast Artillery posts around Honolulu, and Pearl Harbor was even then a great naval base where navy and marine units were stationed. But for a year, Schofield Barracks was almost exclusively a cavalry post.

The area into which the regiment moved was known at the time as Castner Barracks. The main gate on the road from Honolulu, which passed through the reservation and on to the north coast of the island, was known as Castner Gate. Schofield Barracks, planned as the home of the Hawaiian Division, was still under construction at this time. Adjacent to the cavalry area, one infantry regimental area was complete. Extending westward toward Kole Kole Pass in the Waianae Range, additional infantry and artillery regimental areas were under construction. Closer to the pass there were regimental areas of temporary wartime construction, which would be replaced eventually by planned permanent housing. This area of temporary construction was then known as the "Upper Post."

Castner Barracks, as the cavalry area was usually called, was typical of the construction in progress. In the troop areas, the buildings were of concrete, three stories in height, arranged in a quadrangle around an open grass-covered square which was the parade ground. There were access streets to the square at each corner of the quadrangle, and a wide sally port through the Headquarters Building gave access from the quadrangle outside to the area of the officers' quarters. The Headquarters Building housed the regimental headquarters offices; the Headquarters, Supply, and Machine Gun Troops; the regimental guardhouse; and all of the regimental storerooms. Each of the other three buildings of the quadrangle housed one of the three squadrons of four troops each.

The main street from Castner Gate through the post toward Kole Kole Pass went between the Headquarters Building and "Officers Loop." The officers' quarters formed two horseshoes, with the two lines of quarters facing each other across the street. Along the service street in the rear of the quarters there were buildings with rooms for domestics. The outer heels of the horseshoes forming the loop were on the street at the opposite ends of the Headquarters Building, and the Officers' Club was situated between the heels of the horseshoes, directly across the street from the sally port in the Headquarters Building. The club contained a mess for bachelor officers, a small recreation room with billiard and card tables, and a very nice outdoor dance pavilion.

The officers' quarters were of two general types. Troop officers' sets were two stories, stucco, with French doors and windows. Field officers' sets were single houses of wood, two stories, and bungalow type. All were of excellent construction, with large airy rooms and with fixtures of the best quality.

The stables were the same long, low, open models we had been familiar with at the border. The stable area was a prolongation of the troop quadrangle on the side opposite regimental headquarters. Stable buildings were parallel to the quadrangle, with picket lines and corrals at one end. They were assigned in this order from the end of the area near the quadrangle: Headquarters, Supply, and Machine Gun Troops, then the letter troops in alphabetical order. Immediately below the last stable, the road led across the narrow-gauge railroad to the drill field, only a short distance away. This field was a vast mesa, or plateau, bounded on two sides by deep gulches, a marvelous area for training cavalry.

Below the cavalry stable line, between the gulch and the drill field, there was an area of troop gardens and a small village, where Japanese workers employed on the post lived. The garden area, like much of Hawaii, was amazingly rich and produced most of the fresh fruits and vegetables available. There were plenty of papayas, a delicious melonlike fruit for which newcomers usually had to acquire a taste; alligator pears, mangoes, and guavas, famed for their jelly; and of course, bananas. There was little commercial truck gardening for the post market, because pineapples and sugar cane were far more profitable crops and the only ones in which the corporation-owned plantations were interested. The troop truck gardens were important though as a supplement to canned foods, which constituted the basic ration.

The Japanese village provided the gardeners who tended the garden plots, labor for various post activities, and the women who were employed as maids, cooks, and laundresses. There was a small store in the little village, where barrels of dried fish and other Japanese foods were always on display. One could also purchase Japanese goods, such as dishes, tools, and gimcracks of various kinds.

Some food was a problem. Few fresh chickens were raised for sale, and both chicken and eggs were very expensive. Few families could afford a dollar a dozen for eggs, which had been dear on the border at one-fifth that price. Most of the meat purchased in the commissaries was of

Australian origin, shipped in cold-storage, and it was tough, stringy, and tasted of preservatives. Cold-storage eggs from the States also showed the effects of age by the time they reached cookstove and table. Fortunately, fish was plentiful, and Hawaiian mullet was a delight.

The regiment had been reorganized for transfer to Hawaii. It was raised to a strength of fifty-six men per troop, about half its authorized strength, by intensive recruiting. Drafted men had been demobilized, and some of its men were career soldiers, some were Regular Army reservists, that is, men who had enlisted for seven years, four of which would be in the Regular Army Reserve. Many of the latter had been recalled to service, and few had any intention of remaining in when the time came that they could again be furloughed to the Reserve. Most of the others had enlisted for one year just for the opportunity of seeing Hawaii.

Col. John K. L. Hartman was the regimental commander. He had commanded it for a brief period during the war and then, as a brigadier general, had commanded the First Cavalry Brigade. When he was reduced to his permanent rank during the postwar demobilization, he was again assigned to the regiment. Born in Pennsylvania, a graduate of the Military Academy, class of 1888, he had been detailed at times to both the Quartermaster and the Signal Corps. He was a man of medium size, being about five feet nine, stocky build, and slightly stooped, always immaculately dressed with highly polished boots, and always with a riding crop in hand. His grey hair was thinning, and he looked out on the world through bifocals above flowing, slightly drooping grey moustaches, which were a dominating feature of his appearance. He was quiet in manner, somewhat lacking in humor, rather cold on first acquaintance, but warm-hearted and genial when one came to know him. He was greatly respected by his command.

The seventy-five or so officers of the regiment were a mixed lot as to origin. There were eight or ten graduates of the United States Military Academy, only two of whom were lieutenants, the others being of field rank. There were about twenty-five provisional officers from one or the other of the provisional classes, and about an equal number who had received temporary commissions during the war. Most of these were former enlisted men who, though junior in rank, were senior in age and experience.

The first few weeks in Hawaii for the regiment were busy ones for everyone. Horses were drawn from the quartermaster corrals, sorted according to color, and issued to troops. Saddle equipment was drawn and conditioned. Horses had to be exercised, groomed, shod, and conditioned. Neglected barracks were cleaned. There was range practice to complete before the end of the fiscal year. Meanwhile the guarding of the huge post and all of the enormous construction activities then under way added to the normal cavalry functions, imposing a heavy burden on the half-strength regiment. And this burden was not eased in any way by the personality of the general officer who was the post commander at the time. And he was a cavalryman!

Brig. Gen. John W. Heard was a cavalryman of the old school, and he welcomed the return of a cavalry regiment to Hawaii and the opportunity it would provide for further display of his not inconsiderable disciplinary talents. General Heard was a small, almost wispy sort of man, mustached, as were many of the old-time cavalrymen of his day, always immaculately dressed, sandy of hair and complexion—and sandier still of disposition! He was a nervous type and endowed with boundless energy and a vitriolic tongue, which all junior officers and enlisted men held in dread. He was also a great egotist, already memorializing himself by giving his name to buildings, streets, roads, and various other structures. The dance pavilion in the Officers' Club had a large brass plaque, which proclaimed it to be the *Brigadier General John W. Heard Pavilion.* The Post Commander's Quarters, which he occupied when the Seventeenth Cavalry arrived in the islands, were on the *Brigadier General John W. Heard Circle.* Wherever one turned, one encountered the name *Brigadier General John W. Heard* emblazoned on something. He was restless, adventuresome, and courageous. One of his proud boasts was that he required his chauffeur to drive the twenty-five miles from Schofield Barracks to Department Headquarters in Honolulu in twenty-five minutes, and this was over the winding, narrow road, with hair-raising turns and precipitous slopes through some of the deep Hawaiian gulches.

Isolation on an island far from home and fireside and familiar surroundings posed some morale problems among young soldiers when the initial glamour of the romantic island adventure faded. Riding, baseball, swimming, boxing, and all other athletic activities were available on the post, as well as service clubs, local restaurants, and moving pictures. The only civilian community immediately adjacent to the post was the small village of Wahiawa. It was surrounded by pineapple plantations and was the site of a pineapple cannery. It was inhabited almost entirely by workers for the cannery and the fields, most of whom were Oriental. While there was a small hotel, the village had little to offer soldiers in the way of recreation except possibly as a place to purchase that potent Hawaiian distillation, okulehau, an illicit moonshine beverage.

Honolulu was easily accessible by the narrow-gauge railway and by automobile. Few officers and only a very few of the older noncommissioned officers owned cars. However, there were a few automobiles, driven for the most part by Japanese, which were for hire. And there was an occasional bus service, of sorts. In Honolulu there was the famous beach at Waikiki, as well as all of the attractions to be expected in one of the most famous port cities in the world, particularly one standing at the crossroads of the Pacific, where the paths of so many nationalities crossed.

There were excellent beaches on the northern end of the island, in the vicinity of Haleiwa and Waialua, only about ten miles away and easily accessible from Schofield Barracks. There was an attractive small hotel at Haleiwa, but it was more popular with the families than with the single men in the barracks, for that area had little to offer except swimming and golf on a short nine-hole course—and few cavalrymen played golf in those days.

Boxing was one of the most popular spectator sports among the services in Hawaii during this period. Competition was keen between the navy and marines at the great naval base at Pearl Harbor and at the army posts, especially Schofield Barracks. The services had some very able fighters in all classes. Bouts staged alternately at Schofield and Pearl Harbor were extremely popular. The Schofield bouts often drew crowds of five thousand and more, necessitating special trains from Honolulu and Pearl Harbor.

There were the usual track-and-field meets, which were held periodically, as well as the field days that featured mounted races, contests, and gymkhana events. There were occasional traveling shows, which also drew good crowds. Most of them were commercial ventures.

Among the officers, the Officers' Club was the center of social activities, as was usually the case on any army post. There were regimental dances every week or so in the club pavilion. Occasionally there would be dinner dances and bridge parties. Auction bridge was just becoming popular in the services, and a great many of the officers and wives were learning to play. Tables were numbered, and players were seated by place card for the beginning of play. When the rubber was finished, the high scorers advanced to the next table. The result was that at the end of the evening, the poorer players usually found themselves together, enjoying the "aspic salad" which seemed to be a part of the card-table ritual. Some men easily acquired a distaste for such bridge parties and especially for dining in crowded rooms off rickety card tables.

The Officer's Club Mess was operated by a Chinese steward, long associated with Officers' Clubs in Hawaii. And all the mess personnel were Chinese. It was typical of officers' messes, at times very good and at times indifferent, to say the least. It was always popular with married officers and their wives on Sunday night, although there were occasional incidents which interrupted this patronage. For example, the club dining room was crowded one Sunday evening. Soup was served. One young bachelor officer, entertaining married friends, called the waiter and pointed quietly at his plate. The waiter threw up his hands, eyes opened wide, and shrilled in a voice that carried over the entire dining room, "Ooooee! Cockee roach! I get you nudder one!" The waiter may have spoiled the enjoyment of an evening meal for many, but he established a regimental expression for surprised astonishment.

At a later time, complaints among the bachelor officers concerning the quality of the mess reached a point where the commanding officer thought some advice to the young officers was desirable. He charged Col. Charles C. Farmer, who was for a period an additional colonel attached to the regiment, with this duty. Colonel Farmer was another soldier of the old school. A man with independent means, he had spent much time abroad on military attaché assignments and had traveled widely. He was a raconteur of high order and very popular with the officers of the regiment. He assembled them one day to comply with the general's instruction and started by mentioning his great interest in saddle rooms on his travels. He described the saddle rooms of the king of Spain and the shah of Persia, ending by saying that the Spanish was the most magnificent he had ever seen. Then he talked of his interest in kitchens and in the preparation and service of food. Wherever he stayed, he made it a practice to cultivate the manager of the hotels, so that he could have free access to kitchens and pantries. He and Mrs. Farmer had spent some time in one of the most fashionable hotels on the Riviera. As was his practice, he had made friends with the hotel manager and spent time in the hotel kitchens and service areas. One day he had come from the kitchen and was in the service pantry, observing the waiters as they served in the main dining room. While he was standing there, a waiter returned from the dining room with his tray aloft, his coattails swishing. As soon as he was in the pantry, out of view of the dining room, he lowered his tray, spat vigorously into a bowl of soup on his tray, stirred it vigorously, and hoisted it aloft again. Returning to the dining room, he proceeded to a table where sat a richly dressed dowager, whom he obsequiously served the well-spitted soup. She accepted it with evidence of approval and proceeded with her meal.

Colonel Farmer was so shocked that he went at once to the manager to report the incident. The manager told him who the lady was. She had been coming there for years, and few dishes ever placed before her met with her approval until they had been returned to the kitchen at least once. She was vitriolic in her speech to the servants, condescending in her manner, and miserly in her gratuities. There was really nothing the management could do, for ill-treated servants will always find some means of striking back. Colonel Farmer ended his story: "Now when we are dining in a restaurant and Mrs. Farmer complains about the food or service, as she sometimes does, I push my plate aside and eat no more."

His story was effective in reducing complaints among the bachelor officers—within hearing of the mess personnel, at least! But the story in no way interfered with the enjoyment of the mess steward's New Years' Eve party for the officers of the regiment and their wives. The steward, Lee, had been in Schofield for many years and was well known to many officers of the "Old Army" whom he had served. It was his practice to entertain the officers and their wives at dinner each Chinese New Year's. The dinner was always a great event. Tables were placed in the dance pavilion, and the dinner was classic Chinese, with bird's-nest soup, sweet-and-sour pork, Peking duck, fried rice, and all the other vast array of foods that the Chinese love and prepare so well. It was always one of the delightful affairs of the year, with Colonel Farmer's story pushed well into the background of our memories!

Gambling seems to be a very human failing with broad appeal, for the lure of "getting something for nothing" appears to be almost universal and irresistible. In the small bridge games where the stakes were "a quarter a corner" or even a tenth of a cent a point, no one ever suffered greatly from losses. Even the poker and dice games, which were a favorite amusement among the bachelor officers, never caused any great amount of suffering. Married officers rarely joined in these games, but if and when they did, their participation was usually brief, because few could afford the risk of losing more than a very few dollars. Among the troops, however, the poker and dice games were usually continuous around payday until the old, experienced, inveterate gamblers in the regiment had won most of the ready cash. Then the games petered out for lack of customers, to await the next payday.

Because of the convenient location of the Officers' Club, officers frequently stopped by on the way home from Officers' Call or afternoon duties, for a soft drink or for an occasional game of pool or billiards. Several forms of pool were popular among the officers for modest gambling. One was "bottle pool," in which each player drew a numbered ball from a bottle. When, during the game, he dropped the ball with his number on it into a pocket, he would call "Pay me!" and expose his number. Other players would then pay whatever stake had been agreed on, usually five or ten cents, rarely more than a quarter. For the most part these games were innocent amusement and did no harm to anyone. However, two troop commanders who were close friends and both fairly expert at the game, began playing pool for stakes higher than their economic status warranted, at least higher than the expertness of the bachelor member of the duo warranted. Their competition carried on for weeks, with the winner accepting IOUs instead of cash. Eventually, the bachelor member was indebted for several hundred dollars in addition to his monthly pay check, a fact that caused him no small amount of worry and financial embarrassment, to the detriment of his career.

Some of the senior officers purchased automobiles, as did one or two of the bachelor officers of the regiment. Some of the junior married officers bought automobiles in partnership, the two families dividing the use week and week about. Those with cars were very generous with invitations to others. Trips to the beaches: Waikiki, Waimea, Haleiwa, and other popular spots for picnics and swimming. One of the favorite trips was "around the Island," which usually began early on some Sunday or holiday: a swim at Waikiki and a try with the surf boards . . . , then over the Pali, with its breath-taking view from the cliff where Kamehameha I had driven the enemy warriors in his decisive victory that united the islands under his control. . . , down the winding road, with its hair-raising hairpin turns, to Kailua and Hauula . . . , another swim and picnic lunch . . . , on past Kahuku Point and its wireless station to Waimea . . . , another swim and supper at the nice hotel . . . , then back through the cane fields and pineapple plantations to the post, ready to begin another week of work the following morning. Idyllic days, especially for married officers.

Officers of the regiment learned to play polo in Hawaii. None of the younger ones had ever seen a game before coming to the islands. However, it had long been a favorite game on Maui and Kauai as well as Oahu, and they all had fine teams. Officers purchased mallets, balls, helmets, selected horses from the troops, and set about to teach themselves the game. William Cameron Forbes, a former governor general of the Philippine Islands, had written a book for beginners, and the little book, *As to Polo,* was the "bible" for the group of young officers. They had a wonderful time learning the game, to say nothing of getting some very good exercise. However, their progress was slow, as indicated by the outcome of their play in the first of the Inter Island Polo Tournaments in which they participated. They lost to the fine Kauai team by a score of 23 to 1, and to the Maui team by a score of 15 to 0. Several years were to pass, years that brought more experienced players, new ponies to the Polo Stable, and great improvement in individual play before a post team could meet the fine civilian teams on even terms.

Headquarters Hawaiian Department was responsible for all Army installations and activities in the islands, and these were concentrated almost entirely on the island of Oahu. Department Headquarters was located in Honolulu, but the troop complement during the year that followed the arrival of the Seventeenth Cavalry was limited to the following: a few Coast Artillery units, which manned the gun batteries around Honolulu; Tripler General Hospital, at Fort Shafter; some Quartermaster, Engineer, Ordnance, and Signal Corps units; and the post at Schofield. The Seventeenth Cavalry was the only line combat unit, and in consequence, it received an undue proportion of the time of the department's commanding general and his staff.

All senior commanders seem to be somewhat like Louisa May Alcott's philosophers, who

> All on their hobbies they amble away,
>   And a terrible dust they make;
> Disciples devout both gaze and adore,
>   And daily they listen and bake.

Gen. Charles Pelot Summerall, for example, was a martinet of the old school where matters of neatness and cleanliness of the posts were concerned—or "police of the area," as we called it. As more and more privately owned automobiles came into use in Schofield Barracks, there was an increase in oil stains on the streets in front of officers' quarters, where cars stood. These stains displeased General Summerall, and more than one automobile owner was required to restore the street in front of his quarters to its pristine state.

Lack of uniformity in wearing apparel appeared to be the particular *bête noire* of the next department commander, General Morton. He seemed to have an especial aversion to faded khaki uniforms, even the chino khaki which was dear to the heart of the old soldiers who had served in the Philippine Islands. Quartermaster warehouses were filled with stocks of reclaimed clothing left over from the war, and both the War Department and the Hawaiian Department regulations required the issue of this clothing until stocks were expended. There were no monetary clothing allowances at the time, so that issue to troops was on an exchange basis. A trooper turned in his garment for salvage in order to draw a replacement. Since the clothing in the supply stocks had been laundered and relaundered until it was colored from the original olive green to almost white, there were problems.

General Morton was a huge man, with a very large nose which naturally gave rise to the nickname "Nosey," by which he was rather irreverently known among the junior officers. He merited the name for another reason: his meticulous and detailed inspections, which were dreaded by all junior officers. While inspecting a recruit detachment one day almost at the end of their training period, he walked down the line, pointing to the faded and worn clothing and severely reprimanding the young officer for his failure to clothe the men properly. Then he stopped before a terrified recruit, braced at attention, put his finger in some small hole and ripped the shirt from the man's back. Then he placed his hand on the frightened man's shoulder and remarked in a sanctimonious, rather fatherly way: "My boy, you are not responsible for being dressed in rags. Your country does not want you dressed in rags. I have issued orders that you should have proper clothing, but your officers have not carried out my orders. They will, my boy! They will!" And then he glared at the young officer.

Recruits began arriving on the June transport, just two months after the regiment had arrived in Hawaii. There were about four hundred in the first contingent. Instead of assigning them to the troops for training, the regimental commander decided to establish a "recruit detachment," with specially selected officers and noncommissioned officers for instructors. The detachment was established in the temporary artillery barracks in the Upper Post. Here they were given an intensive course of basic training, which would permit them to take their places in the ranks of the troops at the end of eight or ten weeks. Since the regiment was at less than half strength and since a large proportion of the men in the ranks had enlisted for only one year, well over two thousand recruits passed through this camp during the course of the year. They arrived on transports monthly, in groups of one and two hundred. A few of the officers and a large number of the noncommissioned officers remained on that duty during the entire period. It was an onerous but rewarding duty.

There were two products of Hawaii concerning which all newly arrived soldiers as well as the recruits had to be cautioned, for each could cause severe physical discomfort under certain circumstances. Both products had an almost irresistible attraction to those new to the islands. Pineapples and kukui nuts. The vast plantations of pineapples drew soldiers like a magnet when the fruit was ripe—and sometimes when it was not. Soldiers often made themselves ill from overindulgence in the unaccustomed fruit, sometimes requiring hospitalization. Naturally enough, the managers of these plantations did not look with favor upon raids of their crops, and disciplinary action was not infrequent. The kukui (candlenut) tree grows in groves along mountain sides. It is a handsome tree, with a light yellow leaf shaped somewhat like that of a grapevine. The nut itself is dark, something like an English walnut but with a thicker shell, very much like a hickory nut. It has a pleasant flavor, but eaten in any quantity, it acts as a severe purgative, causing diarrhea that can last for two days or more. The old Hawaiians once used the nut oil for lighting and roasted the nut and ate it with salt. Eaten thusly, it was not unpalatable, but few soldiers took the trouble to try them again after their initial experience with them.

For the most part, life moved at a leisurely pace in the delightful climate of the islands. However, time was fully occupied with normal administrative, training, and extracurricular activities. It became even more so after the passage of the National Defense Act of 1920. This act provided that the Army of the United States was to consist of the Regular Army, the National Guard, and the Organized Reserves; and it envisaged a vast school and training system. The act authorized a Regular Army of some 14,000 officers and 365,000 enlisted men. A comprehensive Educational and Recreational (E & R) Program was undertaken, no doubt with the idea of offering greater opportunities in the army and making military service more attractive—all with the hope of encouraging enlistments to maintain such a large increase in our peacetime army. Educational and mechanical courses of wide variety were offered, and practically all enlisted men were pressured into taking some sort of educational or vocational courses. Most officers, noncommissioned officers, and specialists found themselves detailed as instructors in these schools, supplementing the extensive body of civilians who were in charge of the programs. Vocational courses included all the skills common to the service, and others as well. Educational courses began at the lowest level, aimed at eliminating illiteracy;

attendance by the relatively few illiterates was mandatory. Educational instruction included many elementary, grade, and high-school subjects. Many enlisted men elected these courses to avoid the afternoon fatigue details which would otherwise fallen to their lot, and many of these men elected the simplest courses available. There was a great shortage of textbooks in the schools, and the result was that many of the instructors had to prepare lesson sheets, which were mimeographed by the E & R Office.

These programs did not last very long, however, for they were undertaken before the Congress appropriated money for the army of 365,000 men. When the money Congress finally appropriated would only support an army of 150,000 men, most of this ambitious E & R Program fell by the wayside.

Training activities were carried on in much the same way as cavalry had trained since time immemorial—mounted drill and stables in the mornings, troop noncommissioned officers' schools and routine fatigue details and athletics in the afternoons. The only changes to the routine resulted from seasonal variations and interruptions by higher headquarters. The huge grass-covered drill field had space enough for a division. There the troops carried on equitation, squad, platoon, and troop drill and held squadron and regimental formations. There were jumps scattered about the drill area, and these, together with gulches on two sides of the field with their steep banks, provided wonderful facilities for training in cross-country riding. We made the most of them.

The reservation at Schofield Barracks occupied a narrow strip from the crest of the Koolau Range westward across the Waianae Range to the ocean. On the Koolau side of the post, this strip opened to a wedge-shaped formation with a frontage of about ten miles on the coast. The roads and trails in these areas were used for training in reconnaissance and for practice marches. Troops also made extensive reconnaissance of the trails throughout the mountains and along the crests, seeking out trails that led to all the beaches. These rugged mountains of volcanic origin had many tree-covered valleys leading to the sea. Their crests often narrowed to knife-edge paths, with sheer precipices of hundreds of feet on either hand that would test the ability of a mountain goat.

During this first year the regiment conducted the first war game that any of the junior officers of the regiment had ever experienced. The officers were divided into two groups, each representing a regiment and under the command of two senior officers of the regiment. Colonel Hartman was the chief umpire. Each group assembled in an assigned room and spread out the excellent topographical map of the island, which was on the scale of one inch equals four miles. Colonel Hartman passed out the situation and the requirement to the red and the blue commanders. Each group then determined what its dispositions would be at the hour required. One group would then return to the colonel's office and indicate its solution and disposition, after which the other group would do so. So the exercise continued all day, with the colonel making necessary rulings to keep the play in progress. To the young officers, the method seemed very stilted and lacking in action, most probably because they were all completely new to this type of training exercise, which they would see again and again throughout their careers. But it was interesting and worthwhile.

Field training during the first year consisted of a field exercise, conducted under the auspices of department headquarters. The Seventeenth Cavalry was still the only mobile combat unit on the island. "Regimental Notes" in the *Cavalry Journal* for July, 1920, described the maneuver thus:

> The covering of approximately one hundred miles of rugged coast line with a regiment of cavalry, so organized as to repel effectively any attempted landing of troops from transports pending the arrival of reinforcements, was one of the many problems set for the solution of the officers and men of this regiment during the past maneuvers on the island of Oahu. With the exception of the sector in and around the city of Honolulu and Pearl Harbor, covered by the coast defense guns, the entire coastline of the island, which our naval base in the mid-Pacific, was left to the sole regiment of line troops now in this department.
>
> The peculiar features of the island lent themselves in many ways to the solution of the problems. The maneuvers, arranged by Department Headquarters, took cognizance of the fact that the number of troops was limited and the cavalry acted as if unsupported by any other troops other than air service. The "hostile forces" were represented by the submarine flotilla.
>
> Beyond the fact that things were run on the latest systems of liaison and intelligence, the routine features of cavalry maneuvers were little changed. In the three or four days of the preliminary part the customary attention was paid to reconnaissance and intelligence. Command posts were placed at advantageous points, and sectors of defense were organized, so that complete liaison existed over the hundred miles from post to post by means of Very Lights and field telephone lines. Camps

were placed in such localities as would make their observation difficult from the air, and in several tests of these places not one was noted by observers in machines flying at low altitudes.

The question of supply and the rapid shifting of troops was dealt with by taking advantage of the good system of roads on the island and the fact that plenty of motor transportation was available. Inasmuch as the number of horses was insufficient for the men at hand, it was found necessary to transport a part of the regiment in trucks. This feature was found to be of great advantage, although limited in its application.

Another feature of interest to machine gunners was the testing by a cavalry regiment of the infantry machine gun cart, the Machine Gun Troop being issued 17 of these carts for the purpose. As opposed to the pack method of transportation for cavalry, however, it was found that the carts were far inferior. In the first place, when moving at a rapid gait, even over a good road, the light carts bounced about in every direction, and the resultant jolting and jarring proved harmful not only to the guns but to instruments as well. It was also found that ammunition packed in boxes for mule transportation, when carried on the carts, jolted loose from the belts and necessitated almost a complete refilling before going into action after practically a very short march.

When the carts were taken off the road, moreover, they were almost helpless. The narrowness of the trails in the mountains of Oahu precluded their use there. The rough nature of the volcanic ground made it immensely difficult to maneuver, and in going down a mountain pass, easily negotiated by the cavalry and pack animals, almost as much work was entailed as moving a three inch battery.

In the spring of 1920, the regiment had been in Hawaii for more than a year. Men who had enlisted for a year had been returned to the States for discharge, and there were very few reenlistments. Their departure, although their places were taken by others enlisted for the normal three-year period, intensified a serious morale problem. Many of the noncommissioned officers of the regiment were "reservists," that is the men who had enlisted for three years' active service and four years in the Regular Army Reserve. These "reservists" had been recalled when the country entered the war, and nearly all of them now wished to return to civilian life. Although the regiment had brought this problem to the attention of higher headquarters repeatedly, no instruction had been received from the War Department to release them from active service and furlough them to the Reserve in accordance with their original contract. They were becoming increasingly dissatisfied and were beginning to constitute a serious morale problem because of their influence on younger soldiers.

Changes among officer personnel were also causing morale problems. Many temporary officers, especially those commissioned from the ranks, wanted very much to obtain permanent commissions in the expansion that was taking place in the army. Examinations were being conducted, but not many of this group were being selected. Then some of the provisional officers who had accepted permanent commissions were resigning to return to the civilian life they had known, often because their wives disliked military life. All of these factors combined to create a most unusual situation.

Eventually, orders came through, authorizing the discharge of soldiers for the purpose of reenlistment, and a few of the "reservists" took advantage of this authority. In Troop I, the first sergeant, the mess sergeant, the supply sergeant, two duty sergeants, and the first cook were all Reservists. All applied for discharge for the purpose of reenlistment under this authority. Discharge papers were prepared, all administrative work was accomplished, and the discharge certificates required only the troop commander's signature to be effective. Regulations, however, required that discharges be delivered to individuals only after they had reenlisted. The Troop I commander happened to be one of the former provisional officers who had submitted his resignation, and he was in fact awaiting the next transport. On the day before the group of "Reservists" were to reenlist, the first sergeant presented the discharge papers to the troop commander for his signature. He signed them and placed them in his desk for delivery to the individuals when they had reenlisted. However, during the night, the first sergeant removed the papers from the desk, and delivered them to the individuals, whereupon the entire group departed for Honolulu, intending to sail on the next commercial steamer.

Well, there was no small amount of consternation in regimental headquarters at this turn of events. The only noncommissioned officer left in Troop I with any experience was one "Reservist" sergeant, who had refused to enter into the conspiracy, and another sergeant of limited ability. The only thing the "Reservist" wanted in the world was a furlough to the Reserve, to which he thought he was entitled. There was an immediate change of troop commanders, but some weeks were to pass before discipline and organization were reestablished in the disorganized troop. One important factor was the timely arrival of a first sergeant who had remained in Douglas when the regiment had departed for the islands. William A. Davenport was a tough cavalryman of the old school and a successful lightweight fighter in his younger days. Loyal and dedicated, he was still able to impress recalcitrant young soldiers with the meaning of discipline. As for the conspirators, they were immediately arrested in Honolulu and restored to military control before any of them could leave the island. Their discharges, having been obtained through fraud, were of course void. The conspirators were all tried and received sentences which would discourage others from attempting such fraud.

Another incident that occurred in Troop I was indicative of some of the aftereffects of the war which were just becoming evident. The rifle range at Schofield Barracks was almost under the shadow of Mount Kaala, the highest peak on the island, and a magnificent rifle range it was. The firing pits were all on a single line, and the butts, where the targets were mounted, in echelon to the right in successive steps for the 200-, 300-, 500-, 600-, 800-, and 1,000-yard ranges. There were something like fifty or sixty firing points on each of the ranges except the 800- and 1,000-yard ones, which were usually for only specially qualified sharpshooters and expert riflemen.

One day as Troop I was beginning rapid fire on the 200-yard range, the men on the firing order were in place, with coaches beside them, scorers at the tables in rear. The firers had loaded, and the commands "Ready on the right?" "Ready on the left?" had received affirmative signals from the coaches, and the command "Ready on the firing line?" had been repeated to the pits by telephone. Up went the targets, down went the firers, and the crackle of musketry rolled out across the range. Suddenly, one of the recent arrivals bounded to his feet, and with his rifle at the high port, started down the range toward the targets. The range officer whistled, all the noncommissioned officers were blowing whistles, and everyone else was yelling "Cease fire!" at the top of their lungs. The individual turned out to be a soldier who had been shell-shocked in France; he was out of his mind and thought that he was back on the Western Front. After a short period of hospitalization, he was returned to the troop, where he was considered to be a promising soldier. However, any shock, such as a sudden crash or blow or even overindulgence in okulehau, that potent Hawaiian distillation, brought on a mental aberration that made him think he was back in the trenches. He was finally returned to the States for hospitalization and eventual medical discharge. A sad case.

Because of the size of the post and the wide dispersion of installations that required protection against pilferage, and particularly against fire, guard duty imposed no small burden on the regiment during this period. There were usually twelve to fifteen posts requiring a detail of an officer of the day, two sergeants of the guard, three corporals for the three reliefs, and three privates or privates first class for each relief, plus one. The extra soldier was to provide the commanding officer with an orderly, selected by the officer of the day from all the privates of the guard as the best soldier present that day, a detail for which the competition was always very keen. Post Number One and several others at important installations were maintained throughout the twenty-four-hour period. The remainder were maintained only during hours of darkness, and most of these posts required mounted sentries. During the day the sentries from these posts "chased prisoners," that is, guarded prisoners on work details during the day. Since the officer of the day inspected each relief once during its tour, and made one of these inspections between midnight and Reveille, his was a busy twenty-four-hour period.

The regimental guardhouse was on the ground floor of the Regimental Headquarters Building at its southern end, facing the quadrangle. It was modern in every respect and about as secure as any prison. There were never more than about fifteen or twenty regimental prisoners confined in the guardhouse, men either awaiting trial or serving sentences of six months or less. Most of the sentences were for minor offenses, such as drunkenness, violation of orders, pilferage, and absence without leave—A.W.O.L. Men convicted of more serious offenses, such as desertion, larceny, insubordination, sex deviation, and other more serious crimes, were confined in the post prison.

There were always a small number of hardened criminals to be found among the two thousand or more who passed through the regiment in the course of a year or so, a few more in a full-strength regiment. And there were always others who found it difficult to conform to the discipline necessary in any military organization. The post prison was a miniature prison in every respect, a place that provided maximum security and the most stringent discipline. Men convicted of serious crimes and all men serving sentences of more than six months were confined here, as were convicted men awaiting transfer to the disciplinary barracks or a federal prison in the States.

The post prison was of concrete, with cells and guardrooms built around an inner courtyard. Most of the cells were individual, to permit the complete separation of the prisoners, although the open-barred doors did not preclude conversation between adjoining cells. There were a few cells for solitary confinement of recalcitrant prisoners. All in all, this small prison was a self-contained unit that provided effective supervision of the most difficult cases. Guards were all especially selected men, and the prison officer was usually selected for a background of experience in prison work. Men confined here worked at hard labor. Cracking rocks with heavy sledges with pipe handles nicked to ensure that they could be grasped only at the end was normal. Work on roads, garbage details, and all the heaviest and most disagreeable work fell to the lot of the men confined here. Some of them served sentences in the post prison and then were restored to duty, where they made good soldiers. For the most part, however, men confined to the prison were hardened criminals lost to the service.

Formal Guard Mount, usually held several times a week in good weather, was always a colorful formation, witnessed by nearly all the enlisted personnel of the regiment from the porches of their barracks. Guard Mount was one of the most pleasing of bugle calls, and it sounded usually at half past four in the afternoon. First sergeants inspected their details, which were then reported at a designated location to the commander of the guard, who formed them into a platoon. Then, at a signal from the regimental adjutant, the band, already in its place on the parade ground, sounded Adjutant's Call and halted on line between the platoon and the regimental sergeant major, who received the report from the commander of the guard. Then there was the report to the adjutant, the inspection of the guard, the selection of the commanding officer's orderly, Parade Rest, Sound Off—the three cords, followed by the band "trooping the line" and countermarching back into position, and again the Sound Off—all being one of the most stirring of military ceremonial movements. Then the Pass in Review. During the Sound Off and the March in Review, the old and the new officers of the day stood at Parade Rest, but with their arms folded across their chests at shoulder height. Then there was an exchange of salutes between the old and the new officers of the day, the relief of the old guard, and the verification of prisoners in the guardhouse, the formation of the guard into reliefs. Then the report to the commanding officer, with both men saluting: "Sir, I report as old officer of the day," presenting the Guard Report. "Anything special to report?" "No, Sir." Or the reporting of any unusual incidents. Then, "Very well, you are relieved." Then, "Sir, I report as new officer of the day." Salutes. About face.

Midyear of 1920 was to see the end of Schofield Barracks as a garrison for cavalry alone, and midyear 1921 was to see the formation of the

Hawaiian Division well under way. First came the Thirty-fifth Infantry, which occupied the adjoining cantonment area. Then came the Thirteenth Field Artillery Brigade, commanded by Col. Beverly F. Browne, to occupy the old artillery cantonment area of temporary buildings in the Upper Post, where the Seventeenth Cavalry had drilled recruits for a year. Then came the Twenty-seventh Infantry (the Siberian Wolfhounds), and the Fourth Infantry, to occupy other newly completed quadrangles.

Colonel Browne was a graduate of the Military Academy, class of 1901, and a lifetime artilleryman. He was a man of fine appearance, with a most attractive personality and with an abiding love for the game of polo. Through his influence, new mounts were obtained and trained, an entirely new concept of team play was developed, young players were improved, and a new enthusiasm was brought to the game. Through the interest and devotion of this able officer, polo teams from Schofield Barracks were eventually able to compete with the fine civilian teams of the islands on even terms.

After our wars, military authorities have recommended to the Congress which military organization their experience indicated was necessary to ensure national security. The Congress, still under the influence of wartime tensions and with some patriotic emotionalism, has usually looked on such recommendations with favor. World War I was no exception. The National Defense Act of 1920 modernized the military policy of the United States and provided for reorganization of the armed forces, including, as previously mentioned, an army of 14,000 offices and 365,000 men. The single promotion list, which replaced the separate lists for each of the branches of the army, was an important feature of this legislation since it equalized promotional opportunities for all, an important morale factor. The army set about optimistically to reorganize under the provisions of this new military policy. But the rub came when Congress began to consider appropriations for an enlarged military force in peacetime. Appropriations for such a large army were never seriously considered, and there was even doubt that appropriations to support an army of 150,000 would be forthcoming. The result was another reorganization, in which the War Department sought to retain as much of the organization prescribed by law as possible.

The strength of the cavalry was reduced from seventeen regiments to fourteen by inactivating the three regiments with the highest numbers, the Fifteenth, Sixteenth, and Seventeenth Cavalry Regiments. Under the plan of "inactivation," one of the remaining cavalry regiments would sponsor the inactivated regiment, that is it would receive the records, funds, and personnel of the inactivated unit. The hope was that future appropriations might permit reactivation, in which case the sponsoring regiment would provide the cadre, return the records, and share the funds.

Orders were received in due course, transferring the Seventeenth Cavalry to the Presidio of Monterey in California, where the records, personnel, and funds of the regiment would be transferred to the Eleventh Cavalry, which was designated as the sponsoring regiment. So it was that the summer of 1921 was a sad one for the Seventeenth Cavalry. Horses and all government property were turned in to the post quartermaster. Troops disposed of property owned by the troop funds to other organizations on the post. A few of the more recently assigned officers were transferred to other duties in the department. Officers' household goods were packed and turned over to the post quartermaster for shipment. Once more, staff cars carried families to the wharf side, while the railway transported the troops to the city, where they detrained. Troops, baggage, officers and families, unit records—all that was left of the proud Seventeenth Cavalry Regiment—were soon embarked on a sister ship of the transport that had brought the regiment to the islands, the United States Army Transport *Thomas.*

Bands were playing on the wharf . . . , there were leis and flowers aplenty . . . , Hawaiian boys were diving for coins . . . , friends on shore were waving farewells to those on shipboard who were lining the rails. All of the same bustling and movement and confusion were there, but not the gaiety of arrival. There was only a sense of sadness and regret as the ship slowly backs out into the harbor and sails out to pass Diamond Head while the bands on shore play on . . . Aloha!

The Hawaiian interlude had ended.

3. BACK TO THE BORDER

War is a business and must be learned like any other Profession.

—*Napoleon*

1. That soldiers should make it their function to exert themselves to the utmost of their loyalty and patriotism.
2. That they should strictly observe decorum.
3. That they should prize courage and bravery.
4. That they should treasure faith and confidence.
5. That they should practice frugality.

—*Order issued by the emperor of Japan, 1882*

The records and funds of the troops of the Seventeenth Cavalry were soon taken over by the troops of the Eleventh Cavalry, in accordance with the order that deactivated the regiment. The Eleventh Cavalry was also able to absorb some of the enlisted personnel and a few of the officers of the Seventeenth Cavalry, within the strength authorized by the new tables of organization for a cavalry regiment. However, there were several hundred men and quite a few officers in excess of the Eleventh Cavalry requirements. While these extra officers and men were attached to the Eleventh Cavalry for duty, most of them felt that the transferred funds of the Seventeenth were more welcome than they by the Eleventh, and they were left very much at loose ends, awaiting orders for new stations.

The Presidio of Monterey was a very pleasant place to wait. It was another old cavalry post. Barracks buildings, quarters, and stables were of frame construction for the most part, and many were showing signs of wear and tear, and even with the influx of the men of the Seventeenth Cavalry, many of the buildings were unoccupied. The post was pleasantly situated on a hillside overlooking Monterey Bay and the adjacent town of Monterey. The town was close by the post, so that horse-drawn Daugherty wagons, familiar on the old army posts from frontier days, afforded bus transportation for individuals to and from the town. The only really disagreeable feature of life in the Presidio stemmed from the proximity of the sardine factories on the bay side. These wafted rather overpowering aromas over the post whenever the wind was blowing inland, as it often did!

The Monterey area was a great tourist resort. The Del Monte Hotel, a magnificent establishment, was within a few miles. It operated golf courses, tennis courts, polo fields, riding stables, swimming pools, and many other resort attractions. The management extended many courtesies to the officers of the garrison. Pebble Beach, with its golf courses and beaches, was close by the post. There were many miles of pleasant trails through the surrounding woods. And many other resort and recreational areas were within easy reach. The Presidio was a pleasant place to wait for orders, even though those who were recent arrivals from Hawaii were not "taken in to the bosom of the family," so to speak. An amusing incident in this regard occurred some six weeks after the Seventeenth Cavalry arrived on the post. The officers had been assigned quarters in which they "camped out" while waiting their permanent assignment. Col. John M. Jenkins commanded the Eleventh Cavalry at this time. A graduate of the class of 1887 at the Military Academy, he was truly a soldier of the "old school" and one of the senior colonels in the army. He was a small man, immaculate in appearance, with a most magnetic and attractive personality, and he was held in high esteem by all who knew him.

Colonel Jenkins noted a certain coolness between officers of the two regiments. Seeking the cause, he learned that none of the officers of the Eleventh Cavalry had called upon the new arrivals, as tradition and customs of the service required should be done promptly, usually within three days. At Officers' Call one day in early November, Colonel Jenkins dismissed all officers who had arrived with the Seventeenth Cavalry, whereupon he apparently called the officers of the post to account. At any rate, the officers and wives of the Eleventh Cavalry were out in force that night, and calling cards descended like a snowstorm upon the unsuspecting Seventeenth Cavalrymen and their wives during the calling hours of the next several evenings.

It was just at Thanksgiving time that orders finally came from the War Department directing four "Surplus Captains, Seventeenth Cavalry" to "proceed to Douglas, Arizona, in command of 460 surplus enlisted men, cavalry . . . reporting on arrival thereat to the commanding officer, First Cavalry Brigade, for duty and permanent station."

So, it was back to the border again.

Douglas had changed little in almost three years, except that it was not so prosperous and had suffered some loss in civilian and military population. The mountains still frowned down on the mesa where Camp Harry J. Jones stood, but the camp was completely changed. The sea of tents was gone, replaced by a brigade camp of temporary wartime construction, single-story barracks. It stood on the same ground where the tent camp had been and was laid out on the same general plan. Some of the old stables were still in use; others had been removed. A quartermaster, ordnance, and service area had been added, the frame warehouses spreading over a considerable area. The substitution of small wooden cottages for officers' tents and adobe cottages of wartime days and of long low wooden barracks for the long rows of pyramidal tents were the only real changes in the regimental areas. But the camp was far from the beehive of activity it had been during the war.

In the recent reorganization of the cavalry, one squadron of the regiments had been inactivated and the Machine Gun Troop removed from each regiment and concentrated in a Machine Gun Squadron of three Machine Gun Troops. So, in this brigade camp of tar-paper-roofed wooden buildings, the First Cavalry Brigade and the First Machine Gun Squadron found themselves with far more space than they could occupy or even take proper care of. Nothing deteriorates more rapidly than unoccupied buildings of flimsy construction, and such buildings do so even when ample funds and labor are available to maintain and guard them. Such was not the case in these days of severe austerity.

Living accommodations for "single men in barracks," as well as for families of officers and noncommissioned officers, left something to be desired. These structures of green wood had seasoned well in the dry desert heat, leaving cracks through which desert winds whistled and deposited great quantities of dust and sand. Just the upkeep was a great burden. Officers' quarters, except for the commanding officer's set, which was of adobe, were frame, very small, and all of identical plan. One could stand in the kitchen and touch the wall on both sides without moving, and then cover the length of the room in two strides.

The three years had seen one important international change. The border was now open, and one could visit Agua Prieta at will. Since we were experiencing the "great noble experiment," many Americans, both military and civilian, visited there almost nightly. The town had little to offer except for the cantinas and restaurants that dispensed alcoholic beverages of all kinds and Mexican food, which was always popular along the border. Agua Prieta had great attraction for the men in the barracks and for many civilians in the city.

The First Cavalry Regiment was the oldest cavalry regiment in the army. It had been organized in 1832 as a battalion of mounted rangers for service in the Black Hawk War. It was expanded into the Regiment of Dragoons the next year, and in 1836 it was designated the First Regiment of Dragoons when a second regiment was authorized. It became the First Cavalry Regiment in 1861, with the military expansion for the Civil War. The crest of the regiment was a "black hawk rising with wings addorsed (turned back-to-back) on a heraldic wreath of gold, on an eight pointed orange star surrounded by a black dragoon sword belt bearing the motto 'Animo et Fide' (with courage and faith) with the old dragoon belt buckle of 1836."

Col. A. V. P. Anderson commanded the First Cavalry and the brigade. An 1891 graduate of the Military Academy, he was a man of medium height and build, rather short of leg for a cavalryman, and always carefully dressed in well-cut uniforms of superior quality. He was extremely active, very energetic, nervous in movement, had a pleasant disposition but was somewhat lacking in humor. Rather balding, his most prominent feature was a nose, which gave rise to the sobriquet "Hooky." A widower, his family consisted of a daughter who subsequently married a lieutenant of the regiment.

The lieutenant colonel of the regiment was another who brought back thoughts of the "Old Army." Julian E. Gaujot was indeed a personality, and few men had longer service on the border or knew it as intimately as he. He wore the Medal of Honor, which he had won in 1911 when Pancho Villa's forces had attacked Agua Prieta. When Villa's fire was endangering American lives in Douglas, Gaujot had ridden alone across the mesa to inform Villa that if another shot endangered American lives, American troops would intervene at once. Colonel Gaujot was a man of slender build, very dark, almost Indianlike in appearance, with sharp, regular features and penetrating black eyes. He was always immaculate, the perfect picture of a cavalryman. He had a biting and sarcastic tongue which never spared those he considered derelict in their duty, but in spite of this, he was eminently fair in his relations with subordinates and was a brilliant soldier in every respect. He was a frequent visitor to Aqua Prieta, where he was very well and favorably known.

During the early postwar years, the War Department was placing great stress on rifle marksmanship. Although American youth presumably grew up familiar with weapons of all types, the distressing fact was that marksmanship in the army had fallen to a very low level. There were always a very few fine marksmen who distinguished themselves, but they were few in number, and most soldiers were actually very poor shots. In firing a qualification course of four slow-fire and three rapid-fire ranges at 200, 300, 500, and 600 yards, with a maximum possible score of 350 points, the lowest score for qualification was 200, "marksman." "Sharpshooter" required a score of 275, and "expert rifleman," 300. These three scores entitled soldiers who earned them extra pay of $2, $3, and $5 per month respectively. Even with this inducement, which was substantial in those days, the number of men who qualified was distressingly low, and few of the troops ever qualified more than 35 or 40 percent of their men. A figure of 15 to 20 percent was more likely for the troops, even though the army's minimum standard was 80 percent!

In preparation for the "target season," a board of officers was convened "for the purpose of formulating plans for the improvement of the commands in rifle and pistol practice." Nothing much came of this board, but as usually is the case, an individual provided the answer which the board was unable to find in all its deliberations.

Maj. Verne R. Bell joined the regiment that spring of 1922. He had entered the army during the postwar expansion after the Spanish American War. He was one of the finest shots in the United States Army and had won many medals in competition. Major Bell was also a very fine pianist, a talent in which he took great pride. He was a small man of rather colorless personality, and his artistic temperament and talents did not impress themselves much upon young cavalrymen, at least not on first acquaintance. However, he not only knew how to shoot, he knew how to teach others to shoot. And this was a talent that was impressive and one the regiment was sadly in need of!

Major Bell was placed in charge of all range practice. He ensured that the men received the correct preparatory instruction. Then, when range practice began, he used only a small part of the ammunition allowed for the preliminary course. He watched the progress of every individual, and whenever he was sure that a group was sufficiently trained, he had them fire for record. Thus, ammunition was preserved to provide additional instruction for men who required more attention and instruction. The result was that the regiment qualified more than 90 percent of the men for the first time in its history. This was twice as many men as any of the junior officers had ever before been known to qualify.

It was rather sad that all of Major Bell's military qualifications were not on the same level with his knowledge of rifle marksmanship. He had the misfortune to fall under the so-called Class B Law, by which the War Department hoped to eliminate officers with records that were not entirely satisfactory or at least were below the level it hoped to maintain. His fate was evidence that shooting ability and piano playing were not sufficient to make a well-rounded cavalry officer—nor would they ensure success in the military profession.

There was a Junior Polo Tournament held under the auspices of the First Cavalry Division at Fort Bliss in June of 1922. The regiment entered a team, as did other regiments and organizations of the division. There were no funds available for the transportation of horses by rail, at a cost of perhaps two hundred dollars. Nor were there trucks available to transport them by road. So, the polo ponies were marched overland, a distance of some two hundred miles. This little polo detachment of twenty or so ponies accompanied the communications platoons of the First and Tenth Cavalry Regiments, which together formed the First Cavalry Brigade at the time. The platoons were making the march to participate in a division communications exercise. Forage, rations, and occasionally water were delivered at appropriate sidings along the El Paso and Southwestern Railroad for the ten-day march. And to make it all worthwhile, the regimental team won the tournament against the favorites in Fort Bliss. Then the same team won the Senior Tournament, which was held that fall.

The Cavalry School at Fort Riley, Kansas, was just beginning to make its influence felt in the cavalry service at this time. It was beginning its third year in September, 1922, and was offering courses for troop officers, field officers, and National Guard and Reserve officers. It also had courses for such specialists as cooks and bakers, horseshoers, and saddlers. However, only two or three graduates from the first basic course for troop officers had joined the regiment, and they had not made a great impression on us. The great dearth of training material available in the cavalry at this time, the serious austerity, is indicated by a comment of the commandant of the Cavalry School, Col. George H. Cameron, published in the *Cavalry Journal* of July, 1921:

> Many requests are being received for a list of the text books in use at the school. It has been necessary to answer that, except for the

> government manuals on the particular subject, text books are not used. Instruction has been carried out by practical exercises and by lectures and either written problems or examinations. These lectures mimeographed and distributed from time to time throughout the course, become available as texts on their particular subjects. Gradually, this material, which represents research work from varied sources, is being compiled, and next year it is expected that it will be issued in pamphlets of a less temporary nature than the old mimeographed sheets.

The regimental commander, Colonel Anderson, left in March to attend the Field Officers' Course at the Cavalry School. He returned to the command filled with enthusiasm for the instruction that he had received—and also filled with an energetic ambition to transmit his knowledge to the command! During July and August, he turned out all officers of the Camp on most drill afternoons for a tactical ride. At the assembly point, he would outline an assumed tactical situation orally and indicate that solutions would be required at the first "check." Then he would command "Ride in a Flock!" and off we would go, following him at a mad gallop in loose "flock" formation through the hummocks of cactus and greasewood—the real boondocks! At the point the colonel had selected, he would halt, we would gather around him, and then he would call upon various officers for their solution to the requirement he had posed. After hearing them and briefly discussing each, off we would go on another wild gallop, another solution, another discussion, and so on, for a full afternoon and perhaps fifteen miles of cross-country ride.

During the fall of 1922, the War Department decided to abandon Camp Harry J. Jones for two reasons: first, economy, because of the excessive cost of maintaining the temporary construction when a more permanent and far more economical post was available; and second, the desire to move the regiment to Camp Marfa, Texas, where it would be more conveniently located with respect to the Cavalry Division and the Fourth Cavalry at Fort Clark. The two regiments together would form the First Cavalry Brigade. Another reason was the availability of more adequate divisional training areas.

Orders were issued for the change of station. And the change itself would be made by marching—for reasons of economy. Accordingly, we began to pack and make preparations for the move. But political influence in Douglas was brought to bear, and the orders were canceled. Army posts were always an economic asset to the adjacent civilian communities and, at times in our history, had been essential for their protection. The War Department apparently conciliated the civilian opposition to the transfer of the cavalry units by arranging to move a portion of the Twenty-fifth Infantry Regiment from Nogales to Camp Harry J. Jones, for orders were again issued for the immediate departure of the command. The date of departure was then set for Christmas Eve, but whether through the influence of the local merchants, complaining about the effect on the economy of our before-Christmas departure, or simply a softening of some hearts in higher headquarters, a delay was authorized. The command took to the road on December 26, 1922.

The march was made in easy stages, and there were only a few unusual incidents. At the time we were equipped with "trailmobiles." They were hard-rubber-tired, four-wheel vehicles with a capacity of about one and a half tons that had been designed for trailing behind the World War I Liberty trucks. They were also capable of animal draft, and those in use in the command were drawn by mules. Each troop, the regimental headquarters, and the officers' mess had one of the vehicles. As a matter of daily routine, kitchens were struck immediately after the morning meal and loaded on the trailmobiles, which set out immediately for the next campsite. There the camp was laid out, kitchens were set up, and the cooks set about preparing the evening meal. Meanwhile the troops, moving at a more leisurely pace, struck camp, loaded pyramidal tents on the escort wagons, and sent the wagon train off after the trailmobiles. Then the troops cared for animals, policed the campsite, saddled, packed, and took to the road. There was a noon halt, during which animals were fed a light feed of grain and men consumed the lunch carried in their saddle bags. By the time the command reached camp, kitchens were up, and the outline of the camp established. By the time picket lines were erected, animals watered and groomed, the wagon trains arrived with tentage. It was soon pitched, and the command was ready for another night on the winter march.

In midwinter, nights can be very cold in the border area, and this was the case when the regiment set out from Camp Harry J. Jones. Low temperatures caused no small amount of discomfort the first night, and this led to one of the unusual incidents of the march.

The second night on the road, while the regiment was encamped at Rodeo, New Mexico, about two dozen men of the regiment took "French Leave," hopped a passing freight, and headed back westward. Most rejoined us of their own volition after we reached our destination. Others were apprehended in due course and returned to military control at Camp Marfa. There they were all tried for desertion or absence without leave, and all received appropriate disciplinary sentences.

There was a layover in Fort Bliss, the station of the division headquarters and the Second Cavalry Brigade. There our command was inspected by the commanding general, First Cavalry Division, Maj. Gen. Robert L. Howze, and we were entertained by the Fort Bliss garrison. General Howze had organized the division in 1920 and had been its commander since organization. This distinguished officer had served in an Indian campaign, in Cuba, the Philippines, Puerto Rico, Mexico, France, and Germany. He had been awarded the Medal of Honor, two Silver Stars and the Distinguished Service Medal. A broad-shouldered fine-looking man, stocky of build, with rugged features, he was a true cavalryman in every respect, greatly admired by subordinates and respected by superiors. The division reflected his intelligence, initiative, and independence of thought, and his deep and sound military knowledge and high qualities of leadership.

The second half of the four-hundred-mile march was made without incident of particular interest until the final day. The command was camped at Valentine, Texas, a siding on the Southern Pacific Railroad about forty miles west of Marfa. The original plan had been to make this final distance of forty miles in two short marches. However, Colonel Anderson and everyone else were becoming eager to be settled again. Both men and animals were in fine condition, and the weather was good, so Colonel Anderson decided to make the march in a single day. Accordingly, the trailmobiles, with their loads of kitchens, food and other equipment the troops would need on their arrival at Marfa, moved out shortly before dawn. The command marched a couple of hours later, expecting to arrive in Marfa with the trailmobiles.

However, as the day went on, the regiment did not overtake the trailmobiles, and to our horror, they were nowhere to be found when we reached Camp Marfa and were assigned barracks areas. The officer in command of the trailmobiles had taken a wrong turn just after leaving Valentine and had angled off in the direction of Ruidosa, a small town on the border at an angle of about forty-five degrees from the proper direction. How he could have made such an error no one could understand, because the road to Marfa ran alongside the Southern Pacific Railroad. Scouts were dispatched in search of the lost train, but it was near midnight before the trailmobiles, with their important loads, reached camp. They had covered a distance of about seventy-five miles! On the celebration of the regiment's Organization Day in March, the officers celebrated the incident at their party by a verse in the "First Cavalry Dribbles," sung to the well-known war tune "Hinky, Dinky, Parlez Vous:"

> The Trailmobiles on rubber wheels, parlez vous,
> The Trailmobiles on rubber wheels, parlez vous,
> The Trailmobiles on rubber wheels, moved out of camp with
> groans and squeals,
> Hinky Dinky, parlez vous.
>
> And on the road they thought they saw, parlez vous,
> And on the road they thought they saw, parlez vous,
> And on the road they thought they saw Napoleon?
> No! Twas Dicky Gaw,
> Hinky, Dinky, parlez vous!

Lieutenant Gaw was the scout dispatched to find the lost train.

The First Cavalry arrived in Camp Marfa, adjacent to the town of Marfa, Presidio County, Texas, on January 23, 1923. The town was the county seat and located on the Southern Pacific, which cuts across the upper or open end of the Big Bend country of Texas. Big Bend was cattle country, and Marfa was a typical western cattle town. The military post, Camp Marfa, was built as a temporary camp during the war, replacing the tent camps of earlier periods. The camp was constructed mostly of adobe, with cement floors and plastered walls. There was a regimental headquarters building in quadrangular form, with an inner patio upon which the offices opened. The camp guardhouse was close by the headquarters building, and at a short distance the row of a dozen or more low barracks buildings and the parallel line of stables and corrals led away. Barrack buildings were U-shaped, with squadrooms in the wings and a day room across the base. There was a short row of eight or ten quarters for senior noncommissioned officers just below the regimental headquarters.

The main avenue from Marfa to the camp passed in front of regimental headquarters, and just across the street from the headquarters building was a rather nice old farmhouse, which was later to be the quarters of the regimental executive officer. Just beyond, there was the Officers' Club and bachelor officers' quarters, built around a patio. Between the Officers' Club and the troop barracks was the enlisted mens' recreation hall. Up the hill, at some distance and at an angle to the barrack line and at a distance of several hundred yards, was a row of twelve cottages for regimental married officers and a larger set at the top of the hill for the regimental commander. These were all cement-floored, stuccoed adobe and, except for the Regimental Commander's set, of identical design. Between the end of this row of officers' quarters and the Officers' Club, there were several other small cottages, which had been constructed of salvaged lumber, for officers' quarters, the camp hospital, which was also a quadrangle built around a patio, the fire station, and a swimming pool.

The reservation, about a mile square in area, provided ample space for drill and normal garrison training, and the Big Bend to the south provided plenty of room for cavalry marches and maneuvers of all kinds. All in all, Camp Marfa, located as it was on the edge of a nice cattle town, within walking distance of the railroad station, was a very pleasant setup for a regimental post.

Regimental Headquarters Troop conducted an interesting test on a long march. Col. Albert E. Phillips, the foremost authority in the army on pack transportation, considered the *aparejo* totally unsuitable for carrying military loads, especially for use on horses. He had designed a pack saddle which was undergoing tests. The First Cavalry, however, was still equipped with the *aparejo*, and horses were used for pack animals. The Communications Platoon contained two radio sets, one for communicating with higher headquarters and one for communicating with the squadrons, when one was detached. One pack load was the generator, a weighty, top-heavy affair on four legs, which was mounted astride the *aparejo*. The other two loads were the set itself, spare parts, and other equipment, in four rectangular chests, carried as side loads on two horses. The Pioneer and Demolition Platoon had two sections each, with two packhorses carrying axes, shovels and picks in chests as side loads, and two packhorses carrying chests of explosives, chiefly TNT, as side loads. The troop carried these loads the full distance on the long test march, but the prevention and treatment of horses for sore backs and tails required an inordinate amount of time and care. Further, the rate of march was comparatively slow over relatively easy, open roads. The regiment was easily convinced that Colonel Phillips was correct in his belief that the *aparejo* was not suitable for pack transportation with horses in the cavalry troops. The Phillips pack saddle was adopted shortly thereafter as standard equipment for cavalry and artillery pack transportation.

The weather turned bitterly cold immediately after the arrival of the regiment at Camp Marfa, dropping well below zero. Although the stuccoed adobe buildings were far more substantial than the temporary buildings in Camp Harry J. Jones, much damage resulted from the abnormally low temperatures. Kitchens in some of the officers' quarters had mounds of ice three feet high as a result of bursting water pipes and water heaters the morning after the big freeze. Fortunately, few families had yet arrived. There was damage in nearly all the troop barracks in spite of precautions during the night. The facilities of the post plumber were taxed far beyond capacity. However, the soldier's proverbial ability to turn his hand to many arts and crafts stood the regiment in good stead, as did his ability to make do with the limited resources which seemed constantly to be imposed by reasons of economy. Supply sergeants rustled materials, and troop help soon repaired the damage.

Settling into a new station always required a certain amount of adjustment, rehabilitation, and even construction, especially when a camp had stood vacant for any length of time. Funds and materials were always strictly limited and in short supply during this period of postwar readjustment. For the first month or so, these activities occupied much of the attention of the regiment. There was daily drill or horse exercise, care of animals, and a great deal of "fatigue detail," the military term for labor. Then came intense work to complete range practice with rifle, pistol, and light machine gun, and mounted qualification courses with pistol and saber, all so that the regiment could get on with preparations for large-scale maneuvers, which headquarters of the First Cavalry Division was planning for the fall.

Bandits were still active occasionally in northern Mexico during this period, but their raiding across the border had been uncommon for some years, except for occasional cattle rustling. A few months after the regiment arrived in Camp Marfa, however, word came to Colonel Anderson through secret sources of information that a party of Mexicans who were active in the area of Presidio del Norte, some fifty miles to the south, were planning to raid the ammunition magazine building at Camp Marfa during a certain period. It was a large building, encased in galvanized iron, and stood on a ridge at the southern end of a small reservation, isolated from our troop area by something over a half mile. In it were stored large amounts of ammunition and explosives of all kinds used by the troops.

While it is most unlikely that Colonel Anderson considered the danger to be very great considering the distance from the border of some sixty miles, it was within the realm of possibility, and on more than one occasion, cavalrymen had suffered from failure to heed such warnings in service along the border. Accordingly, the colonel directed the Headquarters

Troop to have its Pioneer and Demolition Section fortify the magazine area with wire entanglements, chevaux-de-frise, *fougasse*, and similar field-engineering improvisations such as were used in trench warfare on the Western Front. This was done, and a guard was maintained in the magazine area during the particular "dark of the moon" period, but no raid occurred. Some of the officers thought that the colonel might be trying to impress higher headquarters with his energy and foresight, but even they agreed that it was better to be safe than sorry.

In preparation for the maneuvers that were planned for the autumn, it was necessary to obtain permission from the ranchers over a wide area for camping on and maneuvering over their lands. Maneuvering cavalrymen and their trains required a great deal of space. The area of Presidio County was selected because it provided suitable maneuver space, was less mountainous than Brewster County to the east, and was easily accessible and centrally located for the division. However, those same maneuvering cavalrymen and their trains were just about as popular with ranchers as herds of sheep might have been, and for the same reason: the destruction of grass and the use of water, upon which the economic welfare of the ranchers depended. While the ranchers required no small amount of persuasion for this permission to maneuver over their ranges, encamp in their valleys, and make use of their watering ponds—called tanks in range language—they were cooperative, for troops had always provided protection against marauding bandits. And these ranchers were also patriotic men!

Maj. Adna R. Chaffee was the assistant chief of staff, G-3, First Cavalry Division. He was a member of a distinguished army family, the son of Lt. Gen. Adna R. Chaffee of Spanish-American War and Boxer Rebellion fame. Major Chaffee was a graduate of the Military Academy, class of 1906, the Mounted Service School, classes of 1908 and 1909, School of the Line, 1921, and later, the Army War College, 1925, and also the French Cavalry School. He was tall and slender, a perfect picture of a cavalry officer. He had a fine, strong face, a magnificent bearing, a pleasing manner, and a fine voice. He was considerate of all with whom he came in contact and was very popular among fellow officers of all ranks, who all considered him to be one of the "brains" of the army. His relations with General Howze were close. Chaffee was well known along the border, particularly so in the Big Bend country, where he had many friends. It fell to his lot to conduct many of the more difficult negotiations for the maneuver area. He did, however, receive much assistance from Colonel Anderson, Colonel Gaujot, and other officers of the regiment.

Even while negotiations were in progress for permission to use the lands, detachments from the division engineers, the Eighth Engineer Battalion (Mounted), were busily engaged in surveying the maneuver area and preparing maps for use in the maneuvers.

General Howze considered that the principal reason for having a cavalry division in the army was to be able to concentrate it annually in order to give instruction to commanders at all levels in the handling of their units for protracted periods in the field; to give all officers a visualization of the employment of cavalry under war conditions; and to give instruction to all in the service and supply units as nearly as possible under wartime conditions. Major Chaffee and some assistants visited the maneuver area in June to reconnoiter the area and plan the problems—and to assist further in gaining the good will of the ranchers. Staff officers visited the area in August to fit the details of the problem to the terrain. All arrangements for the maneuvers, scheduled for late September, proceeded satisfactorily.

Shortly before the maneuvers were scheduled to begin, Colonel Anderson was ordered to Fort Leavenworth, Kansas, to attend the Command and General Staff School. Col. Leroy Eltinge succeeded him in command of the regiment. He was a large, robust man, florid of complexion, rather sedentary in habit, but keenly intelligent, studious, and observant, a real intellectual. He had a magnetic personality, with a jovial and pleasant disposition. He had been on General Pershing's staff and was said to have drawn the plan for the Meuse-Argonne offensive that had turned out so well. He had also been on the faculty of the Command and General Staff School, where he had written *The Psychology of War.* All these, together with a most charming wife and daughter, assured Colonel Eltinge of a warm welcome to the regiment.

The First Cavalry Brigade assembled at Marfa on September 22, 1923, all but our regiment having marched from Fort Clark, Texas, a distance of some 260 miles to the east. The Second Cavalry Brigade marched from Fort Bliss at El Paso, covering a distance of about 170 miles to a point about twenty miles north of Marfa, also assembling there on September 22. The first phase of the maneuver found the two brigades maneuvering against each other in extremely realistic situations that provided training in all kinds of combat. In the second phase, the division maneuvered as a unit in a one-sided field exercise designed to afford training in maneuvering as a unit and to show the power of the division artillery and other weapons in an exercise involving the use of live ammunition.

General Howze acted as senior umpire, with members of the division staff as assistants. A troop of the Fourth Cavalry had accompanied the troops from Fort Clark to take care of the very considerable array of visitors and observers. These were quartered in the Officers' Club and the big house across from Regimental Headquarters, as subsequently the quarters of the regimental executive, and in a hotel in town. The group of visitors and observers was taken daily by motor to the area where contact was expected for the day. Troopers of the Fourth Cavalry awaited them there with mounts in readiness.

There was a critique in the field at the Division Command Post near Alamito at the conclusion of the two-sided maneuver and another in Marfa after the division field exercise. The maneuvers were the largest-scale mounted maneuvers heretofore attempted and the largest concentration of cavalry since the Pershing Expedition. It was a most valuable experience and provided much necessary testing of equipment, weapons, tactical concepts, men, and animals.

The Cavalry Division remained encamped in Marfa for nearly a week following the maneuvers. The whole area of the small reservation was a sea of tentage and picket lines. During the week, there was a division parade and review, baseball, boxing, and polo tournaments, a field meet, and a horse show. Relations between the officers and men of the division and the citizens of Marfa were extremely pleasant and agreeable. Many officers' wives from Fort Bliss and Fort Clark were guests on the post, and still others stayed in hotels in Marfa. There were many teas, dances, and other entertainments during the period. It was a pleasant and instructive period, but the First Cavalry Regiment was relieved when guests departed and we were left once more to a peaceful garrison routine.

One of the most enjoyable features of life in the Big Bend was the hunting season. Doves and quail were plentiful and, in season, afforded much sport and many delectable repasts. There was much open range, and ranchers were generous with permission to hunt over their lands. It was possible to make a tour of perhaps fifty or sixty miles during an afternoon, covering a dozen or more ponds which offered good duck hunting most times. One never came home empty handed. About eight miles south of Marfa the San Esteban Dam impounded a lake with an area of perhaps a square mile. It was a favorite spot for hunting and some fishing.

Military life ever changes and ever remains the same. In the cavalry service before the First World War, officers usually remained assigned to one regiment for many years, often throughout their service. If another assignment took an officer away from the regiment for a period of duty, he usually retained his regimental assignment and returned to the regiment when the detail was finished. In the postwar reorganization, however, fewer regiments and their reduced strength required fewer officers for duty with troops, while wider responsibilities in connection with the training of National Guard, Reserve officers, and school and staff duties required the services of a great many. Thus, rotation was necessary to afford officers equal opportunities in the various categories of service. Tours of duty at permanent stations were normally four years. In consequence, every year saw officers depart for new assignments and others arrive to fill their places. Enlistments were for a period of three years. A proportion of professional soldiers always reenlisted when their terms of enlistment expired. Some reenlisted for other stations. Many men, however, left to return to civilian life. Their places were taken by recruits, who usually arrived in detachments once or twice a year. Twenty-one dollars for privates, and thirty dollars for privates first class, and somewhat higher rates for noncommissioned officers were the monthly stipends. The accumulation of wealth, therefore, was never a factor that attracted men to military life!

The unchanging nature of post and regimental life was maintained by the traditions and customs of the service, which are the necessary measure of conformity that any organizational life requires. They recognized the natural human tendency to cling to established habits in the indoctrination that all newly joined members received in the history, traditions, and customs of the regiment and the service. Loyalty and pride in organization were never difficult to create and maintain, for Americans like to be proud members of a superior organization.

Lt. Col. Gaujot, a major, and several captains left the regiment during the summer of 1924 to attend courses at the Cavalry School, for duty with the National Guard, or for duty with the organized reserves. Their places were taken by others, and several recent graduates of the Military Academy joined the regiment during this period.

Lt. Col. Arthur Poillon was the replacement for Colonel Gaujot. Poillon was a wealthy New Yorker who had served in a New York Infantry Regiment during the Spanish-American War and been commissioned in the Regular Cavalry in 1901. He had graduated from the Mounted Service School in 1910, was promoted to captain in 1911, and was thereafter detailed on military attaché duty. He held important attaché assignments during the war with such distinction as to merit the Distinguished Service Medal, and he left an assignment as military attaché in Romania to join the First Cavalry, the only cavalry regiment to which he had ever been assigned.

Colonel Poillon was man of about five feet nine, somewhat inclined to stoutness, for he was a lover of good food, but active, energetic, and jovial, blue eyes always sparkling above a full but neatly trimmed moustache. He was great believer in customs and traditions of the service and was steeped in the history and traditions of the First Cavalry. His glowing personality enabled him to transmit his knowledge and beliefs to the regiment. He was also a great student of the early history of the West and knew much of the old frontier forts. Mounted on Louie, a horse of seventeen hands which he had bought from the regiment as a remount ten years earlier, Colonel Poillon's stocky figure was a familiar sight, recognizable afar and always traveling much faster than the normal rate for either a walk, a trot, or a gallop.

Mrs. Poillon, for whom his pet name was "Tid"—from which the officers of the regiment drew their own somewhat irreverent nickname for him, "Old Tid"—was a lovely, cultured woman, a perfect hostess who brought grace and charm to our social life. The colonel had brought back with the family from overseas a French governess, for their young son, and a French chef. They were no sooner settled into the big ranch house across the street from regimental headquarters and had exchanged calls with the officers of the regiment, than he and Mrs. Poillon began a series of formal dinners, at which they entertained all of the officers of the regiment and their wives. These dinners, with snowy linen, beautiful silver, and glittering appointments, were true gourmet affairs which none of us who had the pleasure of being invited to them will ever forget.

The two of them always entered most wholeheartedly into all regimental activities and social affairs. He shared his knowledge of both the early history of the regiment and of the area with all on many pleasant expeditions and picnics. This delightful couple showed the young officers and their families the beauty of a way of life that few of us had ever known. Knowing them was a valuable and wonderful experience.

Marfa was a pleasant Texas cattle town with a population of perhaps three thousand and was the county seat of Presidio County. It was served by the Galveston, Houston, and San Antonio Division of the Southern Pacific Railroad. Off to the north were the Davis Mountains, with the town of Fort Davis nearby and the ruins of Fort Davis, one of the important frontier posts of the Indian Wars days, nestled in the foothills of the mountains. Twenty-six miles to the east of Marfa was the town of Alpine, the county seat of Brewster County. And south of Marfa were open cattle ranges, broken in places by undulating hills and pitching off occasionally into deep canyons. The rugged, mountainous terrain overlooking the Rio Grande was some sixty miles south of Marfa. There had been some mining in the area but never enough to change its essentially cattle-country nature. One of the uncompleted dreams of the railroad-building era was the "Orient," which was to have crossed the Big Bend and gone through Mexico to the West Coast, ending on the Gulf of Lower California.

Marfa had grown up along the railroad, and one of its two principal streets fronted on the tracks. Main Street, however, unpaved and muddy when the rains came, was perpendicular to the railroad station at the southern end of Main Street, which was a favorite gathering place at train time in the late afternoon. The county courthouse was on the other end of the street. The main highway, which also was unpaved, followed the railroad east and west. The principal north-south road from Fort Davis passed through Marfa and divided south of town, with branches leading off to Alamito and to Presidio del Norte and Ruidosa on the Rio Grande.

Along the two principal streets of the town were the establishments patronized by the military personnel, the townspeople, and the ranchers of the area. Many of the ranchers had town houses and resided there much of the year, especially during the school year. The Busy Bee Café, Popular Dry Good Company, Murphy-Walker, Hans Briam Meat Market, Bailey Novelty Shop, Marfa State and Marfa National banks—all these and others were familiar to the cavalryman of the day.

Marfa, like most other small towns, had its social groupings. One of these was very conservative in its social outlook and viewed military social affairs such as dancing, bridge parties, and cocktail parties with some disfavor. The other group was somewhat more liberal and cosmopolitan in its attitudes and entered into the social activities of the post. Relations between the two groups appeared to be normal, and the relations between the post and both of the groups in the town were excellent. But the differences of opinion did give rise to some interesting and amusing incidents.

Officers of the regiment entertained at dinner and bridge parties in their homes, but the Officers' Club was the center of social activity for the post. Inside the club there were rooms for dancing, mah-jong, bridge parties, and supper parties. There was also a patio, with an outdoor dance floor enclosed on three sides by wings of the building but with one side open, screened only by a lattice. Uninvited guests from the local citizenry, not always the more desirable elements, sometimes gathered on regimental "hop" nights to enjoy the music and view the festivities from which they had been excluded. In those days of prohibition, "the noble experiment," the punch was sometimes spiked with one of the potions ever popular in the border regions, or perhaps even with a little "bathtub gin" to add to the gaiety of the occasion. The dance committee decided that the uninvited kibitzers not only added nothing to the pleasure of the evening, but also were at times a disturbing element. Therefore, the open side of the patio was curtained off with tarpaulins and thus screened from their view. As might have been expected in a small community, this was grist for the gossip mills. Dire rumors circulated of our dark and devious deeds. But they did not effect relations between town and post, and as all rumors do, they eventually subsided.

A considerable portion of the population of Marfa, perhaps as much as a quarter, was of Mexican origin. These people performed most of the common labor in town and on the post and afforded the young wives on the post a source of household help. Most families employed untrained Mexican girls to help with cooking, housework, laundry, and to care for children. Food was always a problem, for little was obtainable from local sources except eggs, chickens, milk, and cream. Lettuce and other garden produce and citrus and other fruits were all shipped in by rail and were available in season. Mexican dishes—chili, tacos, enchiladas, tamales, and others—were as popular as they were in all of the border region. Some of the young wives became quite expert in preparing Mexican dishes for their entertaining. Few who served on the border have failed to acquire a taste for some of this delectable food.

Troops carried on normal training activities, which included the usual equitation, with its slow trotting and suppling exercises; squad, platoon, and troop drill; and squadron and regimental exercises. Only concentrating on range practice and the various qualification courses interfered with the normal training.

In addition, there was always horse exercise, for the cavalryman could not forget his horse, even for a day. This responsibility for something other than himself was one of the features that distinguished the mounted from the dismounted services. Perhaps one day a week, squadron commanders conducted squadron tactical exercises, and there was usually a regimental exercise once a month, in addition to the field-training periods. One of our regimental exercises caused much amusement in the garrison for some time.

The commander of Troop B had bought pigs from his troop funds and was feeding them kitchen waste. The pork would eventually augment his troop mess and fund. He had detailed one man to care for the animals and had promoted him to the grade of corporal. On a day scheduled for a regimental exercise involving a short march and attack in a meeting engagement, the squadron commander was the senior officer present on the post. He accepted the responsibility with enthusiasm. He assembled the officers of the regiment and assured them that he intended to demonstrate how "Riley"—he was a recent graduate of the Cavalry School—conducted such exercises. He explained the assumed tactical situation, and had sent out a detail with flags to represent the enemy. Then he issued orders for the march. When the situation was explained to the troops, the regiment moved out, with Troop B in advance guard, the advance party and point preceding them.

This day happened to be one when even the corporal in charge of the pigs had to attend drill, and it fell to his lot to command the point squad. A few miles west of Marfa, the point signaled "enemy in sight in large numbers." Officers' Call sounded, and all officers assembled at a gallop at the head of the regimental column. The acting regimental commander issued the order for the attack in the approved "Riley" fashion, the officers galloped back to their troops, and the attack was launched in record time. Unfortunately, the "enemy" turned out to be, not the men sent out earlier with the flags to represent the "enemy," but a field dotted with great blocks of white salt for a rancher's cattle. And then the flags suddenly appeared on a flank when the regiment was in a state of total confusion resulting from the error.

The whole exercise was ruined, much to the chagrin of the acting regimental commander, but much to the amusement of the officers of the regiment. When the word got back to the commanding officer of Troop B, who had remained in garrison during the exercise, he asked, "Well, what do you expect when you detail a Hog Corporal to command the point?" The officers never let either the squadron commander or the B Troop commander forget the incident, and the rank "Hog Corporal" was added to the regimental folklore.

The communications detachments of the two squadrons were attached to the Headquarters Troop for administration and training. Normal training exercises involved sending each detachment out along different roads while the Regimental Communications Platoon followed on another. The detachments would practice halting, setting up, and exchanging messages with the regimental sets during ten minutes each hour, which was the normal rest period during cavalry marches.

The Pioneer and Demolition Section of Headquarters Troop consisted of about sixteen men and was organized into two sections to facilitate detailing attachments to squadrons when necessary. In addition to technical training in various aspects of field engineering, this section accomplished a great deal of very practical construction work, such as road repair, building jumps, and similar details.

There was also a Wire Section in Headquarters Troop. It was equipped with about fifteen miles of light wire and the means to lay it from the back of a pack horse, while moving, or from the back of a man, dismounted. A principal purpose of the wire communications was to provide telephone communication between regiment and the squadrons in bivouac and telephone and telegraph communications in defensive situations or in a dispersed situation, such as having an outpost placed out, to give early warning of an impending attack.

Maj. John C. F. Tillson, Jr., commanded the Second Squadron. He was a character in his own right. Of medium size, thin but muscular, rather dark, he was a son of the Old Army, his father before him having been a noted character in the infantry. Major Tillson had attended the Military Academy for two years but had been "found," or dismissed, in 1906. He had then enlisted in the army and had eventually passed examinations and received a commission as a second lieutenant of cavalry in 1909. He had completed the first year-long course at the Mounted Service School in 1914. This course, devoted almost exclusively to equitation, horse training, and activities and crafts connected with the horse, had given Major Tillson consuming interest in such activities and a very sound knowledge of the training and conditioning of race horses and polo ponies. He loved polo, jumping, and all horse activities, although he was never an outstanding individual performer. He could exhibit a warm and pleasing personality when it suited him to do so, but he could be mean and sarcastic to his juniors. He was critical of his superiors, whom he discussed freely with individual officers at times almost to the point of seeming disloyal.

The polo field at marfa was dirt and located on a nice flat just below the stable area. Major Tillson conceived the idea of constructing a half-mile race track around it. He also constructed jumps about the reservation to permit steeple chases of two miles or more. With labor provided by the Pioneer and Demolition Section of Headquarters Troop, occasional fatigue details from each troop, and borrowed road graders and salvaged lumber, we created an exceptionally nice fenced race course, complete with a small clubhouse that provided pleasure for everyone.

To celebrate the completion of the course, the regiment invited a polo team from the Fourth Cavalry at Fort Clark and organized a full-scale race meet, field meet, and gymkhana. There were steeple chases; flat races at various distances; cossack races, in which soldiers stood in their saddles; roman races, in which soldiers stood with one foot on the back of each of a pair of horses; and gymkhana events of all kinds. Occasions such as this were enjoyed by all.

The officers of the regiment saw their wives elect a sheriff of Presidio County—almost. In doing so, they created a disturbance in the civilian community that bordered on physical conflict, muddled plans of higher headquarters to the extent that planning for an important maneuver was almost wrecked, and caused a storm that rumbled across Texas, with echoes and reverberations all the way to far-off Washington. And all without the knowledge of even their husbands.

The town of Marfa and Presidio County, like other cities of much greater size than their nine or ten thousand souls, had political rivalries. Like other communities in the South, the rifts were concentrated in the only party worth mentioning in Texas of that day, the Democratic party. In most western counties the office of Sheriff—with a capital S—is an important political plum and much sought after. It was so in Presidio County that spring of 1923, and the race was so close it seemed that a mere handful of votes might determine the outcome. Members of the rival factions were engaged in a bitter political battle, with no quarter asked and none given.

One of the factions, which was supporting the incumbent sheriff, was the more conservative social group of the town, in which Mr. Brite, the most important rancher in the area, was most influential. In the other faction, Mr. Tom Snyder, who was prominent in the more liberal social group, was very active. The officers of the regiment were quite aware of the political struggle, because both Mr. Brite and Mr. Snyder had daughters married to officers in the regiment. However, it was considered to be a local affair, only of cursory interest to army officers concerned with their own responsibilities and activities.

In this early summer month of 1924, the regiment was hurrying to finish target practice preparatory to intensive preparation for field training. The rifle range at Camp Marfa was less than a mile from the post, just over the hill from the commanding officer's quarters and across the presidio road from the southern edge of the small reservation. Range practice usually began as soon after dawn as visibility permitted and stopped at noon, when afternoon winds and mirages made shooting difficult. Besides, there were many activities incident to military life to occupy the afternoon hours—care of animals, troop schools, administration, courts-martial, and the like. So it was that married officers were nearly always home for lunch. Returning from the rifle range, they stopped at Regimental Headquarters for Officers' Call, which included orders and details for the following day, and for personal mail. Then home for lunch.

On this particular day, I entered the kitchen of our quarters at the northern end of the Officers' Row, where my wife was putting finishing touches to the noon meal for our two small children and ourselves. She was bubbling with suppressed excitement, and I was greeted gaily!

"Guess what?"

I admitted that I could not imagine the cause for her excitement.

"I voted!"

"You WHAT?"

"I voted!"

Then the story unfolded. Mr. Tom Snyder and his wife, whose family included two attractive daughters married to officers of the regiment, entered into all the social activities of the post and were immensely popular. They had come out to the post during the morning, collected nearly all of the wives, and taken them in to Marfa to vote in the election. Mr. Snyder explained that while the laws of Texas excluded "felons, insane persons, and members of the Regular Army" from voting, this ban did not apply to wives. Since they had resided in the state more than a year, in the county more than six months, and in the precinct more than thirty days, they were eligible to vote. And it so happened that there was no law then requiring prior registration. So, nearly all the wives on the post had been taken to the polling place, where they had cast their vote in the Democratic primary. And my wife added: "And after I voted, I asked, 'Now where is my cigar?'"

My heart sank, for I knew the fat was in the fire. All of the husbands felt rather sheepish and somewhat disapproving, but the deed was done, and there was nothing we could do about it. There was much amusement over the incident, especially when it appeared that the votes of these women were just enough to nominate the challenging candidate.

But it wasn't over! The state of relative calm was short- lived. Mr. Brite was not one to stand idle in the face of such a challenge, even though his daughter and a niece had "jined the cavalry." The wires soon began to hum. Some of the ranchers indicated that they were withdrawing permission for the troops to use their ranges for maneuver purposes. Marfa was in an uproar. Appeals were made to the commanding general, First Cavalry Division, and to state authorities. There were continuing discussions with Colonel Poillon who was in temporary command of the regiment.

There was a special Officers' Call to deal with the matter. What had seemed quite a lark to the young wives took on a far-more-serious aspect. The colonel undertook to "read the riot act" to the assembled officers, and undertook to give special attention to Lieutenant "Breezy" Hudson, who was Snyder's son-in-law. But Breezy came right back: "Heck, Colonel, I am not responsible for what my mother-in-law does." And there did not seem to be anything the regimental commander could do about that!

Officials descended on the little post—Inspectors General, judge advocates general, and civilian legal authorities. Officers were lectured on family responsibility, public relations, and their general responsibilities as officers of the United States Army. There was considerable confusion for a few days. Eventually, of course, legal authorities ruled what should have been apparent to the election officials in the beginning: wives of army officers could establish residence and voting rights only in the legal residence of their husbands. Since none of the officers were legal residents of Marfa, or of Texas for that matter, their wives had no more right to vote in a Texas election than did "convicted felons, insane persons, and members of the Regular Army."

For a while, all of this put somewhat of a damper on the social activities and our general relations with the town. However, we all set about mending public relations with as much charm as we possessed. Memories of distaff dabbling in local politics receded into the past, and relations were soon reestablished on the old basis. Officers stationed in Marfa during this little political storm learned thoroughly that it is not well for the military, even its distaff side, to undertake to influence the selection of candidates for political office, particularly in a local election.

Colonel Eltinge was promoted to brigadier general during the summer of 1924, and he left the regiment. He was followed in command by Col. Charles E. Stodter, an 1896 graduate of the Military Academy. He was also a distinguished graduate of the Infantry and Cavalry School in 1907 and of the Army Staff College in 1908. He was interested in sports and joined us in polo. He loved hunting and was a very fine shot. He surprised us by hunting ducks on San Esteban lake with a .22 rifle, drilling them cleanly through the head! His personality was not particularly impressive, since he was somewhat lacking in humor and very inclined to be impatient with anyone who failed to accord him the deference he considered his position as commanding officer warranted.

Sometime after he assumed command, the regiment invited the polo team of the Eighth Cavalry, the division senior champions, to Marfa for a series of games. This team was headed by Maj. Harry D. Chamberlin, the finest horseman in the army and a distinguished polo player. He was a Military Academy graduate, class of 1910, of the Mounted Service School Classes, the French Cavalry School at Saumur, and the Italian Cavalry School at Pinerolo. He was instrumental in introducing the "forward," or Italian, seat into both the American services and the American horse circles for jumping and cross-country riding. He was tall, handsome, a magnetic personality—the very beau ideal of a cavalryman.

We planned to take advantage of Major Chamberlin's presence and have him discuss team play in polo with the officers, and we wanted to use the Officers' Club for the discussion. However, we had not obtained Major Chamberlin's agreement on using the club in advance, and the regimental polo team had also made the mistake of defeating the Eighth Cavalry team in a hard-fought game. So he was unwilling to conduct the "skull session" in the club and suggested that we assemble on the picket lines, where we could talk horse.

Messengers were sent out to notify all the officers. However, when Colonel Stodter reached the picket line, where the officers were assembled, he was very wroth indeed and left no doubt that he thoroughly disapproved of having one of his officers alter any program without his approval. Major Chamberlin's assumption of responsibility for the change, however, his discourse on horses, and his experiences in the various schools he had attended removed the sting, and even the colonel was pleased.

Another incident during Colonel Stodter's tenure had a most disruptive effect on morale among officers and their wives, and it cast quite a shadow over social activities on the post. Officers' wives had a bridge club, which met once a week for an afternoon of bridge and tea. There were never more than four tables. The ladies played progressive auction, with the very high stakes of "a quarter a corner." The high score thus took home less than four dollars on any day, and the low score always received a "booby prize," provided by the hostess for the day. The colonel's wife was president of the club, but there was no formal organization, since the ladies entertained in turn.

Mrs. Stodter was a large woman, not unattractive in appearance, but rather humorless, as was her husband. She felt the responsibility and prestige of her position as the "Colonel's Lady" very keenly. She was strait-laced in her attitude toward social activities, and since she disapproved of "gambling," she took exception to the practice of playing for a quarter. One day when she did not attend, Mrs. Stodter sent word by one of the ladies that there would be no more playing for money in the bridge club.

Well, "Hell hath no fury like a woman scorned" hardly describes the commotion in the bridge club when a dozen or more were scorned—and by one of their own sex. The discussion was a bit on the riotous side as the ladies endeavored to solve the problem of maintaining their rights in the face of this directive. One of the ladies even hopped up on a chair at one of their meetings and in a spellbinding fashion proclaimed, "Mrs. Stodter is a mighty fine lady, but she makes damned poor tea!"

The meeting broke up without the ladies having arrived at any agreed-upon plan of action, and one of the gossips—every post always had at least one—carried the story of the meeting, in detail, to Mrs. Stodter, who was very hurt and upset by the reaction of the ladies of the club. There was much talk for several days in an effort to smooth ruffled feathers, but the Ladies Bridge Club of Camp Marfa, Texas, after an active and agreeable life of some two years, was regretfully laid to rest.

In July of 1924, Brig. Gen. Ewing E. Booth, recently promoted to the rank, assumed command of the First Cavalry Brigade. He divided his time almost equally between the two regiments at Fort Clark and Camp Marfa. This distinguished officer had served in the Spanish-American War in the First Colorado Infantry and had been commissioned in the Regular Cavalry in 1901. He was an honor graduate of the Infantry-Cavalry School, class of 1903, the Staff College in 1905, the General Staff School in 1922. He had been closely associated with Gen. J. Franklin Bell, who had so much to do with establishing the school system in the army. General Booth had much experience as an instructor in the schools and in staff work as well. He was an officer of profound professional knowledge and the author of the text on "Methods of Training," in use at the Command and General Staff School.

General Booth knew exactly what he wanted in the way of planning and conducting training, and he set about carefully and deliberately to indoctrinate the officers of the regiment in correct methods. These were simple enough in outline: compute the training hours available in the training year, based on the training days available, and the hours available each day; subtract the hours reserved by higher headquarters for training larger units, inspections, ceremonies, and all other necessary activities which would interfere with training; what was left were the hours left for training the unit. List all subjects in which training is required and allot an appropriate number of hours for training in each subject. Use this master schedule in preparing the weekly training schedules, and record on it the training in each subject as it is carried out. It sounds very simple and easy, but the troop commanders had their troubles meeting the requirements of this meticulous perfectionist. General Booth was always quiet and patient, but he knew what he wanted. He persisted until the troop commanders fully understood precisely what he wanted of them. All of this was one of the most instructive and valuable experiences any group of troop officers could have.

He had another principle, which he preached on all occasions: "Never use sarcasm when dealing with juniors, especially enlisted men." He maintained that when a superior used sarcasm in correcting individuals of lower rank, he was taking an unfair advantage. He believed that sarcasm hurt feelings because the subordinate could not answer back on even terms, and that men never forgot hurt feelings. It was an illuminating concept, coming as it did from one who had spent so many years in the service when such sarcasm was almost a way of life.

In the winter of 1924/25, the Regimental Polo Team played in the Mid-Winter Polo Tournament in San Antonio. A great many teams from all along the border participated, and several tournaments were played. Among these were the Circuit and the Twelve Goal championships, both of which were limited to teams with a total handicap of no more than twelve goals. The winner in the Circuit Championship was to compete in the national Inter-circuit Championships, to be held in Philadelphia in competition with winning teams from other circuits in the United States. The First Cavalry team lost the Circuit Championship to the Fort Bliss team, headed by Major Chamberlin, but subsequently defeated the same team for the Twelve Goal Championship. The success of the team was the occasion for quite a celebration when we returned to Marfa. Most of the garrison, with the regimental band and many of the townspeople, were out to greet us.

Shortly after we returned to the regiment, we learned that my name was listed with several other captains who had been selected to attend the Troop Officers' Course at the Cavalry School beginning in September, 1925. All were pleased, because it was becoming obvious that such training was essential to an officer's career.

Major Chamberlin was anxious to have me play in the Inter-circuit Championships with the Fort Bliss team, which would represent the First Cavalry Division in the national matches in Philadelphia. In order to meet the eligibility rules for play, I had to be a bona-fide member of the Fort Bliss garrison. Since we were to leave the regiment during the summer in any case, the transfer was not objected to by the regiment. In June, I was transferred to Fort Bliss, assigned to the Eighth Cavalry, and then to the command of Troop E of that regiment. Meanwhile, our household goods were packed by the quartermaster for shipment to the Cavalry School at Fort Riley in the fall.

Mrs. Chamberlin, known as Sally to almost everyone in the cavalry, was truly a lovely woman in every way that a woman can be. She was tall, graceful, blond, lovely looking, athletic, a wonderful horsewoman, and she was loved and respected by all who knew her. She found a furnished house for us near the post, one belonging to an officer who was away on leave for the summer and who wished to rent it for the income. The agent was willing to let it to us for the two months we required. We paid the rent and moved in.

Toward the end of the month, the Express Company telephoned to say our trunks had arrived, but we assured them there must be a mistake, as we were expecting no trunks. The next morning, several large trunks were deposited on the front porch, and these were all stenciled with the name of the officer who was on leave and whose house we were living in. Then the agent informed us that the owner had decided to return from leave and was expected within the next day or so.

After much scurrying around, we found a small brick house in a new development which was under construction. It had been finished, but neither water, gas, electricity, or phone had been connected. The agent rented it to us furnished, and it was, with a grand total of the following: two beds, two bureaus, a dining-room table and four chairs, a small living-room table and three chairs, and all of the kitchen utensils and dishes piled in a dishpan in the kitchen sink. In with them was a sales slip for a total amount for the lot—the enormous sum of $3.47. We were not overburdened with housework, but we managed well enough for the month.

I had the normal duties of a troop commander during a summer training period for the mornings during those two months. Afternoons were devoted to polo practice.

So passed the summer.

4. THE LIFE OF RILEY

I'm Terence O'Reilly, I'm a man of renown,
If they'd let me, I'd have Ireland free,
On the railroads, you'd not pay any fare,
I'd have the United States under my thumb,
And I'd sleep in the President's chair.

Is that Mr. Reilly, can anyone tell?
Is that Mr. Reilly that owns that hotel?
Well, if that's Mr. Reilly, they speak of so highly,
Upon me soul, Reilly, you're doin' quite well.

—*"Is that Mr. Reilly?"**

There had been a mounted officer's school at Fort Riley from shortly after the Spanish-American War until the time of the Pershing Expedition into Mexico in 1916. The Mounted Service School, as it came to be known, had established an enviable reputation in its field, and its graduates were held in high regard by all cavalrymen. The courses there were devoted almost entirely to equitation, horsemanship, and the various arts and crafts associated with animal management. The reorganization of the army under the National Defense Act, in modernizing our national military policy, established a comprehensive, modern school system for the army, and the effects of these schools upon military thought and military training were becoming more and more evident with each year that passed. Officers were coming to realize that graduation from the service schools was im-

*According to *Bartlett's Familiar Quotations*, this anonymous 1882 poem is assumed to be the origin of the phrase "Leading the life of Riley," meaning to have an easy time.

portant not only to the development of their careers but also to their academic standing at the school. They were anxious to have the opportunity to attend their branch school, and they were anxious to do well there. This was the next step on the military educational ladder and therefore in a successful military career.

The "Life of Riley" had already become almost a legend in the tales of the Mounted Service School, which were recounted by graduates for the edification of all young cavalrymen. Its resurrection as the Cavalry School had already, in the first few years of its existence, added to the legends to such an extent that the laurels earned by the prewar makers of legends and tellers of tall tales were endangered. All officers certainly approached their first assignment there with anticipation but also with some uncertainty.

Fort Riley was established in 1852 for the protection of immigrants to the Pacific coast and for the morale effect on the powerful Indian tribes who inhabited the West. It was here that the immigrant trails divided, one going northwest to Oregon, the other westward toward Colorado and Utah and then southwest through New Mexico and Arizona to California. The location selected was just below the point where the Smoky Hill and Republican rivers unite to form the Kansas River, which then flows almost due east for another hundred and fifty miles to empty into the Missouri River at Kansas City. These rivers, which form the southern boundary of the United States Military Reservation at Fort Riley, meander through a flat alluvial plain of incredible fertility. The plain, from two to six miles wide in the area of the reservation, is bordered by precipitous cliffs nearly two hundred feet high. These escarpments are marked near the top by a clearly defined outcropping of a stratum of white limestone characteristic of the area. It is known locally as "The Rimrock."

Just below the confluence of the Smoky Hill and the Republican, the Kansas River forms a horseshoe-shaped bend about one and a half miles in diameter. Three flat-topped ridges extend from the foot of the escarpment into the wide bend for about two-thirds of a mile, then pitch off another lower escarpment into a flat tree-covered bottom. The main line of the Union Pacific Railroad follows the curve of this bluff along the river bottom through this part of the reservation. It is on these three flat-topped ridges that the post of Fort Riley was built, but the construction of the three areas was completed in different periods.

In September, 1925, the post consisted of three principal areas: the westernmost, the Cavalry School proper; a central part, the regimental area of the Second Cavalry Regiment, which acted as school troops; and the easternmost area, in which were Godfrey Court and Rileyville. The area of the Cavalry School, the oldest part of the post, was originally a cavalry regimental area. It was triangular, sitting between two dry water courses leading off the escarpment to the northwest, with the base of the triangle along the lower escarpment overlooking the railroad. Along this lower escarpment were some fifteen or sixteen stables that housed the animals of the school, the veterinary hospital, the horseshoeing shops, and the Horseshoers' School. Then, around the parade, were the barracks for the Ninth Cavalry, the black regiment which was the school detachment, the Bakers' and Cooks' School, the Administration Building, the Academic Building, the Book Department, and various shops and activities. Then came the officers' quarters on Sheridan and Forsythe avenues, which were broad, tree-lined streets with single and double sets of stone quarters; Arnold and Carr Halls, which were bachelor apartments; the Post Chapels; and across Highway U.S. 40, which cut through the post from east to west along the foot of the upper escarpment, two stone apartment buildings known as "The Flats."

The central area of the Second Cavalry, Sherman Circle, was horseshoe-shaped, with the open end overlooking the lower escarpment. Around the semicircle were single and double sets of stone officers' quarters. Troop barracks faced each other across the heels of the horseshoe, and the stable area extended across the heels, overlooking the railroad and the river bottom. This area had been built originally as an artillery post beginning in the late 1880s, and there was still one battery on station as part of school troops. There were accommodations here for a full-strength cavalry regiment. Opposite the tip of the bend in the horseshoe, between it and Highway 40, were Sumner and Waters halls, bachelor quarters of temporary wartime construction. Across Highway 40 from the Second Cavalry area was the Post Hospital.

Godfrey Court was centered in the southern part of the eastern area of the post. Built as a two-thousand-bed hospital during the war, it was of the standard light frame construction, laid out in rectangular form, used for all temporary hospitals of that era. There were four parallel rows of two-story ward buildings, three buildings in each of the two outer rows, two in the inner rows. In the central court between the inner rows, there was a Red Cross building in the shape of a cross, which contained a large room, used for receptions and dances, and two very small apartments. Across the northern end, midway between the end buildings of the outer rows, were the mess halls and kitchens. The forty wards in the ten main buildings had been converted into forty sets of apartments for student officers, so that Godfrey Court housed forty-two families. Rooms in these apartments were made of Beaverboard partitions some seven or eight feet high, that is, little more than half way to the ceilings. Bathrooms were the original ward washrooms, toilets, and showers. There was a row of wash basins and toilets more than ample to take care of the largest family simultaneously. The ten main buildings had full-length porches upstairs and down, and all were connected with the central mess hall by covered runways.

"Rileyville" was about a half mile northwest of Godfrey Court across Highway 40. Between Rileyville and the Post Hospital and on the same side of the highway was the Post Fire Station, conveniently located to the most inflammable buildings in the entire post. Rileyville was a sort of shantytown, a collection of noncommissioned officers' and married soldiers' quarters of temporary construction, to which had been added many others built of salvaged materials. Here lived the married noncommissioned officers and married soldiers of the Ninth Cavalry. These men worked in the various shops and offices, cared for the many animals used in the classes at the school, and performed certain maintenance and janitorial work in buildings and quarters. Many of the wives and daughters were employed in the officers' messes and in the quarters of the officers of the garrison and the school.

The reservation, some twenty thousand acres in area, was roughly an irregular oval in shape, about nine air-line miles from east to west and seven north to south. Except for Smoky Hill Flat, an area of about two square miles in the river bottom south of the post and between the Smoky Hill and the Kansas rivers, the reservation lay north of the Republican and the Kansas rivers.

To the west of the post, the Rim Rock escarpment ran almost due east and west and overlooked a broad bend in the Republican River known as Republican Flats. Here were located polo fields, rifle ranges, pistol ranges, and a race course. North of the Rim Rock, the whole reservation was rolling, grass-covered prairie, broken only by steep-walled canyons in the lower reaches, but with few other areas that checked galloping cavalrymen.

From east to west, the names Three Mile Creek, Packers Camp, Wolf, Coyote, Magazine, Pumphouse, Rock Spring, Governor Harvey, and Breakneck canyons will ever be nostalgic memories to cavalrymen. Names of other landmarks on the reservation were also household words: Sumner

Hill, Morris Hill, Redoubts 1 and 2, Four Way Divide, Pawnee Point, and Sherman Heights.

In the eastern end of the reservation, on a broad flat between the escarpment and the Kansas River, Camp Funston had been the home of the Eighty-ninth Division, National Army, during the war. In 1925, the camp was completely demolished. Paved streets and foundation stones were all that remained, reminding one of a great cemetery, more so because of the Funston Monument standing at the entrance. Just east of the reservation boundary lay Ogden, Kansas, and a few miles farther to the east the thriving little city of Manhattan, which was the site of Kansas State Agricultural and Mechanical College.

South of the reservation, at the tip of the bend in the Republican River and just four miles from Fort Riley, was the town of Junction City. Here most of the post shopping was done, and many post children attended Junction City schools. Eisenhower's Drugstore, Good Eats Café, the First National Bank, Miller's Drugstore, Davis and Meseke—Army Grocers—were just a few of the names familiar to us during those days. And just ten miles upstream, along the banks of the Republican River, was the little village of Milford, about which more later.

Brig. Gen. Ewing E. Booth, somewhat irreverently known as "Briney," had been transferred from the First Cavalry Brigade at Fort Clark to command the Cavalry School. His background, experience, and knowledge of training particularly fitted him for this command. In the organization of the Cavalry School, the commandant occupied a dual role, for in addition to being commandant of the school, he was commanding general of the post. An executive officer, an adjutant, a personnel adjutant, a quartermaster, and a surgeon comprised the staff for post administration. He directed the activities of the school through the assistant commandant, who was assisted by the school secretary and four directors, who headed the school departments.

The assistant commandant was Col. Robert J. Fleming, an 1891 graduate of the Military Academy. This outstanding officer was quiet and reserved in manner and speech. He was rugged in build, and his craggy features and grim mouth gave him a stern appearance that led student officers to refer to him as "Old Death." He was, however, pleasant, active, energetic, an excellent horseman, and devoted to hunting.

Like General Booth, Colonel Fleming thought that cavalry training in the past had placed too much emphasis upon horsemanship and mounted activities and not nearly enough on the use of weapons and the tactical employment of cavalry—cavalry combat. As one edition of *The Rasp*, the student yearbook, put it: "He says we ought to use these heavy Springfield rifles we been carting about for years. This idea kinda startled people here at first who always thought you could lick anybody by just shouldering-in and two-tracking." Few errors in classes, indoors or out, ever escaped his alert eye, but his corrections were always considerate and thoughtful. He was held in high esteem on all sides. His contribution to the development of the Cavalry School was a very material one.

There were three full-year classes during this period: Advanced, Troop Officers, and Advanced Equitation. There was also a National Guard and Reserve Officers Class, of three months' duration, for officers of troop grade, and an Advanced National Guard and Reserve Officers Class, of six weeks' duration, for field-grade officers.

These classes ended in June. From time to time the school conducted refresher courses for senior officers. Besides these classes for officers, the school conducted schools for horseshoers, bakers, cooks, and saddlers. These specialists schools were usually of three or four months' duration, and were administered separately from the officers' courses.

The Advanced Course, for field-grade officers, usually about twenty-five in number, emphasized the study of tactics in the employment of the combined arms in preparation for the Command and General Staff Course at Fort Leavenworth. The entire class was usually sent there directly, and it was supposed to be an exceptionally tough course. However, the Advanced Course also included thorough instruction in the employment of cavalry, in automatic weapons, musketry, methods of training, military history, and field fortifications—not to mention horsemanship, which occupied a goodly portion of the time.

The Advanced Equitation Class consisted of twelve officers, selected from the Troop Officers' Class of the preceding year, for special training in horsemanship for the purpose of developing instructors in the subject. This class received almost no academic instruction, but devoted the entire time to equitation, horsemanship, and related subjects. Each officer was assigned four horses: a remount, a green jumper, and a green polo pony, selected from among the horses schooled in the classes during the preceding year, and an old jumper. The year was naturally a very pleasant one to which all members of the Troop Officers' Class aspired. There were always some keen disappointments at missing it by many in the Troop Officers' Class when final selections for the next year were announced in the spring.

The Troop Officers' Class of 1925 consisted of about fifty-six officers, mostly captains with a few lieutenants. It was divided into two platoons, to facilitate instruction in horsemanship. One platoon used the East Riding Hall and stables nearby; the other, the West Riding Hall and stables across the street. Platoons changed riding halls and horses, except remounts, at midyear. Each officer was assigned a remount, which he was to train during the year. Each platoon had other horses for training in equitation, jumping, cross-country riding, use of weapons mounted, and for riding to hounds or hunting. Except for remounts, the assignment of horses to student officers rotated, so that all officers had the experience of riding practically every horse in the Department of Horsemanship at some time during the year, and under many different conditions. Some of these horses, such as Potomac and Harry Chamberlin, were spoiled, hard-mouthed beasts that could be counted on to give any officer who happened to be astride a wild ride whenever the instructor commanded "Ride in a Flock!" and set off at a gallop across the reservation.

The Department of Horsemanship also conducted courses in animal management, horseshoeing, and pack and wagon transportation for all classes. The senior veterinarian usually conducted the classes in animal management. The course included the study of breeds, the selection of horses, feeds and feeding, first aid, and other knowledge essential for the care of animals in the field. Classes in horseshoeing included both theoretical and practical instruction. It was conducted by the Horseshoers' School, which also did the horseshoeing for the Department of Horsemanship. The theoretical instruction was given by the senior instructor in horseshoeing, Frank Churchill, a civilian government employee who was an instructor of many, many years experience. He fancied himself as an authority on the subject, which, in practice, he was. Few officers who attended his lectures will ever forget the monotone of his voice, well larded with participles, which led students to dub him "Old Putting and Taking." Churchill made spurs and steel horseshoes of fine quality and special design, and he was the author of a small book *"American Methods of Horseshoeing."* At least one pair of Churchill spurs and a copy of the book were considered almost mandatory by all students who hoped to stand well in the horseshoeing course.

The Department of General Instruction taught subjects that could not logically be included under tactics, weapons, and horsemanship. These included: map reading and sketching; methods of instruction; aerial photograph reading; pioneer duties; military history; leadership; discipline and psychology; Army of the United States; mess management; mobilization plans; and riot duty. Military history consisted of lectures on the employment of cavalry in the World War, emphasizing the tactical principles illustrated by cavalry operations in the campaigns. The Army of the United States course was to fit officers for duty with the various components such as the National Guard.

The Department of Cavalry Weapons was responsible for instruction on automatic weapons and the rifle. The course emphasized instruction in the operation, characteristics, power, and limitations of machine guns and automatic rifles and the use of fire-control instruments. It covered principles of tactical employment only in a general way, since the Department of Tactics had responsibility for the subject. The department carried on a great deal of experimental work pertaining to weapons and instruments and worked closely with the Cavalry Board, about which more in a moment.

The Department of Tactics included instruction in the organization of cavalry units; estimate of the situation; mechanics of solving problems; preparation and issue of combat orders; writing messages; cavalry liaison; logistics; movement by rail; combat intelligence; the preparation of problems and exercises; squadron regimental and brigade staff functions; the employment of cavalry in the field; and employment of other arms and services with which the cavalry might be associated in brigades and smaller units. Each subject was presented by conference, conference problems, map exercises, demonstrations by school troops, map problems and terrain exercises.

Military schools suffer from an ailment common to Americans and especially common to governmental institutions and activities—the impulse to change. However, General Booth's background and experience were eminent qualifications for effecting the best organization for accomplishing the school mission and for ensuring the most complete coordination among all its elements. The year 1927/1928 did see a radical change in the organization of the school, however. The departmental system was done away with, and in its place the instructional staff was divided into seven sections, each headed by a chief of section. A director of instruction became the principal assistant to the assistant commandant in the management of the school, supervising the general plan for instruction in all the classes. These were the sections:

1. Training: taught an assortment of subjects, including training management; the solution of problems; map and aerial photograph read-

ing; Army of the United States; mobilization plans; administration; drill; transportation; and riot duty—for a total of some 192 hours.

2. Employment of Cavalry-Combat was responsible for instruction in offensive and defensive combat; field fortifications; cavalry organization; estimate of the situation; and combat orders—for 48 hours.
3. Employment of cavalry, security, and information handled an assortment of subjects, such as reconnaissance; raids; outposts; positions in readiness; river crossings; and liaison, in some 109 hours of instruction.
4. Other arms taught logistics; command and staff; artillery; infantry; aviation; medical service; chemical warfare and engineers, in a total of 179 hours.
5. Dismounted Combat was the old Department of Cavalry Weapons, which was now responsible for teaching cavalry combat to include as low as squad and platoon. It specialized in musketry; machine guns; machine rifles; rifle marksmanship; and pioneer duties, totaling 289 hours.
6. Horsemanship taught 455 hours of horsemanship; 70 of animal management; 40 of horseshoeing; and 8 of transportation, pack, and wagon—all totaling 573 hours.
7. Publications and correspondence conducted no instruction but was responsible for editing all Cavalry School publications and material, for preparing cavalry correspondence courses, and for maintaining the Instructors' File, where copies of all lectures, notes, exercises, and problems were filed for future reference.

Forty-eight hours of instruction were required for terrain exercises, and 53 for graduation events. Thus, troop officers that year were subjected to 1,402 hours of instruction of one kind or another.

Every Friday afternoon during most of the year, there was a map problem, in which the students spent the afternoon solving tactical situations on a map. The one used was usually a topographical map of Gettysburg and vicinity, scale 1:21,210, so well known to students of all the military schools. Solutions were graded by instructors and were usually returned to the students in one or two weeks. They were marked with letters indicating superior, above average, average, satisfactory, and unsatisfactory. Marked problems were usually returned on Friday afternoons, perhaps to allow the students to have the weekend to celebrate or recover from disappointments—there was usually reason for one or the other. The marking system caused so many morale problems when students began debating among themselves the merits of their and the school's solutions that it was eventually discontinued. Problems were then returned marked only "S" or "U." The school maintained a class standing, but the student could only judge how well he had done by comparing his solution with the "school solution" and by the tone and amount of instructor comments on the paper—unless, of course, his mark was "U."

The Cavalry Board's activities were closely related to the work of the school, but it functioned directly under the chief of cavalry. It consisted of the commandant, the assistant commandant, and from three to five officers designated by the chief of cavalry. Its purpose was to consider subjects pertaining to the cavalry that were referred to it by the chief of cavalry and to originate and submit to the chief of cavalry any recommendations looking to the improvement of the Cavalry Branch. It considered and tested weapons and equipment of all kinds as well as matters of cavalry tactics. The normal procedure was to obtain expert opinion and recommendations from the appropriate school departments and other specialists, to consider it with information and recommendations received from other sources, and then to make its own formal recommendations to the chief of cavalry.

The school operated on an eight-hour day, five days a week, but academic assignments were such as to require several hours study each night. About half the daytime hours were devoted to academic subjects; about half to horsemanship and related activities. In the academic departments, the employment of cavalry occupied about half the time; instruction in other subjects, the remainder. Lectures, conferences, conference problems, map exercises, and written tests of one kind or another occupied most of the mornings except Friday. Since Friday afternoon was usually devoted to map problems, the morning was spent with the horses.

Instruction in animal management and horseshoeing was scheduled as convenient during the year, but equitation and horse training occupied most of the day's periods allotted to horsemanship. Indoor instruction in equitation was designed to develop a correct military seat for riding, training horses, and jumping. Outdoor instruction was to develop boldness in riding and to show the capabilities of animals across country, over obstacles, jumps, down steep slides, up steep slopes, and the like. Instructors in horsemanship also taught the use of cavalry weapons mounted—that is, the use of pistol and saber.

Outdoor riding was carried on throughout the year in all kinds of weather. Riding in deep snow, for example, always provided many thrills. In remount training, each officer had the experience of taking a green horse, gentling it, and carrying it through the various stages necessary to develop it into a first-class cavalry mount.

Mounted work was by far the most popular part of the course, even though it may not have been the most profitable from a professional viewpoint. It was the horse, of course, that distinguished the cavalryman from the other branches, even the artillery, because of the manner in which they used them. It made the cavalry an elite branch of the service, and it was in horsemanship that most of the legends of the school originated. The horse doubled the work of training cavalrymen in comparison with that of training the dismounted branches, and it was the horse that increased the sense of responsibility of cavalrymen, for they could not forget him for even one day.

Saturdays and Sundays always found cavalry officers, students and instructors alike, taking a "postman's holiday," riding: exercising remounts, hunting, playing or practicing polo, or riding for pleasure with members of their families. The reservation at Fort Riley was a horseman's paradise: wonderful bridle paths around the wooded "Island" . . . along the Republican River . . . up Magazine and Pumphouse canyons . . . and miles of open country where one could gallop for hours without drawing rein. And there were varying degrees of rough going: steep slides . . . jumps of every kind scattered about . . . ditches . . . and wonderful footing for horses everywhere. For the horseman and the horsewoman as well, a detail to the Cavalry School was in every sense "leading the life of Riley"!

Social activities began with a reception and dance where the commandant, the assistant commandant, and school officials received the student officers and their families. All officers wore name plates to facilitate coming to know one another. After passing through a receiving line, officers and their ladies took their place in the line to greet others following. Then there was dancing until late, and after this ball, and all others throughout the year, many impromptu parties where congenial groups assembled to talk horse, discuss personalities and activities of the school, sing some songs, and even perhaps imbibe a bit of the brew which was still forbidden. Such impromptu gatherings were normal after receptions and dances in Godfrey Court and elsewhere on the post as well. Formal receptions were held to honor all visiting dignitaries, such as the chief of staff of the army, the chief of cavalry, and others. Dances were held weekly. Important occasions such as Halloween, Christmas, New Year's, and Valentine's Day were always occasions for celebrations with masquerades, costume parties, or other special balls.

Army authorities were making efforts to reestablish the social customs and traditions of the service, which had meant so much in military life before the war, and to indoctrinate the large number of officers who had joined the officer corps during and immediately after the war. This effort was especially evident in the cavalry, and particularly so at the Cavalry School. Officers who had been assigned in England during or shortly after the war brought back special cloth and patterns for riding breeches and gave them to a local tailor. He became famous for making them. There was a period when every cavalryman aspired to owning "Faber Breeches." Later one of his tailors became almost as noted as: "Albert More—Breeches for Cavalrymen." Another change in uniform which resulted from the war was the abandonment of the old tight-fitting, high-collared blouse in favor of a lapel blouse of English type. The dark, olive green blouse, pink breeches, shining Sam Browne belt, and riding boots—always worn with spurs, of course—together made an extremely presentable uniform. And all new arrivals at the Cavalry School were *encouraged*—to put it mildly—to turn themselves out to best advantage.

The paying of "calls" was a mandatory social requirement and a major problem on a post like the Cavalry School, where so many officers were stationed. Nevertheless, it had to be done. On selected nights, officers and their wives set out with cards arranged in order, two for the officer being called upon and one for his wife—and performed their devoirs. If they were "fortunate" and found that many of the individuals they were calling upon were "out"—perhaps out performing the same duty—they might on occasion make as many as fifteen or twenty calls in the course of an evening. When the couple returned to their own quarters they were sure to find a pile of cards under their own door. A dozen or so evenings, though, and the social task was done.

Dinner parties were usually on the formal side, that is, one dressed for dinner, officers either in uniform or tuxedo, their wives in long dresses. Even so, this was a post of "gay young cavalrymen" willing to try anything, and never willing to back down on any dare. At a small dinner party one night when the subject of conversation was horses, as was usually the case at any party at the school, jumping was under discussion. In this instance, however, the question was bareback riding and whether or not one could ride a horse bareback over a five-foot jump. A challenge was issued when the discussion got particularly hot and heavy, and since the host was an instructor in horsemanship and in charge of one of the class platoon stables, all talk ended, and the dinner party adjourned to the East Riding Hall, horses were brought from the stable nearby, jumps were set up, and the contestants proceeded to ride bareback, with only halters to guide the horses over five-foot jumps. Clad as we were in tuxedos, it was quite a midnight show. When the activity began to gather quite a host of spectators who were on their way home from other parties, lights were turned out, horses returned to the stables, and members of the party wended their way homeward, agreeing that "a pleasant time was had by all." And the serious problem was resolved to the satisfaction of all!

Godfrey Court was a unique way of family life. In each of the ten two-story frame buildings, there were four apartments, two upstairs and two down, all with full-length porches. These forty apartments housed forty families, with an average of three children each. All buildings were connected with each other and with the central mess by a wide covered passageway, through which stretcher cases, wheelchairs, and food carts had once passed, but through which children on tricycles, bicycles, and roller skates now thundered and through which families passed on their way to meals in the mess.

In the mess hall, a T-shaped affair, smaller families were seated together, two or more to an ordinary troop mess table designed to seat ten soldiers. Large families had a table to themselves. The Ninth Cavalry, the school detachment, provided the cooks, and the waitresses were the wives and daughters of the Ninth Cavalry soldiers. There were highchairs for the small children and an area for parking baby carriages for those too small to be left alone at home. With more than a hundred children and eighty adults, most with strong personal feeling about food, diet, and taste, mealtime at Godfrey Court often approached a state of pandemonium. Meals were ample and wholesome as a general rule, but the menu was characteristic of such mess halls, where there is no room for personal choice. Few who were patrons of the mess will every forget Mess Steward Bradshaw and the great commotion on the day when steel wool was served in a dish of spinach.

School authorities expected student officers to be under intense pressure throughout the school year because they appreciated the great importance of the training in the officers' future careers and its value in the national-defense effort. Throughout the year, measures were taken to relieve students of as many extracurricular responsibilities and pressures as possible. Elementary schools and kindergartens were operated on the post, and special arrangements were made for older children to attend schools in Junction City, including special rates on the interurban, which ran from the post to the city. Ladies clubs, bridge clubs, book circles, riding classes for women and children were all available, and families were encouraged to participate. All through the year, while instruction in academic subjects and horsemanship continued apace, there was a continuous round of activities which offered both officers and their families the pleasures of being either spectators or participants.

Riding to hounds had long been popular at Fort Riley, although the dry and windy Kansas climate was not favorable for fox hunting. There were no foxes on the reservation, but in earlier days, fox hounds had been used for hunting coyotes. A pack of eight hounds—wolfhounds and greyhounds—was still maintained for chasing jack rabbits and coyotes by anyone who wished to do so. Since 1921, the Cavalry School Hunt had been admitted to the Master of Fox Hounds Association and had been recognized by the United Hunts and Steeplechase Association. Drag hunts were held three times a week, one day being for noncommissioned officers and soldiers of the command. Hunting was always popular, and the fields in attendance were usually large, especially on Sunday, when student officers were able to attend.

Polo was popular during the fall, spring, and summer, although among student officers, only the members of the Advanced Equitation Class had the time and opportunity to play. Nevertheless, there were numerous teams and frequent trips to tournaments in Colorado, Leavenworth, Kansas City, and elsewhere. All through the winter, there were informal horse shows to afford student officers experience in horse-show riding as well as the opportunity to see fine performers, both horse and man, in action. Cavalry School mounts and cavalry officers usually formed the hard core of Olympic riding teams, and in the years between the games, a nucleus of horses and men were maintained at Fort Riley in training. When the year of the games approached, other candidates arrived, team organization developed, and intensive training got under way.

In 1927, for example, the War Department directed the formation of the Army Horse Show Team to prepare for the international competitions in the Olympic Games of 1928. Brig. Gen. Walter C. Short, one of the exceptionally fine horsemen of the cavalry, was designated as team manager. He had been one of the original instructors in the old Mounted Service School and had long been associated with horsemanship activities. The general had made an immense contribution to the development of equitation and horsemanship in the army and was highly respected by everyone. Maj. Harry Chamberlin and Maj. Sloan Doak were outstanding, among other fine horsemen on the team. The entire post of Fort Riley profited by seeing this fine team of outstanding riders and horses in action over an extended period. Student officers were particularly fortunate to get this "dividend." The team won acclaim and made many friends for the army on its visits to the various eastern horse shows and eventually acquitted itself well in the Ninth Olympiad in Amsterdam.

The Cavalry School even supported an "undergraduate" newspaper, the *Standard*, so named for the flags carried by cavalry units on horseback. Flags carried by dismounted troops are called "colors," and it is interesting that this distinction is noted in General Orders for Sentinels in the "Manual of Interior Guard Duty": "To salute all colors and standards not cased." The paper, of four sheets, came out every Wednesday and was avidly awaited by everyone, for it was always irreverent, and no one—from the commandant to the junior officers on the post—escaped its well-aimed barbs. The paper provided a useful safety valve by exploiting the humorous side of more serious incidents, by gently pricking inflated egos, and by keeping classmates from straying too far from the accepted norm of student conduct.

One year, the Air Service, then in its barnstorming heyday, put on a most impressive demonstration of aerial bombing and gunnery for the school. As a finale for this big show, targets representing a troop of cavalry in a dispersed advance formation were set up on Republican Flats, along the road leading north from Junction City. Then, at the appropriate time, wave after wave of bombers came over and dropped bombs upon the column, and other waves of fighters swooped low to strafe the troop with machine-gun fire. A huge crowd, both civilian and military, watched the exhibition from the heights of Campbell Hill, more than two hundred feet above the Flats and less than a half mile from the target. The air officer, who was describing the attacks, called attention to the fact that nothing could live under such a bombardment. But just as the bombs from the leading wave began to fall, a soldier's dog dashed into the midst of the target area and began to chase from one to another of the falling bombs. All through the demonstration, the dog ran from target to target, pursuing the bursting bombs, giving tongue with all his might. He escaped unscathed. Even though he detracted somewhat from the effectiveness of the demonstration, the airmen sent him a collar engraved with recognition of the incident.

Graduation week at the school was known as June Week, and it had all the aura of romance and excitement of June Week at West Point, from which both the name and the aura were inherited. This was the important period of the year, when the skill, prowess, ability, and mental alertness were tested in a series of events that would try individual collective proficiency and at the same time provide entertainment and excitement for families, friends, and other interested spectators. Since the contestants were all husbands, the anxiety, excitement, and anticipation were perhaps higher among the wives than among the competitors themselves. June Week concluded with the graduation exercises in the traditional fashion of schools. Diplomas presented then indicated mental and professional knowledge, just as June Week events tested physical fitness.

While there were the usual jumping and schooling horsemanship events, many of the others were unique to June Week. A typical June Week might begin with a squad pistol-firing competition. In this test, squads of eight officers from the platoons made two runs of six shots each, firing three shots while riding in close order at targets stretched on a cable overhead, then deploying as foragers and firing three shots at targets arranged as skirmishers on the ground.

As a young cavalryman, Gen. George S. Patton had been master of the sword at West Point and then an instructor in the use of the saber at the Cavalry School. When he left the school, he presented a cup for competition in the use of the saber, mounted, to be competed for annually by the Troop Officers' Class. It was known as the Patton Cup and was one of the most sought-after prizes in all of the mounted competitions. The course was a winding one, with twenty dummies and four jumps: post-and-rail, log, ditch, and brush. The dummies were boxlike affairs, placed to the right and left of the path to be followed by the contestant. Each one had a "head," made of burlap stuffed tightly with straw, which was held erect by a weight suspended in the box. This would bring the head back erect after the charging saber had penetrated and been withdrawn. One minute and thirty seconds was allowed for the course, and a bonus of points for less time assured that the course would be taken at maximum speed. It was an exciting course and one that was supposed to demonstrate the value of the saber in combat.

Another June Week competition involved the use of both pistol and saber mounted. In this course, each officer fired five shots at mounted, standing, prone, and kneeling targets at distances from five to fifteen yards; then returned pistol, drew his saber, and attacked five dummies with the saber. The course also included obstacles like those on the Patton Cup course. One minute was allowed for this course.

There were point-to-point competitions for remounts that the student officers had trained. These were over measured courses of five to eight miles, flagged for walk, trot, and gallop, which the officers rode without watches. They were to be completed in specified times—a test of gaiting. There were also courses over jumps.

In other courses, remounts were tested in the use of saber and pistol mounted; in jumping indoors and out; and in a schooling competition.

The Standard Stakes, a cup presented by the *Standard* with prize money from the entry fees, was perhaps the sportiest event of the week. This event was open to all officers on the post and was a *must* for all student officers. The total of all one dollar entrance fees was divided among the win, place, and show places. In the first phase, horses of indeterminate disposition and unknown to the contestants were tied on a picket line three hundred yards from the start line, with saddles and bridles on the ground behind them. Each contestant ran the three hundred yards to the horses, saddled and bridled them, rode down a course of jumps along the Republican River, and to a saber course, which was the second phase. Seizing a saber on the run, he attacked three dummies and then continued to the pistol range, the third phase. Here he dismounted, took a pistol, and fired at a bottle marked with his number from a range of twenty-five yards until the bottle was broken. Mounting again on any horse, he proceeded to the Republican River, forded it, dismounted, and led his horse for a mile to a second ford, mounted, forded again, rode to the foot of Sherman Heights, dismounted, and led it up a steep climb. At the top, he mounted again, galloped to the rifle range, and again dismounted. Here he seized a rifle, fired at a bottle marked with his number, again at a range of one hundred yards, until it was broken, when he mounted again and rode to the finish line. Penalties were awarded for failure to break bottles, missed jumps, or missed saber dummies. It was a grueling course.

Another grueling and exciting competition was the Night Ride. It was a course of about sixty miles, usually laid out in a figure eight, with the West Riding Hall as the center and three stations on each loop, and outguards as checks at other points. Four contestants started at intervals of two or three minutes on each of the four legs of the loops. They were provided with a sketch map, showing the route and instructions on time permitted between stations. No watches were carried, so that the contestants estimated rates in order to reach stations at the proper time. Penalties were awarded for exceeding time between stations, and horses had to be serviceable when inspected the following afternoon. The distance was usually covered in from five to six hours. When rain added to the dark of the moon, the Night Ride was a *real* test of horse and man.

No June Week was ever complete without a big horse show, and there was always a series of polo games with an outside team, such as Fort Leavenworth or Kansas City. And there was always a Graduation Hop. It was a happy and exciting period. No cavalryman ever walked across the stage in the War Department Theatre and received his diploma without a thrill of pride in being a cavalryman and in knowing that he was a better one for having "been to Riley." And no officer of one of the other branches who had been a student with us and walked across that stage did so without a thrill of pride that he was a better army officer for having been to Riley and graduated from the Cavalry School.

The Cavalry School classes also published a year book, the *Rasp.* All school annuals can be thought of as precious, historical documents, for on their pages are the record of happy associations, humorous events, and memorable occurrences, together with photographs, cartoons, wit, humor, and sound common sense—all to enable us to recall the period in the future. The *Rasp* was produced by student officers, and there was always plenty of talent. The intense activity of the classes and the association we had with horses provided a wealth of material in amusing incidents—and some that were not so amusing! Some editions of the *Rasp,* like that of the Mounted Service School Class of 1914, are collectors' items.

In addition to the official events and entertainments, each class during June Week had class parties, usually at the Bridge Tea Room, and individuals exchanged many cocktail parties, dinners, and buffet suppers. Many new friendships had been made and older ones cemented. All were better for having attended "Mrs. Riley's School for Boys."

Fort Riley and the Cavalry School were fortunate in the character of the neighboring towns. There were actually only two that had any bearing on the way of life at Riley. Ogden, on the eastern edge of the reservation, had been a booming town in the days of Camp Funston, but it now had faded into a sleepy Kansas village. Ten miles upstream on the banks of the Republican River, the village of Milford had a fame of sorts. Located there was one of the most powerful radio stations in the United States and also the hospital that promised to work wonders for men past their prime. Both belonged to "Doctor" John R. Brinkley, a most controversial figure in medical circles. Over the radio station, which reached a vast area of the country, Doctor Brinkley exhorted men to come to Milford to recapture their lost youth or to purchase one or the other of the various elixirs he dispensed. When they came to Milford, as they did in numbers, he was supposed to restore their virility by a quick transplantation of goat glands from a herd grown on the grounds of the establishment. No cavalryman required the glandular rejuvenation, and none desired the sleepy tranquility of Milford.

Junction City was a typical Kansas town. Its streets were laid out in the square formation so typical of the West, where settlement followed survey. The town's name stemmed not only from the junction of the two rivers that formed the Kansas River but also from the junction of the immigrant trails northwest to Oregon, westward toward Colorado, and southwest toward Arizona and California. The main street, Washington, ran due south from the bridge over the Republican River on the reservation boundary. Along this street were most of the establishments patronized by the post. The First National Bank, La Shelle Shoe Store, Shane Book Store, and Waters Hardware were all familiar to us. On one cross street was the previously mentioned "Albert More—Breeches for Cavalrymen." On another, Davis and Meseke—Army grocers, who supplied fine groceries, friendship, information, and advice. And many others. Few evening drives were complete without pulling up in front of Eisenhower's Drugstore for a malted milk or stopping by Miller's for one of their special sodas. Junction City was the place where most day-to-day shopping was done, and the businessmen were friends of the army.

Manhattan was only twelve or fourteen miles to the east, and the only paved road in central Kansas connected Junction City with Fort Riley and Manhattan. The latter was two or three times the size of Junction City and had more shops. It was also the home of Kansas State, with far more undergraduates than students in the Cavalry School—and younger. So Manhattan was a college town—Junction City, a farm and cavalry town.

Kansas City was about one hundred and fifty miles to the east, and it offered all the advantages of a big city. There were beautiful shops and merchandise from all parts of the world. Officers and their wives visited the "Big City" occasionally and made use of the shops, for the credit of Regular Army officers was always good. And we often suffered from these visits for many paydays thereafter!

Brig. Gen. Charles J. Symmonds succeeded General Booth as commandant. Symmonds graduated from the Military Academy in 1890. A man of medium build, he was very reserved and quiet, dignified in appearance, and sedentary in habits. His most distinctive physical feature was a flowing, bushy moustache; his most inseparable companion, a pipe. He was unusual for an officer of his length of service in that he had no record of attendance at service schools. He had, however, distinguished himself in command of the post of Le Havre in the American Expeditionary Force, for which he received the Distinguished Service Medal. The *Rasp* of the year 1928 gave this slightly disrespectful but affectionate description of him: "We got a General here who aint like a general. He's a B.G. but he don't act like he wanted to be a M.G. because he don't bother nobody by prying around and making people unhappy. He had charge of the biggest pile of castor oil in the world during the war and if it wasn't for him as mayor of Jerve our doughboys would of starved and gone about in rags. Anyways everybody here says they hope he is Chief of Staff and stays on here at Riley writing poetry."

As young men will, it was not uncommon for one to call another in off-duty hours and announce on the phone: "This is General Booth," or "This is Colonel Fleming." It was an idle prank and never done with an intent to deceive more than momentarily. Capt. E. M. Daniels was the officer temporarily in charge of several officers and the Horse Show Team. Their duty was to keep the horses in condition and put on exhibitions for visiting dignitaries. One night after a dinner party at his house, the phone rang after he had retired for the night. He answered in the prescribed manner: "Captain Daniels quarters, Captain Daniels speaking." The answer: "Captain, this is General Symmonds. I want you to put on an exhibition at half past seven tomorrow morning in the West Riding Hall, and I . . . ." But Daniels interrupted: "Well, I'm the Prince of Wales, and I have just . . . ." There was a splutter in the receiver, then: "Captain, what is the matter with you? I'm coming right over there to see what condition you're in!" Bang!

It *was* the general! He had an unexpected visitor from Washington who was to leave early the following morning. He was anxious to see the Horse Show Team. And Daniels suddenly realized it probably was the general. He dressed in record time, was at the curb when the general arrived in minutes, and explained the misadventure and apologized. General Symmonds was mollified, and there were no repetitions of that prank thereafter.

Brig. Gen. Abraham ("Abe") Lott, class of 1896 at the Military Academy, followed General Symmonds as commandant. Lott was rather tall, somewhat angular in appearance, and none too impressive in personality—at least as far as the lower ranks were concerned. He had attended most of the army schools and had served several tours on the General Staff in Washington. He made no great imprint upon the Cavalry School during his period as commandant, but his two principal assistants certainly did: Col. Bruce Palmer, the assistant commandant, and Col. Charles L. Scott, the director of instruction.

Colonel Palmer was commissioned from the ranks in 1900 after cavalry service in the Spanish-American War. He was a graduate of the Infantry-Cavalry School and the Army Staff College. He had served on the General Staff from 1920 to 1924 and had become thoroughly familiar with problems confronting the cavalry and with the attitudes of others toward it. He had a keen, alert mind, was active and energetic, and was an enthusiastic horseman. He came to the school with an ambition to modernize the branch by developing tactics and techniques, organizations, and methods of employment that would make maximum use of armored vehicles and motor transportation. He and Colonel Scott also wished to demonstrate that horse cavalry had endurance far greater than was generally recognized. Colonel Palmer was a great believer in realistic field exercises and field maneuvers as a means of experimentation and teaching. Like most cavalrymen of the period, he was accustomed to austerity in the cavalry and the army and therefore was accustomed to improvising.

There was not a *single* modern tank or armored car in service in the army at this time, although other nations had continued to develop them after the war. There was much discussion in the service and out, and many articles were written in service journals on the subject of motors, armor, and mechanization. In 1928, the army organized one Armored Car Troop at Fort Meade in Maryland and sent it to join the First Cavalry Division at Fort Bliss for testing. In equipping this troop, several different makes of cars—Dodge, La Salle, Auto, and some others—were used as bases, and on them, "armored" bodies made of boiler plate and light armor plate had been built, some by the Ordnance Department, some by troop mechanics. The cars were armed with machine guns and equipped with radios for communication. Since the vehicles were intended primarily for reconnaissance, these improvisations were sufficient to emphasize the need for armored vehicles and for developing methods for their tactical employment. The experiment was sufficiently successful to warrant the organization of a second troop at Washington Barracks in 1930 as part of an intended Armored Car Squadron. The Cavalry School did not actually see much of these armored units, but that did not stop Colonel Palmer.

In field exercises and maneuvers for the instruction of the classes, Colonel Palmer made use of a dozen or so old White reconnaissance cars of World War vintage. They had been designed for the transportation of artillery reconnaissance parties, and each could carry about ten or twelve soldiers. They were used about the post mostly for transportation of personnel, and Colonel Palmer used them to represent armored cars in field exercises. Usually two or three students represented the crew, and powerful hand flashlights were used to represent fire from the vehicle. Each carried a flag to indicate whether it was in or out of action. The vehicles always carried their normal enlisted driver and usually an instructor, who served as umpire. These old trucks lumbered about the reservation and surrounding countryside. They did not look like armored cars, but all concerned obtained some conception of the capabilities and limitations of the armored vehicles they were supposed to represent—without their ever firing a shot. We also learned about the appropriate employment of such vehicles.

Colonel Palmer was ably assisted by his director of instruction, Col. Charles L. ("Scotty") Scott. He was rather small in stature, active, energetic, and had strong opinions on most subjects and voiced them freely on all occasions. He was a 1905 West Point graduate, the Mounted Service School of 1912, and had just finished the Command and General Staff School. He was an able horseman, enthusiastic, one of the best judges of horseflesh in the army, had been in the Remount Service during the war, was largely instrumental for its organization after the war, and served as its first chief. He was also one of the prime movers in establishing the American Remount Association and was widely known throughout the country. He came to the Cavalry School filled with enthusiasm for the development of cavalry along modern lines to exploit fully the capabilities of armored vehicles to enhance the power of cavalry. He and Colonel Palmer made an excellent team.

Another innovation of the Palmer-Scott period would have disturbed some cavalrymen of earlier generations—a "hundred mile march in twenty-four hours." It was a demonstration and test in which a provisional squadron of some 210 men and officers and more than 260 horses marched one hundred miles over a measured course in twenty-four hours carrying full field equipment. All student officers and instructors of the Cavalry School made the march with the squadron. It was a completely successful demonstration of the marching capability of cavalry, as well as of proper cavalry marching technique. Careful inspection after a brief rest within twelve hours of the finish showed that the squadron was fit to continue. Colonel Scott, with his vast knowledge of horses and horsemanship, was one of the prime movers in the organization and conduct of this march. Strange to say, perhaps, he was also one of the most enthusiastic advocates of mechanization for cavalry.

These were still prohibition days in the nation, and Kansas had been "dry" long before the rest of the country. Indeed, a daughter of Kansas, Carry Nation—and her hatchet—contributed to this state of aridity. However, moonshine could be found in Junction City and was obtained there by members of the garrison, as well as the local civilians. One of the local purveyors even concealed his stock in the sand dunes on Republican Flats on the reservation. Much was imported from Leavenworth and vicinity, where it was distilled, one bootlegger making the run about once every week. Once, on being asked the age of one demijohn by an interested customer, he replied, "Well, Cap'n, all I know for sure is, it's about a hundred and thirty-five miles old." The price was about ten dollars a gallon.

During much of this period a farmer who lived on the south side of the Kansas River below the site of old Camp Funston converted a portion of his corn into a liquid form. This potent distillate he dispensed to a select clientele of customers, mostly officers on the post, for the very reasonable price of six dollars a gallon. There was great distress when increased prosperity drew attention to his activities, with the result that this source of supply was terminated.

Another source of liquid refreshment characteristic of the period was "home brew." The local grocer, who was widely patronized by service families, stocked sugar, malt syrup, bottles, bottle caps, capping machines, and would even confide to certain customers the "receipt" he used. However, instructions for brewing were not hard to come by, for nearly everyone had a favorite formula he was willing to disclose. Sunday nights were always a good time for bottling, because the brew could then be ready when classes let out on Friday afternoon.

While all of this was not only contrary to the law but also to post orders and regulations, it was characteristic of the social mores of the country. Few looked upon the violation of prohibition laws as a crime, and many viewed all of it very much as a game. The "noble experiment" was not very popular, and it was not very successful in denying beverages to those who wanted them. There were not many scandals caused by what abuse there was of the law. There was one incident, however, that created a sensation and provided much conversation for a considerable period of time. It is reflected in a memorandum published at the time:

THE CAVALRY SCHOOL
FORT RILEY, KANSAS

February 16, 1931

MEMORANDUM:

The following is published for the information and guidance of this command.

About 8:45 p.m., January 19, 1931, a soldier in civilian clothing was observed to approach the East Section of Carr Hall, and, a few minutes later, to come therefrom carrying a demijohn of intoxicating liquor.

Upon being apprised of the above facts, the Commandant ordered the Post Executive to search Carr Hall and vicinity, beginning at the East end and continuing until he found intoxicating liquor or until a complete search disclosed that none was present.

As a result of the search, two demijohns of intoxicating liquor of identical type and content with the one in the hands of the soldier were found in the quarters of an officer in the East section of Carr Hall. The liquor was confiscated and the search discontinued.

These facts appeared to establish a prima facie case against the officer of violation of law, Army Regulations, and post orders. They also created a strong presumption that the liquor found in possession of the soldier was introduced into Carr Hall with the liquor found in the officer's quarters.

The soldier submitted to investigation, trial, and conviction by Special Court-Martial for possession of intoxicating liquor and introducing same on the military reservation in violation of the 96th Article of War, without giving any information concerning the liquor found in the officer's quarters or denying knowledge of same.

Investigations of the case of the officer disclosed that at least one of the demijohns was observed in his quarters on the morning of the day of the search, which was made about 2:00 p.m., and that the officer had spent the night of January 19–20 in his quarters, except from about 6:45 p.m. to about 7:45 p.m., and from about 8:15 p.m. to about 9:45 p.m.

However, the officer has stated in writing, under oath with reference to the liquor found in his quarters, that it was there without his knowledge, without his consent or permission, wither tacit or direct, and that he does not know who put it there, or why it was put there.

This is a very comprehensive statement, and if it is to be believed, would present a complete defense to any intentional misconduct. While the officer is an interested party and his statement must be considered with that in mind, as a general rule, the sworn statement of a commissioned officer can be taken as speaking the truth. Nor does it seem likely that a commissioned officer would jeopardize his commission in order to escape a relatively light punishment.

In view of the above, no further action has been taken. This is not to be considered as indicating any departure from the expressed attitude of the Commandant with reference to such matters. There should be a desire on the part of members of the command to assist in the prevention of a repetition of such occurrences not only as a protection to the good name of the post but for their own protection. The Commandant expects the cooperation of all concerned to that end.

By order of the Commandant:

R. M. Campbell,
Lieutenant Colonel, Cavalry
Executive.

OFFICIAL:
Distribution: F.

One reason there was no more trouble with alcoholic beverages in connection with entertaining done by classes and other members of the garrison, was the "Bridge Tea Room." This nice little establishment was located at the southern end of the bridge over the Republican River leading toward Junction City. It was just across the river from the reservation and was very conveniently located with respect to the post. Class parties and other entertainments involving any considerable number of persons were usually held there whenever alcoholic beverages were to be served. Cavalry officers for many years enjoyed the hospitality of the Bridge Tea Room and lifted their voices in song without fear of disturbing neighbors, for there were none. Since it was off the reservation, it was outside the jurisdiction of the commandant.

Just across the Kansas River and within a mile or so of the post there was a lake formed by what had once been part of the river bed. Whiskey Lake, it was called. It was perhaps two hundred yards wide and a mile in length in normal weather. It was one of the favorite duck-hunting places, and competition for hunting rights on it was usually keen every fall. It was also a favorite place for ice-skating enthusiasts from the post and Junction City when it was frozen over, as was usually the case for several weeks each winter. The farmer who controlled the lake had been retired as steward of the Cavalry Club for many years during the days of the Mounted Service School, when Fort Riley was both an artillery and a cavalry post. He was a bit partial to cavalrymen, and cavalrymen had little trouble obtaining hunting rights on Whiskey Lake. He was the subject of a famous cavalry song:

Ha! Ha! My Levi!
Oh, it's twelve o'clock by the village clock,
And the artillery's in bed,
When the Cavalry rolled in all full of gin,
And to old Levi said:
Chorus:
Ha! Ha! My Levi! We want rum, give us some.
Ha! Ha! My Levi! We want rum, give us some!
When you get that funny feeling,
Shoot the lights right out of the ceiling,
Then you know the Cavalry has come, sure come!

Hunting was popular with many officers. There were occasional mallards during the season on some of the small water courses on the reservation and surrounding country. Doves were plentiful during the season and could be found along the country roads. There were always areas where quail could be found, but they were not plentiful. One form of hunting was unusual. Hunting rabbits at night. Driving along country roads the headlights of the car would disclose rabbits feeding in the fields along the roadside. They could also be found on the polo fields on the Pump House and Republican Flats at night. Few of us returned home without an adequate bag.

Another winter sport was popular where there was snow, and there were usually two or three good snows during a winter: bobsledding—but not the wild ride down the mountainside course of Alpine popularity. When the weather looked promising for snow, a couple of officers who were handy with tools would construct a bobsled of suitable size. When the snow came, this sled would be loaded with six or eight enthusiasts sitting astride it. The driver then passed a long rope through the bumper of an automobile that was properly equipped with chains. When towed at speed along the snow-covered roads and streets of the post and across the parades and drill fields, this sport guaranteed thrills for many a winter's afternoon and evening.

These were troublesome days for the cavalry branch of the army, for it was becoming evident that there were increasing numbers who opposed the branch and did not wish it well. Some of these were among the earth-bound who have ever viewed the man on horseback with envious suspicion. Some were among those contending for the limited appropriations provided for the support of the under-strength army. Some others were among those of whom Maj. Gen. Leonard Wood had warned in 1926 when he wrote: "In considering the questions of Army reorganization it is vitally important that the determination of policy be not largely in the hands of those who look at warfare from the standpoint of the Western Front alone. Especially is this important in matters pertaining to the cavalry arm. In normal warfare, cavalry still has its role to play, a role quite as important as in the past." General Wood, obviously appreciative of the cavalry's mission, was not a cavalryman. But the troublesome fact was that the "determination of policy" had been almost entirely in the hands of individuals such as he spoke of since the end of the war.

The first postwar reorganization of the army in 1920 had provided for nine hundred and fifty officers and twenty thousand cavalry enlisted men in seventeen cavalry regiments. But in 1922, Maj. Gen. Willard A. Holbrook, chief of cavalry, had remarked: "The cavalry has been particularly at the mercy of the 'economists' because an immediate result of the World War in France was to cause a certain amount of doubt in the minds of those familiar only with the operations there as to the future value of cavalry." Another reduction in strength followed.

When Maj. Gen. Herbert B. Crosby, chief of cavalry, came to the Cavalry School on his final visit before leaving the office at the end of his four-year term in March, 1930, he made a farewell address to the assembled officers of the Cavalry School, which was a classic in its way. His remarks were apologetic in tone because he had not been able to do more to protect the interests of the cavalry in a way that would satisfy everyone. At the same time he was defiant and scornful of those cavalry officers whose views on reorganization and equipment of cavalry differed from his own. He clearly reflected his great frustration at the lack of understanding and cooperation he had encountered in the internecine warfare being carried on in the halls of the War Department.

General Crosby had begun by saying that when he had assumed the office of chief of cavalry four years previously, the first paper on his desk was "Major Project Number 1," which was to reduce the strength of three and one-half cavalry regiments by one-half. He went on to explain that the reorganization which he had directed was in the effort to save as many regiments as possible within the appropriation allowed for the cavalry. He had achieved it by coming to an organization in which the regiment was, in effect, the old four-troop squadron, heavily reinforced. He added: "There is no use beating about the bush, because there is no doubt that the cavalry is on the defensive at the present time. . . . We are fighting for our lives and we have to keep fighting all the time. If they let us do it we will certainly be in the picture at the beginning of the next war. If not, we will not be in the picture anymore." He added that "it doesn't pay to fight too hard in the end, because somebody may get mad and make an arbitrary cut."

General Crosby criticized cavalrymen on maneuvers for making mounted charges, saying that they did so when they "could not think of any thing else to do," and observers always criticized cavalry charges. He also criticized officers who opposed mechanization, saying: "Another line is mechanization. People seem to think mechanization is an enemy of Cavalry. It is the greatest friend of cavalry just as the air service is. . . . Mechanization will create a greater demand for Cavalry than ever before. It would certainly save a tremendous lot of horseflesh and that is a big thing for us to remember in war time."

General Crosby ended his address by saying that when he asked for all the pamphlets on the subject of training, two men came in with a pile of papers as high as a desk and certainly as big. He told them to take them out, for he was too old to be able to go over them all in his lifetime. He added that his office was trying to cut down to what they had had in 1916, before the war, and he added: "I really believe that we could have a whole lot better Army if we would go back to what we had in Ninety-eight and then see what we really had to have instead of picking over what we have and retaining so many things."

This farewell address caused no small amount of commotion in Cavalry School circles. Most instructors felt very much let down. They thought that they had been loyally carrying out the policies laid down with respect to cavalry organization and employment as directed by the War Department through the chief of cavalry. But the instructors were left in no doubt that during these past four years, the chief of cavalry had been a most frustrated man.

The organization of the armored-car troops was only an indication of the army's increasing interest in mechanization. There were almost no funds appropriated for research and development as such, so that whatever was done had to be accomplished at the expense of other activities. An experimental mechanized force was established at Camp Eustis, Virginia. Soon after Gen. Douglas MacArthur followed General Summerall as chief of staff of the army in March, 1930, he decided that the missions contemplated for the Mechanized Force were cavalry missions and that it should be a cavalry responsibility.

It was not long after this until the oldest and youngest of the active cavalry regiments turned in their horses. The First Cavalry from Camp Marfa and the Thirteenth Cavalry from the Cavalry School turned in their horses, moved to Fort Knox, Kentucky, and together with certain supporting units, were organized as the First Cavalry Brigade (Mechanized).

Colonel Palmer and Colonel Scott both supported the trend of mechanization in the cavalry, as did all of the instructors at the Cavalry School with the possible exception of an occasional one in the Department of Horsemanship. Most thoughtful officers in the branch also supported the trend. However, there were many who supported the views expressed by a distinguished cavalryman of former days, Maj. Gen. James A. Parker, USA, Retired. In a letter to the editor, published in the *Cavalry Journal* of September–October, 1932, General Parker asked:

> Can this be so?—when they well know that the strength of the Cavalry arm has already been reduced below what it should be. Why should not they, as well as the War Department, make proper representation to our legislative bodies and request that sufficient men be authorized for mechanization purposes, rather than having mechanization at the expense of existing arms, especially the Cavalry arm—all of which are now reduced to the irreducible minimum for proper national defense?

General Parker criticized "our American proclivity for new things" and deplored our inclination to "follow our British cousins in uniform, weapons, and equipment." He discussed at some length what he considered to be limitations of motorized and mechanized forces and the excellence of our own cavalry in 1918. Then he added:

> Finally, as a nation whose vaunted policy is defense, we should employ our wits not so much in the invention of proper use of mechanized warfare devices as on the best way of destroying these engines in war. That should be easy, because that line of thought has not hitherto been much followed. The Germans made a start at it by using anti-tank artillery, thermite and other bombs, attacks on caterpillar treads, gas, traps, caltrops, etc. Let us use a little American inventiveness, and machines will be useless in war as the German submarines and Zepplins had become in 1918.

General Parker was considerably out of date, but even in the face of the progress that had been made in the ten years since the end of the war, there were still a few cavalrymen who shared his views.

Such was the "Life of Riley"!

5. BRAVE RIFLES AND THE SOCIETY CIRCUS

> I suppose society is wonderfully delightful. To be in it is merely a bore. But to be out of it is simply a tragedy.
>
> —*Oscar Wilde,* Lady Windermere's Fan

> Must we drag on this stupid existence forever,
> So idle, and weary, so full of remorse,
> While everyone else takes his pleasure and never
> Seems happy unless he is riding a horse?
>
> —*Edward Lear*

In the year 1931, Fort Myer, Virginia, had been the station of the Third Cavalry Regiment—Gen. Winfield Scott had called it "Brave Rifles" when it stormed the Halls of Montezuma in 1846—since it returned from France and service in the American Expeditionary Force at the end of World War I. Myer was a small post and was primarily cavalry, since the regimental commander was also the post commander. The Sixteenth Field Artillery Battalion was the other line unit on post—for a total of four troops of cavalry and three batteries of artillery. The post had long been the station of ceremonial troops for the nation's capital, which also provided a measure of security in case of need. The normal functions of the garrison involved funeral escorts for the burials in Arlington National Cemetery, participation in parades, escorts of honor for the president and visiting dignitaries, ceremonial parades and reviews on the post, exhibitions, and the normal peacetime training of troops.

Fort Myer seemed to be a proving ground for colonels of cavalry, for all who commanded there were usually promoted to general-officer rank in due course. With about eighty colonels of cavalry competing for the cavalry share of some eighty brigadier-general appointments in the entire army, and with vacancies occurring only by reason of death or retirement at the age of sixty-four years, rivalry for the assignment was keen. The chance of lightning's striking was perhaps better near the eye of the Washington storm center, where colonels were under the immediate notice of the chief of staff of the army. For he made the recommendations for promotion, and the president made the appointments, with the "consent" of the Senate. So Fort Myer was desirable, especially for the senior ranks. And an essential requirement for assignment to command the delightful post seemed to be an individual's ability to maintain the pace of the Washington diplomatic social whirl without undue financial embarrassment.

An outstanding list of cavalry colonels had commanded the Third Cavalry during the twenty years from the demobilization in 1919 and the start of another mobilization in 1939/40. William C. Rivers, Hamilton S. Hawkins, William J. Glasgow, Harry N. Cootes, Jonathan M. Wainwright, and George S. Patton—all commanded during the period, and they were to garner a goodly collection of stars. The commanders of the Cavalry Squadron and Artillery Battalion were also marked men. Both Maj. Alexander D. Surles and Lt. Col. Charles P. George, who commanded the units in 1931, were to achieve general-officer rank, as were many others who served there. Fort Myer was indeed a most desirable post!

There is always a certain amount of sameness about military posts—as there is with college campuses, and prisons! And yet each one has its own peculiar atmosphere and individuality. In the years from 1931 to 1934, only one general officer had quarters on the post at Fort Myer, and he was not part of the garrison. He was the chief of staff of the army, and he occupied Quarters No. 1, which was reserved for him.

Geographically the post is almost an integral part of the Arlington National Cemetery, which stands on the high ground south of the Potomac River overlooking the capital. The small reservation is a triangle, little more than half a mile wide, tucked against the northern side of the cemetery, with a strip about a quarter of a mile wide extending along the western side. The red stone walls of the cemetery, familiar to so many Americans, are a part of the post. Four gates lead into the post. One, the north, toward Georgetown and Rosslyn; the west toward Clarendon; the south leading toward Columbia Road; and the Fort Myer, on the northwestern corner of the cemetery.

Approaching the post from Rosslyn at the southern end of the Key Bridge, the road led up a hill, through the north gate, past the chief of staff's quarters, and on the same side of the street, past three other double sets of quarters also facing south toward an open parade ground, the bachelor officers' quarters, and the post's quartermaster area. The main street, though, turned left at Quarters Number 1. On its right was a row of four red-brick double and single houses for the senior officers of the garrison. The last house on the southern end of this row, with a wonderful view looking out over Washington, was the quarters of the regimental commander. The road turned right there, past the parade, and on the left was a row of six double houses. Then a cross street. Left down it led to the Fort Myer Gate of the cemetery, with five more double sets of quarters and the post hospital on the right and several new houses on the left. If one turned right at the intersection, the street skirted the parade and went to the quartermaster area; and if one went through the intersection, on the right was the headquarters building and the chapel. It was here that formations for funeral escorts were almost continuous. In the west edge of the building were the offices of the regimental commander, the adjutant, the sergeant major and noncommissioned staff, the regimental executive, and the squadron commander. Upstairs in the building was a large hall where formal receptions and dances were held, and next door and on the same side of the street were the Guard House, the Regimental Supply Office and the Post Office—all of which looked out on the polo field.

Further down the street there was another intersection, with the Headquarters Troop Stable and the Veterinary Hospital on the right and the Riding Hall and the horseshoeing shops on the left. The west gate led off the post just a little further on. The stables were off to the right of the intersection by the Riding Hall, and if one turned left or south there, with the Riding Hall on the right, the Post Exchange and Service Club were on the left, then on the right the Cavalry Barracks, the Artillery Barracks, and the Artillery Stables. Down on the left, opposite the Artillery Barracks, were several sets of noncommissioned officers' quarters and the post laundry, just inside the south gate. Down opposite the end of the street, at the far end of the polo field from Regimental Headquarters, was the drill field, a flat cleared area about a half mile long and a quarter of a mile wide. Such was the post at Fort Myer from 1931 to 1934.

There was much open space in the country round about. In the broad river bottom between the cemetery and the Potomac River was the United States Experimental Farm, operated by the Department of Agriculture. This area was crisscrossed by miles of excellent graded pathways between the various experimental plots. They made wonderful bridle paths for riding, where one could go for hours and gallop at will with good footing. The Memorial Bridge was completed during this period, and it provided the most direct route from Fort Myer to downtown Washington through the Fort Myer gate into the cemetery and out through the McClellan gate across the bridge.

West of Fort Myer, between the post and Clarendon, housing developments were in their infancy and just starting to take over farms. One of the officers on duty in the Office of the Chief of Cavalry lived in a white-frame farmhouse just outside the west gate. From the south end of the cemetery a wide four-lane road had been graded due west past Bel Air and Glencarlyn for a distance of about eight miles. No pavement had been laid, and during these years it was a wonderful route for riding. All of the area between Fort Myer and Camp Humphreys (now Fort Belvoir) retained the rural atmosphere that had characterized it for many years since the Civil War. It was also a delightful area for riding along country lanes.

Col. Harry N. Cootes was commanding officer of the Third Cavalry in 1931. He was a fine-looking man, a courtly Virginian of the old school, charming in manner and pleasing in personality. Having ample means and a most attractive wife, he had done the usual stint of aide, military attaché, and similar assignments. He was not the studious type who sought to impress a command with his military knowledge, but he knew well how to delegate authority and responsibility and to draw loyalty from subordinates. He was most anxious that all officers present the best possible appearance. He left no doubt that he expected officers of the Third Cavalry to own and wear the blue uniforms that had recently been authorized for optional wear on all appropriate official and social occasions.

Colonel Cootes was followed in command in 1933 by Col. Kenyon A. Joyce. This poised and dignified officer had served in the National Guard during the Spanish-American War and was appointed a second lieutenant of cavalry in 1901. He was a distinguished graduate of the Infantry-Cavalry School, class of 1905, and of the Staff College in 1906. He was a graduate of the Command and General Staff School and the Army War College and had served tours on the General Staff Corps. He had also had diplomatic experience on military-attaché assignments. A handsome man, always impeccably dressed, he was reserved in manner but possessed a keen sense of humor. He impressed all with whom he came in contact. Interested in all horse activities, he was very popular with the hunting and horse-show circles in the Virginia and Washington areas.

Like Colonel Cootes, Colonel Joyce knew how to delegate responsibility and authority. Both of these able men left most of the tedious administrative details to their able subordinates, Maj. George S. Patton, Jr., executive officer, and Maj. Alexander D. Surles, the squadron commander.

The Third Cavalry had been reorganized in the last reduction of both the cavalry and other branches to provide personnel for the expanding air service. The chief of cavalry had decided to retain the regimental designations while reducing the number of troops in them. The regiment was therefore the equivalent of a strongly reinforced squadron of four troops, the same as a squadron that had existed when a full regiment had fifteen troops. The regiment now consisted of the Regimental Headquarters and Headquarters Troop, one Machine Gun Troop, and two squadrons of two troops each. The first squadron, with troops A and B, was stationed at Fort Ethan Allen, Vermont, and troops E and F were stationed at Fort Myer. All troops were at full strength, and each rifle troop consisted of three full-strength platoons and a light machine-gun platoon.

Major Surles, the squadron commander, was a graduate of the Military Academy, class of 1911. This brilliant officer was a graduate of the Cavalry School Advanced Course, the Command and General Staff School, and the Army War College. He had served two tours on the general staff, was well known in Washington, and was generally regarded as one of the outstanding army officers of his age. He was of medium size, slender of build, sandy of hair and complexion, active, energetic, studious, thoughtful, and considerate of juniors and seniors alike. He was not a polo player, and he took little personal interest in horse show exhibitions, although he was a very strong supporter of both activities. For relaxation he preferred golf, and day-to-day, most of the administrative load of the regiment and the post fell on his willing and able shoulders.

The troops of the Third Cavalry were unusual in the caliber of their noncommissioned officers, practically all of whom were professional soldiers of long experience. Some of them had been commissioned officers during the war. First Sgt. William B. Moffatt of F Troop, for example, had been a captain and had distinguished himself. Some who could have been officers had been unwilling to accept commissions. When the regiment was ordered from the border overseas to join the Expeditionary Force in 1917, the noncommissioned officers of Troop E promised each other to remain with the "old troop" throughout the war, come what may. They lived up to this pledge, refusing opportunities to attend officers' training camp and even refusing to accept commissions when they were offered. It was a demonstration of the wonderful esprit that often motivated cavalrymen in the professional army, even though it may not have been the best way for such able men to have served their country during the war. Fifteen years later, members of this able group of soldiers still occupied the key positions in the troop to which they had pledged themselves and each other. There was little about soldiering that these noncommissioned officers did not know. Thoroughly competent in every respect, they presented a challenge in leadership to any officer assigned to command the troop.

As a footnote, this group of noncommissioned officers was still in the service when the Second World War came along. All of them were commissioned. The first sergeant, William Lawrence, was a major of cavalry with General Wainwright on Bataan and Corregidor and was a member of the general's personal party. He died as a result of hardship following General Wainwright's surrender.

Funeral escorts had been an important function of the Fort Myer garrison from the time Arlington National Cemetery was established. During the years following the First World War, the duty was particularly heavy. Families were exercising their option of having the dead returned from France, and a great many of them were buried in Arlington. Scores in a single day were not uncommon when this movement was at its height. The duty was not lightened by the critical attitude of officials and other personnel, both military and civilian, toward the ceremonies.

Service regulations prescribed the details of funeral escorts and ceremonies. While the details were similar, each service had its own traditions and customs. Further, funeral and burial services varied according to the religious service involved. Many persons seemed to think that because some of the customs and traditions of military funerals were of ancient origin, the rites were as fixed as the laws of the Medes and the Persians.

Several customs peculiar to military funerals have developed over the years. The firing of volleys is supposedly from the ancient Roman funeral rite in which casting earth three times on the casket constituted burial; it was then customary to call the dead three times by name, which ended the ceremony, after which friends and relatives pronounced the word "*Vale*" (farewell) three times as they left the tomb.

The black horse following the casket, caparisoned in mourning with black boots reversed in the stirrups, was an appropriate cavalry adaptation of the medieval practice in which the knight's charger in mourning followed the knight to his last resting place, with boots and saber reversed to show that his war days were ended. The use of the caisson for transporting the soldier's remains in a flag-draped casket also originated in a mounted service, the artillery. The sounding of Taps, the most beautiful of all bugle calls and the most impressive part of any military funeral, is perhaps the most recent in origin of all the customs. It is supposed to have been adopted by the Army of the Potomac during the Peninsular Campaign of 1862 as a formality for all military funerals. It was used earlier when the military situation made the firing of volleys inadvisable. Then the custom spread throughout the army and was eventually confirmed in orders. It is known, however, that some regiments used the call during the Mexican War in 1845/46. There can be no more fitting honor to a departed comrade or to the end of a funeral ceremony than this call which recalls the words:

Fades the light,
And afar,
Goeth light,
Cometh night,
And a star,
Leadeth all,
Speedeth all,
To their rest.

Regulations prescribed funeral escorts according to the rank of the deceased: from one squad for a private soldier to all troops and organizations that could be assembled for a high official such as a chief of staff or the president. Procedures were laid out in detail for forming escort and its conduct, from the arrival of the casket at the chapel until the sounding of taps at the grave side and the departure of the escort from the cemetery. In those days, every veteran seemed to feel that he was an expert in military ceremonies, whether he was or not. In consequence, whenever a funeral escort made any error whatsoever in action or appearance, criticism from the high command, veterans and veterans organizations, members of Congress, retired officers, and sundry others was likely to rain down on the post commander. And woe betide any firing party that let off a volley that did not sound like a single shot. And many did not!

Naturally enough, all new arrivals at Fort Myer were thoroughly indoctrinated with all the legends and tall tales pertaining to funerals in Arlington and were duly impressed with the importance given to such ceremonies. Consequently, newcomers studied manuals and understudied others to acquire the knowledge necessary to avoid the mistakes that might bring criticism of the command. However, over the years, the command had simplified the procedure by standardizing the sizes of escorts and firing parties and also by developing a method of rehearsal that minimized any chance of error. One young officer reduced the advice for newcomers on the conduct of the escort to a single, cardinal rule: "When the stiff's in motion, Present Arms!"

Headquarters detailed a "funeral officer" each month. He was responsible for arranging services, coordinating with the cemetery officials, supervising the escort, reconnoitering the route to the grave site, and all other details to ensure that the ceremony proceeded smoothly. On days when there were a dozen or more funerals, as there frequently were, he was a busy man. Troops and batteries were rotated weekly for providing escorts and firing parties. For high-ranking persons, though, the entire command might be required as escort. The duties had become so standardized by 1931 that they were not unduly onerous, except for long marches to distant grave sites and religious services of exceptional length on hot, humid days in midsummer.

No one could follow these processions at the slow funeral pace of the "Dead March," with its beautiful, stirring strains, without deep emotion and an abiding respect for a departed comrade. All burials in Arlington were attended with all the solemnity and respect that could have been accorded to members of one's own organization, family, or friends. Chaplains were always as deeply concerned as any pastor could be for a personal friend or devoted member of his own flock. A military funeral is a beautiful and impressive ceremony, and close association with Arlington was a wonderful experience for the officers and men stationed at Fort Myer who participated in them. One learns that there is beauty in death and in the respect accorded the dead by the nation and those who live on after them. And when the band turns away, leaves the cemetery, and strikes up a sprightly quickstep to lead the escort on to other duties, it is a symbol that the living must carry on.

"Regimental Notes" in the *Cavalry Journal* issues of early 1922 mention the initiation of activities that came to dominate the life at Fort Myer for a goodly part of the year:

> The severe winter weather has made the ground impracticable for much outside work and most of the training has, therefor been in the riding hall. Exhibition drills have been given each Friday afternoon, and will continue during March. The program consisted of a

> close and extended order drill by Troop E armed with the saber; a rough riding exhibition by Troop F; a "monkey drill" by Troop G; an exhibition of four-line team-driving by the Service Troop or a period or two of indoor polo; a battery drill by the 3d Field Artillery, and a jumping exhibition by the jumping squad. These rides are well attended by the people of Washington and have been witnessed by a number of distinguished national and foreign personages.
>
> The season of riding hall drills was closed April 7 by two performances of a "Society Circus" for the benefit of the post athletic fund.
>
> Exhibition drill squads from the troops of the squadron have attended the various horse shows throughout Virginia and have been most enthusiastically received. . . . The demand for attendance of troops at horse shows and fairs has been very much increased this year, and one or two squads could well be kept busy during the summer, to avoid considerable disappointment to some towns.

Over the years, each troop developed one or more spectacular drills or exhibitions and brought them to the highest state of perfection for what had come to be known as the Winter Rides. Innovations and refinements were continuous. Competition was keen among the troops and batteries to present an exhibition that would demonstrate the greatest professional skill and afford the most thrilling and spectacular entertainment for the benefit of the audience.

The Machine Gun Troop specialized in "monkey drill"—acrobatics on horseback—and had developed an exhibition that would have been a credit to professional equestrian acrobats of the circus world. The troop also demonstrated on occasion a drill by a machine-gun platoon with pack horses in complex movements ending with going into action and firing. It was particularly spectacular in the enclosed space of the Riding Hall.

Troop E developed a musical ride, with twenty-four riders, that involved many intricate movements executed with the greatest precision. They were all demonstrated in unison at various gaits and exhibited a marvelous state of training of both horses and men. The twenty-four soldiers, perfectly uniformed and mounted on well-groomed chestnut horses with legs bandaged in white and each trooper carrying a guidon with its fluttering pennant all together, presented a beautiful sight. The troop also developed a very exciting and startling jumping exhibition. A platoon performed over a series of jumps, two on each of the long sides of the Riding Hall, one midway at each end, and a square pen placed diagonally in the center. The platoon took the jumps in pairs and fours and then executed a series of intricate movements, with pairs jumping the obstacles and single troopers passing between them in the opposite direction. With all men topping jumps simultaneously, it was a thrilling sight. The exhibition ended with trios of riders crossing through the square pen jump in the center of the hall from each of the four directions in a perfectly timed and coordinated movement. The final maneuver appeared to be so dangerous to the spectators that it was performed only on special occasions.

Troop F specialized in a breath-taking exhibition of rough-riding, usually costumed in western dress. A squad of sixteen men rode "cossack," standing in their saddles, picked up handkerchiefs from the floor with their teeth as they galloped by, vaulted from side to side of their horses, rode through flaming hoops, and were dragged behind horses, all at breakneck speed. The troop also specialized in a tandem driving drill in which mounted troopers drove two horses before them, in tandem. Black horses with white harnesses, bandages, cockades, and lines, performing daring drills to music was always one of the most beautiful of these many exhibitions.

Each artillery battery had also perfected a drill with four gun carriages and caissons that was usually the finale for the Friday-afternoon shows. The drills, with their six-horse teams performing at high speed in the limited space of the Riding Hall, were spectacular. When the drill ended with the guns going into action and firing off salvos of blanks, they filled the hall with sound, smoke, and the smell of powder and provided a fitting climax to the afternoon's military exhibition.

The Riding Hall had upper and lower galleries at each end, with a total seating capacity of about eighteen hundred. The south gallery was reserved for invited guests and was equipped with special theater-type seats; the north gallery was for post personnel and, on occasion, general admission. Admission was by ticket, although there was no charge. The commanding officer invited the guest of honor for each Friday event from among the official, diplomatic, political, and social groups in the capital. The exhibitions became so popular that there were often six thousand applications for the eighteen hundred seats available on a Friday.

Preparation for the shows—a large portion of winter training!—occupied the Riding Hall fully throughout each working day on a very closely timed schedule. Then, on Saturdays and Sundays, it was always fully occupied with riding for individuals, classes for ladies, girl scouts, boy scouts, and similar activities.

Fort Myer was an outstanding station for "gay young cavalrymen"—and artillerymen—who were bachelors, and the young lieutenants assigned there were almost invariably bachelors. The White House social calendar has always set the pace for the diplomatic and social whirl of Washington and of Washington "society." It turned about the various scheduled receptions and dinners which were always "white tie" affairs in this period. These would include some or all of the following: a judicial reception, a cabinet dinner, a diplomatic reception, a New Year's reception, the vice-president's dinner, an army and navy reception, a House of Representatives reception, a dinner for the chief justice and the Supreme Court, and some state dinner or reception each week. Young army and navy officers were required in considerable numbers for these functions as guides, escorts, ushers, and similar duties. Dressed in "blues" with gold braid and shoulder knots, these aides added a touch of color that offset the somberness of white tie and tails. Accordingly, the units at Fort Myer and others in the Washington area were always assured a full complement of lieutenants to meet the demand for "White House Aides." It was a popular and sought-after assignment.

Washington also happened to be a place where the concentration of diplomatic and political power and personalities watered down the power of wealth and lineage usually in control of the portals of "Society"—always with a capital "S." The sacred precincts of society were perhaps easier to penetrate in Washington than in most other large cities. Washington debutantes were a most important part of Washington Society, and the same White House aides were much in demand as escorts and in seeing that stag lines were properly filled. Between the demands of their White House duties and the social whirl, the lieutenants were left with few evenings to devote to social life on the post—and few concerned themselves with what there was of it! However, it was this aspect of social life in Washington that was responsible for the development of the "Society Circus," which became a means of raising funds for the support of the post's athletic activities and various post and army charities.

The basic concept of the Society Circus was simple—to encourage the debutantes, children, and all others who had been thrilled by the Winter Rides to take an active part in an exhibition similar to the ones they had witnessed. Since the rides were more military in nature and performed mostly in uniform, a variation in setting was sought for the Society Circus. A theme was selected each year, and special drills and exhibitions were developed for the participants. Similarly, each of the troops developed special drills, in keeping with the theme, and performed in costume. The "Circus" was always a most colorful show as well as a profitable one for the post and the army charities it supported.

In the year 1933, "technocracy" was a word much in the daily press and conversation. That year it was selected as the Society Circus theme—a pageant portraying equestrian and other events from various periods of the world's history. The time was to be the year 2933. The place, the city of Technocracy. The scene was the control room of the dictator, Technor. He and his right bower, Machinor, and several other Technocrats were present in a room represented by a platform suspended over the center of the Riding Hall, in full view of the spectators in the galleries at each end of the hall. The scenery consisted of huge panels painted on beaver-board, which lined the walls of the hall above the knee boards. These scenes were all painted by enlisted men from the regiment and the artillery battalion, among whom there were a number of talented artists and cartoonists. The scenes were all of a technical and imaginary nature, a sort of Jules Verne type of illustration to suggest Technocracy and the dictator's control room. The personnel in the control room—the announcers and their technical assistants—were costumed to caricature "the technocratic man."

The circus opened with Technor talking to Machnor—over the loudspeaker—telling him he wished he'd lived in the days when "men were men, ladies were beautiful, and they all rode horses." Then they discussed that era, which the events that followed supposedly represented: a grand parade, in which all participants entered the hall; then a series of events in which both the men of the troops, the debutantes, and personnel from the post, such as the Cub Scout Troop, all took part. There were variations from the Friday Rides; for example, the Troop E Musical Ride now represented a march of the crusaders; F Troop's rough riders were now cossacks; and the debutantes performed the F Troop tandem ride. The evening was full, with a total of ten events and a grand finale. It was a grand success, one of the most important parts of the year for the garrison, a truly fitting climax for the season of Winter Rides.

While the social life of the bachelor lieutenants was full with the demands upon them as escorts, the most senior officers of the post were involved in the "cocktail and dinner party circuit" of official and diplomatic entertaining. Their involvement with the social life of the post was limited for the most part, involving only the official interchange of calls, an annual reception then required by the customs of the service, and the official receptions following the rides and exhibitions. The remaining officers of the post were left to their own resources, along with their families. Cocktail parties, buffet suppers with their song fests after the Friday Rides, picnics, and other similar activities were the normal social life.

Until prohibition was repealed in 1933, gin of our own manufacture was the most common beverage. Newcomers to the post soon acquired a telephone number and name in one of the Maryland suburbs. A person called the number, identified himself, and remarked that he could "use one (or more) on such and such an evening." On the designated evening a nice-looking car stopped in front of the house, and a well-dressed, pleasant-mannered man delivered the appropriate number of one-gallon tins of pure alcohol, each with a small vial of "drops." These, mixed into the alcohol with an equal quantity of water, provided a very satisfactory gin of excellent quality.

In Virginia, officers occasionally procured "corn whiskey" in gallon glass jugs. This was very satisfactory if aged in charcoal kegs or with the sticks of charcoal that could be purchased in drug stores and added to the bottles. However, the "corn" usually ran about ten dollars a gallon, while the pure alcohol was only six, and the latter produced two gallons of gin. Needless to say, gin was the most popular drink on the post.

Fort Myer was a difficult station in which to plan and carry out a broad and effective training program because of the nature of the special duties required of the garrison. We troop commanders followed the system we had learned years earlier by computing the total number of hours available for the year, based on the normal eight-hour day, deducting from this the time reserved by all higher headquarters for their organizational training, then deducting the hours reserved for parades, ceremonies, escorts, and inspections. What was left was available for training in such subjects as mounted and dismounted drill, equitation, marksmanship, scouting and patrolling, interior guard duty, manual of arms, dismounted combat, and numerous other subjects. The time required for escorts, parades, and funerals could never be foreseen; it could only be estimated by comparison with hours consumed in previous years. And since the dates and hours could never be anticipated, training schedules had to be very flexible.

During the winter, the Friday Rides dominated all training activities. Each troop and battery devoted its period in the Riding Hall each day to improving, developing, and perfecting its exhibitions and in training understudies. The periods of about an hour each were rotated among the troops and batteries. The Riding Hall period assigned was therefore the controlling factor in the daily training schedule. Since the drill teams usually included nearly all of the noncommissioned officers of the troop, they and the troop commander were not available for regular training during the Riding Hall hour and, of course, the time immediately preceding it and following it. This was not necessarily a disadvantage, however, for it forced us to develop understudies for all of the noncommissioned officers in the troop.

The small size of the outdoor drill field at Fort Myer was somewhat a limiting factor in troop training, particularly for those of us accustomed to the wide open spaces of the Southwest or the vast expanses of the military reservations at the Cavalry, Artillery, or Infantry schools. The small Myer drill field was usually congested, because it had to serve for the outdoor drilling of the four troops and three artillery batteries. But the Regular Army soldiers always had to "make do," and the garrison at Myer always did so.

Much of the short-range target practice was carried on within the confines of the post. In a ravine between the cavalry stables and the quartermaster area, the regiment had its "thousand-inch range" for the firing of light and heavy machine guns, small-caliber rifles, and pistols. During the spring and early summer there was always a continuous clatter of firing there, and it caused no small amount of disgruntlement in the residences of Clarendon and Arlington. For regular range practice, we used the rifle range of the District of Columbia National Guard at Camp Simms in the Anacostia area. Combat firing was done on the reservation at Camp Humphreys—later Fort Humphreys, and now Fort Belvoir. This was a favorite spot with the troops, for they liked to traverse the country roads between Humphreys and Myer. Troops especially liked an exercise that permitted troopers to return to the post in pairs over the twenty miles or so of winding country roads—a valuable training exercise.

Participation in fairs, parades, horse shows, and celebrations of various sorts were always very much a part of cavalry life, and the preparation was an important part of it. The year 1931 marked the one hundred and fiftieth anniversary of the siege of Yorktown and the surrender of Cornwallis there on October 19, 1781. To commemorate the event, Congress established a committee of senators and representatives to give direction to the "Celebration of the Sesquicentennial Anniversary of the Siege of Yorktown, Virginia, and the Surrender of the Forces under the Command of Lord Cornwallis," and Congress appropriated funds for the celebration to be held at Yorktown, October sixteenth to nineteenth, 1931. The state of Virginia also established a commission and appropriated funds to assist in the celebration. To supplement the work of these two commissions and to act in a capacity in which these federal and state commissions could not function, still-another committee of public-spirited citizens was formed—the Yorktown Centennial Association. Other states followed the lead of Virginia and created commissions to assist in preparations for the celebration.

That same year the National Park Service, pursuant to an act of Congress, had established the Colonial National Monument, which embraced the Yorktown Battlefield, Jamestown Island, and Williamsburg. This work of the Park Service contributed greatly to the preparations for the celebration, including clearing the battlefield and much of the planning of the grounds on which it would take place. Several hundred army troops from Fort Monroe spent weeks building roads, paths, docks, clearing parking spaces, and erecting tents. Practically all government departments, states, patriotic organizations, and even some foreign governments were involved in the preparations in one way or another.

The purpose of all of this was purely patriotic. It consisted of five principal parts: the Colonial Fair and Exhibition; concessions; entertainments; music; and military drills and exhibitions. The grounds were laid out in a rectangular area about a mile in length and half as wide just south of the village of Yorktown. They consisted of a pageant field, which was an arena laid out in the form of a horseshoe with grandstands seating twenty thousand spectators; sixty or seventy huge tents adjacent, for exhibitors from the various states, patriotic shows, and societies; the Colonial Fair and offices; and finally, a camp nearby for army units. Surrounding the whole area were parking lots and taxicab stands.

The four days of the celebration were: Colonial Day, Revolutionary Day, Religious Day, and Anniversary Day. The programs for each presented appropriate addresses by distinguished citizens; various historical pageants appropriate for that particular day; exhibition rides and drills by the cavalry troops and an artillery battery from Fort Myer; antiaircraft demonstrations by coast-artillery troops from Fort Monroe; and band concerts by service bands. Ships of the American and French fleets were anchored in the York River and were open for visitors. Special entertainment included Punch and Judy shows, concerts, tilting tournaments, marionettes, old-time fiddlers, dancing, and many other colonial-type amusements appropriate to the times represented.

Exhibits included National Park Service paintings, photographs, and models of national parks; naval exhibits of ship models; army exhibits of weapons of the colonial period; and an Indian village. The army camp was open to visitors, the fleets entertained them, and the frigate *Constitution* was anchored in the York River and received visitors daily. The celebration culminated on Anniversary Day with an address by President Hoover and the presentation of General Pershing and Marshal Pétain, who was the distinguished foreign guest for the occasion.

The cavalry troops from Fort Myer were called upon all during the celebration for their usual ceremonial, parade, and escort duties, as well as for their exhibition drills. With the arrival of so many distinguished guests and dignitaries, there were two exhibitions, afternoon and evening, and a constant stream of visitors through the camps—busy days, but days that always appealed to the cavalrymen.

One factor that particularly appealed to us in those days of austere peacetime budgets was that even for the comparatively short trip, we were moved by rail from Fort Myer to Yorktown, men, horses, and all of our equipment. The cost was probably charged to funds appropriated for the celebration, rather than to funds budgeted for military transportation, otherwise the command would doubtless have made a practice march going and coming! It was an experience thoroughly enjoyed by all.

During the winter of 1931/32, the gloom of the Great Depression was settling over the nation, despite presidential assurance that "prosperity was just around the corner." The words had a hollow ring to the increasing millions of unemployed who could find no work. Desperation drove many of these unfortunate people into "hunger marches" in their demand for employment or other assistance in their hour of need. Press and radio reflected an atmosphere of unrest in the land, and there were occasional clashes with police. It was expected that groups would descend on Washington to petition Congress or the president for aid. Recognizing that disorder was always possible, as a precautionary measure, the commanding general of the Third Corps Area directed that all officers be given a thorough review course in officers' schools in "The Military in Domestic Disturbances." Accordingly, the legal and tactical aspects involved in the use of federal troops to assist civil authorities in maintaining or restoring order in riot conditions were thoroughly reviewed in schools during the month of January. No one dreamed during the instruction the circumstances under which the knowledge would be put to use.

Among the millions of unemployed in the nation, there was one group that considered it had a just claim which the government should settle and thereby afford them direly needed economic assistance. This group, the veterans of the World War, held "Adjusted Service Certificates," which represented the bonus that Congress had voted as partial recompense for their wartime service. The certificates were actually bonds, which were to mature in twenty years, or about the year 1945. To the veterans in need, it seemed only just and reasonable that the Congress should authorize the immediate payment of these certificates in this period of distress. In fact, most veterans believed that the bonus should have been paid in cash in the first place.

So, as winter passed, press and radio began reporting groups here and there across the country heading for Washington, with the avowed purpose of petitioning the Congress for the immediate payment of the bonus. The first veterans that came to the notice of the troops at Fort Myer, however, were not members of these organized groups, but rather were indigent individual veterans seeking food, shelter, and work. As was to be expected, the soldiers were very sympathetic toward these unfortunate men. As a relief measure, the troops employed a few of them as kitchen police and stable police, each man in the troop contributing a small sum each month to afford them a very modest wage. The arrangement was popular with the men, for each would willingly contribute a dollar a month to escape the drudgery of the kitchen and stable-police duties. Besides, they felt they were helping unfortunate comrades. Troop commanders were pleased because the arrangement provided more soldiers for training. But it was not to last.

Early in May, veterans began arriving in Washington, at first in individual driblets, and then in more or less organized groups in ever increasing numbers. Almost spontaneously, or so it seemed, movements began in various parts of the country, all converging on Washington, reminding one of "Coxey's Army" of an earlier period of national economic distress. Like other movements of the sort, it gathered momentum as it was widely publicized in press and radio, as agitators redoubled their efforts, and as economic efforts continued to worsen. And there were a few Communist and radical elements which sought to exploit the movement to their own ends.

Municipal and state authorities met these veterans with sympathy as they crossed the country in bands of varying sizes. However, they presented problems beyond the capabilities of the local authorities. Thus, they hurried the groups on their way, often providing trucks to transport them to the boundary of whatever town, city, or state was involved. Thousands more rode freight trains, without interference on the part of the railroad authorities—in fact, with their acquiescence. The people of the nation sympathized deeply with the veterans.

The trickle that began flowing into Washington in May, then a city of a little more than 450,000, soon swelled into a flood that reached an estimated 20,000 or 25,000 at its peak. And many of these men had their families with them. The civilian authorities in the District of Columbia were not prepared to handle any such influx of indigent persons, even though there was great sympathy for them. In fact, the policy of the administration was not to accord official recognition to the movement or to provide any official assistance in the way of housing, food, or other conveniences, lest by doing so, Washington should become the mecca for floods of other unemployed throughout the nation and thus impose an intolerable burden upon the community.

Gen. Pelham D. Glassford, U.S. Army, Retired, the chief of police, on his own responsibility and against the wishes of the District's commissioners, made valiant efforts to assist these veterans as a measure of preserving public order. He was even elected treasurer of the initial organization of veterans in Washington. The veterans took over and occupied numerous empty buildings scattered about the downtown area, some that were already condemned and awaiting demolition as a part of the development of the Mall project. They also established camps in various parks and open areas in the city. The largest of these was in the Anacostia Flats, on the east bank of the Anacostia River north of the Naval Air Station. At the height of this veterans' movement, this camp housed some twelve to fourteen thousand persons—men, women and children—in a shantytown of nondescript tents, shacks, and hovels of the most primitive kind, constructed from scrap lumber, packing cases, and tin salvaged from various dumps.

The veterans organized themselves along military lines into the Bonus Expeditionary Force (BEF) and elected a commander, Walter W. Waters, the leader of the California contingent. The BEF was further divided into regiments to facilitate administration and control. It adopted regulations for conduct and control, and it organized its own "military police" to enforce them. The vast majority of the veterans belonged to this organization, but there were two or three groups, totaling several hundred, led by two well-known Communists from Detroit, who remained outside the major organization and pursued their own reactionary and obstructionist course.

Benefits were staged to assist the veterans, and private donations from the sympathetic citizenry of Washington and other parts of the country also aided in sustaining them. The veterans themselves resorted to all sorts of money-raising devices, from selling apples to staging exhibitions. As Camp Marks—the name given to the huge camp on the Anacostia Flats—grew in size, it attracted many sightseers and curious persons. One of the favorite money-raising schemes was to bury an individual who was to remain underground presumably until Congress authorized payment of the bonus, but actually for periods of a few days. The coffin had an aperture through which the buried individual could be seen, and curious spectators paid a fee to see him!

One of the special attractions in this "buried-veteran act" was Joe Angelo. During the war he had been the orderly of Maj. George S. Patton, Jr. When Major Patton was seriously wounded while on a patrol, Joe Angelo had dragged him into a shell hole, sheltered him under heavy fire, and had then got him back to the American lines. For this heroic deed, Angelo had been decorated. The fact that Major Patton and the Patton family had done everything possible for Angelo during the years following the war did not prevent others from exploiting him and his heroic deed.

For the most part, this mass of veterans was disciplined and law-abiding even though the Communist-led groups sought to create dissension and discord. Nevertheless, thousands of idle men, roaming the streets of downtown Washington, trying to force neckties, shoe laces, pencils, apples, or gimcracks of various kinds on passers-by, were never pleasant to experience, and unescorted women soon avoided downtown streets. Then too, the thousands of veterans, living in half-demolished buildings, rude tents, huts, and hovels under the most primitive of conditions, presented the city with a sanitary problem of great magnitude.

As the number of veterans increased in the various camps, pressures on Congress intensified. Thousands of veterans thronged the Capitol grounds almost daily when Congress was in session, and there they heard sympathetic addresses by various members of Congress. Bills introduced to appropriate funds to assist in feeding and caring for the veterans were opposed by the District's commissioners and the administration for fear of encouraging further "marches" on the city. And the Congress took no action on the legislation that was introduced, nor did it act to authorize payment of the Adjusted Service Certificates, which the veterans advocated. Waters, the commander of the BEF, was violently anti-Communist, as, indeed, were the vast majority of the many thousands of veterans. The

Pace and Stembler communistic groups, however, increased their agitation. Tempers flared now and then, and there were occasional clashes with the police, although the District police were most sympathetic and sought to aid the veterans in every way possible. There was a feeling of unease in official circles, and a restless, troubled feeling throughout the city. No one knew what to expect.

This feeling of uneasiness was reflected at Fort Myer, for the officers and men of the garrison were soon restricted to the limits of the post. Individual officers and men could leave only with permission of the commanding officer, and then only for brief periods for urgent reasons. Meanwhile, troops were being thoroughly trained in the tactics of riot duty and the techniques of handling riotous crowds. Day after day, one troop, equipped with pick handles, slickers, blankets, and noise-making implements of various kinds, would take position behind a shoulder-high corral fence. Another troop would ride its horses up against the fence in the face of waving slickers and blankets, shouting and noise of all kinds, and the beating of sticks—all possible actions of a disorderly mob. These exercises were repeated day after day, until horses and men were thoroughly accustomed to the sound and fury and would advance into any crowd, regardless of any action it might take.

These activities did not escape the notice of the veterans, for while the garrison was confined to post, there was no restriction on access to it. People came to and from the post as usual. One indication of the notice that the Communist agitators were taking of the training in progress was the handbills that were surreptitiously distributed on the post during this time. They were found in barracks, stables, and other places frequented by the soldiers, but none of the distributors was ever apprehended. Practically all of the papers immediately found their way to the desks of the troop commanders, for the solders were irritated by such clandestine activities. One of the handbills on ordinary newsprint about eight and a half by eleven inches read as follows:

TO ALL MARINES ON DUTY IN WASHINGTON
TO ALL ENLISTED MEN AT FORT MYERS, [*sic*] VA.

SOLDIERS AND MARINES:

The higher Army and Navy authorities, acting for the Wall Street–Hoover government are taking steps to use you against the Ex-servicemen who are now in Washington. Your officers expect you, if the government considers it necessary to club or shoot down the Veterans to prevent them from carrying on their struggle and getting the bonus.

The veterans demand their bonus which is due them. The "heroes" of 1917 are now facing unemployment and starvation together with the rest of the 15,000,000 unemployed workers. The vets are fighting not only for the bonus but for unemployment insurance for all the workers. Only unemployment insurance will give proper relief to all the workers. The bonus is but a drop in the bucket. The unemployed workers are tired of starving. Your folks back home are getting tired of slowly starving to death.

The government has billions for the bankers but not one cent for the unemployed or for the Vets. It has not done anything to increase the miserable pay in the service. It has even cut the ration allowance.

Only a few weeks ago you marched in memory of the dead. Now the bosses want you to club and shoot these same ex-Servicemen who fought in the last war. Did you ever stop to think how many of you will be killed in the next war? The last war was fought for the bankers, for Morgan and Rockefeller, and the veterans got nothing but promises and police clubs. Now preparations are going on for a new war project to protect the bankers' interests, to destroy the only country where unemployment has been abolished by its workers' and farmers' government—The Soviet Union (Russia). You servicemen will be among the first to go. What will you get when you get out of the service? You will be treated the same way they are treating Vets today.

The bosses want you to do their dirty work for them. They want you workers and farmers in uniform to protect their profits for them. Soldiers! Marines! You are workers! No real red-blooded American soldier will allow himself to be used to shoot down fellow workers,—his war-time buddies,—his father or brothers who are unemployed.

Servicemen—Fraternize with the Vets! Help them get their bonus! Tell your officers en mass [*sic*] that you will not be used against the Vets! Organize Committees in every single company to support the Bonus! Refuse duty if you are ordered out against the bonus marchers and the unemployed!

SUPPORT THE FIGHT FOR UNEMPLOYMENT INSURANCE!
JOIN THE YOUNG COMMUNIST LEAGUE,
P.O. BOX 28, STATION D,
NEW YORK, NEW YORK

WRITE TO THE YOUNG COMMUNIST LEAGUE,
P.O. BOX 28, STATION D,
NEW YORK, NEW YORK
(All names will be strictly confidential)

YOUNG COMMUNIST LEAGUE OF THE
UNITED STATES OF AMERICA
P.O. Box 28, Station D New York City

Another of these handbills, about ten by thirteen inches in size, also printed on ordinary newsprint, was headed: "Refuse Duty against your People!" It was addressed: "To all men in the U.S. Army, Navy, Marines, and national Guard; Workers and Workers in Uniform." This sheet had a small cartoon in the upper left entitled "Heroes of 1917" and another in the lower right entitled "Bums of 1932." The text was an appeal along the lines similar to the one quoted above. This one ended:

"REFUSE DUTY AGAINST WORKERS AND FARMERS!"
FIGHT FOR UNEMPLOYMENT RELIEF!

ORGANIZE ENLISTED MENS COMMITTEES
IN EVERY OUTFIT!

"(Printed by Union Labor) Issued by a group of servicemen"

There were many more of these handbills, but their only effect on enlisted personnel was to create a feeling of anger and impatience with those responsible for distributing such crude appeals.

Congress adjourned on July 16 without authorizing payment of the bonus. Before adjournment, however, it did authorize veterans to borrow against their Adjusted Service Certificates for funds for transportation to return to their homes. Several thousand availed themselves of this authorization, and several thousand others departed as they had come. But the hard core of veterans, some ten thousand or so, refused to depart, insisting they would "stay till 1945 to get the bonus." Their chant was "Bonus or a job." This group was of course symbolic of the vast army of the unemployed throughout the country. But it presented a special problem for the Administration and the District authorities.

As numbers of veterans departed during the ten days following the adjournment of Congress, tensions of the past weeks appeared to lessen, and the dangers seemed to recede. On July 27 the restriction on post personnel was lifted, and officers and men were permitted to leave the post for the first time in a number of weeks. A day or so before this, the District's commissioners ordered that a group of condemned buildings on Pennsylvania Avenue at Third Street be cleared for demolition, so that development on the Mall could be continued. Veterans who were occupying the buildings refused to vacate them, assaulted police with bricks and pieces of concrete, tossed General Glassford down a flight of stairs, and took away his pistol. In the course of this rioting, two veterans were killed by the police. Then the commissioners appealed for federal troops to quell the rioting and restore order. Their use was authorized by the president.

About two o'clock on the afternoon of July 28, Maj. George S. Patton, the regimental executive officer, telephoned the troop commanders at their quarters, saying the squadron was ordered into Washington to quell riots and that the troops were being alerted by the sergeant major. He also dispatched a messenger for Major Surles, who was absent from the post for the first time since the restriction was originally imposed. Troop commanders hurried to join their troops, which were soon saddled and formed up along the stable line. Major Surles joined shortly, and the squadron then pounded down through Arlington National Cemetery, over the recently completed Memorial Bridge, and halted on the Ellipse south of the White House at about half past two o'clock. Then there was a long delay while the squadron waited for the arrival of the infantry battalion, coming by steamer on the Potomac from Fort Washington. Eventually the battalion docked near the War College and joined the squadron on the Ellipse by truck. Then we formed the column.

The squadron moved out in a column of platoons, followed by the infantry battalion with a few of their old World War tanks, and swept down Pennsylvania Avenue from the Treasury Building at Fifteenth Street toward the Capitol—the reverse of the direction normally followed by parades. Simultaneously, so it seemed, every office building and business establishment in downtown Washington discharged its occupants onto the streets. This parade was indeed witnessed by thousands, and a tense atmosphere of excitement pervaded the scene.

At Third Street and Pennsylvania Avenue, opposite the half-demolished buildings where the rioting had occurred earlier and which were still held by the veterans, there was another delay. Cavalry troops isolated the building, for thousands were converging on the scene—both veterans from other camps and spectators. The spectators often caused more difficulty than the veterans and provided some incidents more amusing in retrospect than the soldiers appreciated at the time. For example, one cavalry corporal kept applying the flat side of his saber to the rear of a pompous, stout individual who kept maintaining loudly that he was a member of Congress. Since the corporal was denying permission to cross Third Street, he won the argument.

General MacArthur, the chief of staff of the army, conferred with military, civilian, and police authorities on the scene. Eventually, the infantry moved into the building and asked the veterans to disperse. They were met with ribald refusal and some opposition. However, a few tear-gas grenades soon emptied the premises of hundreds of veterans. The cavalry troops pushed them along Third and Fourth streets to Missouri Avenue, about a block from the vacated buildings where they halted to permit the veterans to disperse and to await further orders.

Spread out in a single thin line for several blocks, faced with the veterans just expelled from the emptied buildings and thousands of others who were now pouring into the area from other camps, the situation became more and more tense by the moment. One group of veterans gathered in front of Troop E, where they recognized 1st Sgt. William Lawrence and some of the other noncommissioned officers they had served with during the war. The group began baiting Sergeant Lawrence and the other noncommissioned officers as only men who have also been soldiers can do. But Sergeant Lawrence and the other soldiers sat like statues and answered back not a word. Their only action was to apply the flat of a saber whenever individuals tried to slip through the thin lines. Theirs was a magnificent illustration of Regular Army discipline.

But the tensions increased, and eventually the mob became bolder in the face of seeming inaction on the part of the cavalry. A few bricks and stones from the rubble heaps were thrown. Several soldiers were struck, and at least two were knocked unconscious. Then word came to disperse the mob. The cavalry troops moved forward, with drawn sabers in hand. There was a hail of bricks and stones. But not one drop of veterans' blood was shed, although many felt the flat of troopers' sabers and some few were threatened with the point. Many veterans sought refuge in shacks they had built along the Mall or in trucks parked along the streets. A few blows with the pommel of a saber on the tin roofs or the thrust of a saber through cracks soon emptied the shacks and trucks, though, and the veterans continued their flight.

It went on across the Mall to the vicinity of Twelfth and D streets, where the communistic-led veterans were housed in vacant buildings. These were soon emptied. Then, after some delay to allow the veterans time to disperse, the troops turned toward the big camps on the Anocostia Flats.

Shortly after nightfall, they crossed the Anacostia Bridge and were on the flats on the edge of the camp by about half past ten. The squadron halted, to allow the veterans time to vacate the area. The Infantry Battalion moved in to clear it. It was soon a mass of flames. By morning, the veterans were gone, and the huge primitive camp was a smoldering mass. No one knew who set off the first fires, but it was the complete answer from both a sanitary and disciplinary point of view.

About nine o'clock on the morning of July 19, while the now-almost-vacant camp was still smoldering, trucks arrived from Fort Myer with forage for the animals, much needed picket lines, and kitchens for the troops. Horses were soon fed and groomed. Kitchens were set up, and the aroma of coffee soon contended with the smell of the smoldering ruins. Once fed, the troops waited patiently—and waiting is not at all unusual in the army.

While waiting, the senior officers of the squadron gathered around one end of the picket lines. There, seated on bales of hay, they gossiped over events of the afternoon and night and wondered what the next move would be. Time passed, and a tall sergeant of the Twelfth Infantry approached, with a small civilian in tow, and asked for Major Patton, saying that the man claimed to be a friend of the major's. When Major Patton saw them, his face flushed with anger: "Sergeant, I do not know this man. Take him away, and under no circumstances permit him to return!" The sergeant led the downcast man away.

Then Major Patton turned to the small group of officers and said: "That man was my orderly during the war. When I was wounded, he dragged me from a shell hole under fire. I got him a decoration for it. Since the war, my mother and I have more than supported him. We have given him money. We have set him up in business several times. Can you imagine the headlines if the papers got wind of our meeting here this morning!" Then he added, "Of course, we'll take care of him anyway!"

The only duties performed by the squadron that night were rescuing some army tentage from fires set by the veterans. Troops bivouacked on the ground until nearly four o'clock in the afternoon of July 29, except for the detachments of Headquarters and Machine Gun Troops which were guarding the Eleventh Street and Pennsylvania Avenue bridges. They were kept busy. About four o'clock, the squadron and the Infantry Battalion assembled and marched back into the city, visiting areas on Pennsylvania Avenue at Second and A streets northeast, the area between Maine and Maryland avenues, a small part of which had not burned the preceding day, and finally back to the vicinity of Twelfth and D streets southwest, with the mission of mopping up stragglers. Almost none were found.

At Twelfth and D, word came that the emergency was over. Troops were to return to their stations. The squadron was back at Fort Myer, with horses and equipment cared for, by half past five o'clock, ready for the evening meal. The emergency indeed was over. The remnants of the BEF were streaming out of Washington, as one correspondent described it: "The bonus army, bedraggled, hungry, shabby, moved out along the roads that led away from the Nation's Capital. . . . The BEF had died in the same confusion in which it was born."

For a few days, news reports in the papers followed the progress of these remnants. But the great Bonus March was ended. And never again would such a movement be repeated in Washington. Cavalry training and special training for riot duty had paid off. The unruly mob had been dispersed, without bloodshed, without animosity, and with comparatively little trouble. For the troops, the following day was duty as usual.

There was never much partisan political feeling on military posts, even during years of presidential elections. Military people lived for the most part in small garrisons, where the economic status was established by the military rates of pay, and social life was dependent largely on local resources. The military were isolated from the political rivalries that seem to characterize most American communities and to arouse personal and political animosities on occasion. Then too, Regular Army officers were sworn to uphold and defend the Constitution of the United States of America, like the president himself, and being an arm of the executive branch, regular troops carried out orders regardless of the political party in power—as they had done in the BEF riots. Further, few officers maintained voting residence, and absentee voting was relatively rare at this time. In the depression winter of 1932, interest among the personnel at Fort Myer in the forthcoming change in the administration was largely economic. The vast army of unemployed was growing. Bread lines and soup kitchens could not alleviate the hunger and distress. There were reports of food riots. Various states were declaring bank holidays to meet emergency financial stresses. Like the rest of the nation, people on the post at Fort Myer hoped that the new administration would find some way to restore the economic situation. The year 1933 was to be an eventful one in more ways than one. And the Cavalry Squadron was to have an important part in initiating the change in regimes.

Third Cavalry "Regimental Notes" in the March-April issue of the *Cavalry Journal* reported:

> The 2d Squadron commanded by Major A. D. Surles acted on March 4th as the Presidential Escort for the journey from the White House to the Capitol and return from the ceremonies incident to the new President taking the oath of office. The squadron marched in column of platoons at a trot which made a very effective formation. . . . Machine Gun Troop, Third Cavalry, with Machine Gun Troop Tenth Cavalry, made up a squadron, commanded by Captain Clyde D. Garrison, which formed the Cavalry component of the Inaugural Parade later in the afternoon.

It was the last time perhaps that a presidential inaugural would see a cavalry squadron as a presidential escort. Mounted escorts had long been traditional for important personages, and the presence of mounted troops, accoutered in all their best military trappings, always added to the pomp and glamour of such events. This particular escort, however, was something of a case of "a bad start maketh a good ending."

Before eleven o'clock that morning of March 4, the squadron was booted, spurred, pipe-clayed, and polished to the Nth degree and in place along Pennsylvania Avenue in front of the East Pennsylvania Gate leading from the White House's front entrance. The presidential party was to leave from that entrance at half past eleven. A White House aide was to signal Major Surles when the party was ready to leave. The squadron would then present saber, while the trumpets rendered the honors, then wheel to the left in a column of platoons and lead the presidential party at a trot down Fifteenth Street and Pennsylvania Avenue to the Capitol. The squadron had rehearsed this procedure on the drill field at Fort Myer until all was letter perfect.

The squadron had dismounted, adjusted equipment, tightened cinches, removed the last specks of dust, and otherwise ensured that nothing would mar the perfection of its performance. It was not yet half past eleven when the squadron had remounted, reformed ranks, and drawn saber in preparation for the initial ceremony. Suddenly, to the amazement of everyone, the limousines, with the secret-service escort, swept out from the North

Portico, through the gate in front of the squadron, and turned into Pennsylvania at a good clip! It was the presidential party!

There was no time for rendering honors, and for a moment, all was a confusion of limousines and motorcycles and horses. At command, the squadron wheeled to the left in column of platoons, pounded down the avenue at the gallop, crowded past the presidential party on both sides as it turned from Fifteenth Street into Pennsylvania Avenue, and gained its proper position. Then, with guidons fluttering and sunlight flashing on the gleaming sabers, the squadron led the president and the president-elect to the Capitol. There the squadron wheeled into line and rendered the honors as the limousines discharged their passengers. Then it dismounted and, from its vantage point on the Plaza in front of the Capitol steps, viewed the inaugural ceremonies. When these had ended, the squadron remounted and escorted the new president back to the White House without further incident. But it had been a hectic experience.

Most Regular Army officers of that day had established satisfactory and pleasant relations with banks in various parts of the country where they had served earlier in their careers. As a matter of convenience, we had the finance office deposit our pay checks in those banks. Few lived on a cash basis; most used monthly credit and paid bills monthly by check. Even the commissaries and post exchanges were operated on this monthly credit, but all such post bills were paid by the tenth of the month—or else.

Sighs of relief at the installation of the new administration turned into worry only a couple of days later, when the president directed a bank holiday, or moratorium, which was to extend to March 9 or later. All banks closed their doors, and our pay checks were in them. The moratorium was extended to March 13, when some of the banks began opening doors for normal business. Officers who had deposits in these banks were fortunate. Other banks began opening their doors for new business but paid off old depositors in driblets at rates of 5 and 10 percent every few months. Officers who had accounts in these banks suffered, but those who had accounts in banks that did not reopen were indeed unfortunate.

But the worst was yet to come!

One of the early "recovery" measures of the New Deal was the Economy Act, which lopped $500 million from the salaries of government officials, civilian and military, veterans' compensation, and pension funds. In the military services, this 10 percent reduction in pay was across the board. It was a severe blow, because many were drawing less than they had drawn a dozen years earlier, although family and financial responsibilities had multiplied.

The application of this pay cut involved some rather interesting complications in the military service. Rates of pay for government employees by grade were fixed by law and by a mass of regulations broadly based on an eight-hour day and forty-hour week. Most civil-service employees received extra pay for required overtime work, but not in the military. It was decided that government employees could not be required to work the hours represented by this 10 percent cut in pay. Therefore, a system of compulsory leave was adopted, and individuals were required to take leave each month for the days and fractions thereof representing the 10 percent that had been deducted from their pay. The system involved a great deal of unnecessary paper work on the post, for each officer had to report the specific days he would take leave each month. But of course the leave schedule had to ensure the presence of officers for important duties at all times. Many officers turned in these reports each month and then continued with their normal duties. There was never very much that officers and families could do with these fractional periods, even if they could have afforded it—which few could!

Meanwhile, President Roosevelt and the "brain trusters" and the Congress were struggling desperately to combat the "Great Depression" during the spring and summer of 1933. One after another of the alphabetical agencies—the NRA, PWA, AAA, CCC, etc.—were created and entered into the realm of controversy. Aside from having numbers of unemployed men raking leaves and leaning on shovels about the post for a brief period, the only agency that affected our lives was the CCC, the Civilian Conservation Corps.

The Congress established the CCC as a recovery measure designed to give useful employment to many thousands of idle young men, to provide assistance for their families through allotment of pay, and to perform valuable reforestation and other work in the national forests and parks. It was one of the most valuable of the New Deal measures.

It fell to the lot of the army to establish the organization and to administer it during its formative period and, later, most of its existence. Troops were stripped of officers, noncommissioned officers, cooks, and other technical specialists to organize the camps, conduct recruiting, provide tools, transportation, and equipment, and, finally, supervise the work. However, "pacifistic" sentiment was strong in the country in those days; this, added to the traditional American antimilitary sentiment, vastly complicated the problems of getting the camps under way. Any form of military drill, semblance of military organization, or military command and discipline was forbidden.

During most of the summer, troops and batteries at Fort Myer were left with only a single officer and were bereft of many noncommissioned officers and other soldiers while post duties continued at their normal pace. They were troublesome days, but Fort Myer was better off than many posts where even a greater proportion of officers were taken from their normal duties. Eventually, reserve officers were called to active duty, and gradually these able men assumed responsibility for operating most of the CCC camps. The army's Corps Areas, however, were left with the responsibility for administering the camps through various districts. By November, nearly all Regular officers had rejoined the command at Fort Myer.

FIRE CALL! Always a dread sound on any post but particularly so on a cavalry post because of the stables. But it was not a stable that caused the call to sound that bitter cold night in February, 1934. It was the Riding Hall—one of the most important buildings on the post.

The winter was a cold one. Most of the motor transportation on the post was old; much of it had been in service since the World War. The post quartermaster was having trouble starting engines on the cold winter mornings and was having much trouble with frozen radiators and frozen oil. It seemed logical to park the vehicles required for daily post administration in the Riding Hall during the hours of darkness, especially since it had a heating system that provided a measure of warmth. So it was used during this spell of bitter weather.

When the fire was discovered, it was already too late, for the gas and oil had turned the interior of the hall into a raging inferno. Post and Arlington fire departments were unable to save the building and, indeed, were fortunate in being able to prevent the fire from spreading to nearby barracks and stables. The Riding Hall was a total loss. However, the cavalrymen were able to salvage bricks from the destroyed walls for the construction of storerooms and other alterations in the troop barracks. And Major Patton salvaged an iron horse's head that had hung over the main entrance!

The hall had occupied such a vital part in the life of the post that its loss cast a pall of gloom over us that was to last for days. No more Friday Rides. No more Society Circus. No one knew where the funds would be found for reconstruction during these depression days. But somehow funds were found, and the army engineers set about the business of rebuilding.

The *Cavalry Journal* of January–February, 1935, describes the opening of the new Riding Hall:

> With the Secretary of War as the guest of honor, the new riding hall at Fort Myer, Virginia, was opened with two performances of a military pageant on January 12, 1935. With every seat sold nearly a week before the show, the officers and men of the garrison under the direction of the post commander, Colonel Kenyon A. Joyce, 3d Cavalry, set a new high standard of colorful and thrilling entertainment before two audiences which included the Secretary of State, the Assistant Secretary of War, and many members of the Diplomatic Corps.
>
> The first event on the program was a pageant "The History of the United States Army" written and directed by Captain H. W. Blakely, 16th F. A. With a musical setting by the mounted regimental band of the 3d Cavalry, which played music of the period represented by each unit, groups of soldiers were presented armed, equipped and uniformed as were their predecessors in 1776, 1812, 1846, 1861, during the Indian Wars, 1898, and 1918. The final group to enter the hall showed the highly trained technicians who are the soldiers of today with their radios, automatic weapons, and scout cars. The music of this modern group was appropriately, "There's Something about a Soldier."
>
> The new riding hall replaces the one destroyed by fire in February, 1934. The ring is one hundred by two hundred feet, and there are seats for 1800 people arranged in stadium fashion on three sides. There is also a sound-proof control booth with a loudspeaker system, light and signal bell controls, and telephone communications.
>
> The regular Friday afternoon exhibition rides were resumed on January 18, the guest of honor being Major General Hugh A. Drum, Deputy Chief of Staff.

Brave Rifles were back in business again at the old stand and ready for the next Society Circus!

6. IVIED HALLS ON THE WILD MISSOURI

For seven long years, I courted Nancy,
Heigh! Ho! The rolling river,
For seven long years, I courted Nancy,
Hah! Ha! I bound away
To the Wild Missouri!
—*Cavalry Song*

The city of Leavenworth, Kansas, is situated on the west bank of the Missouri River about thirty miles northwest of Kansas City. The military post of Fort Leavenworth adjoins the city of Leavenworth on its north side. The military reservation is about three by four miles in size, roughly rectangular in shape except for a wide bulge eastward, caused by a broad bend in the Missouri River. A long, steep, wooded ridge extends the full length of the reservation along its western edge. In the period before the Second World War, Fort Leavenworth was the home of what was perhaps the most important military institution in the United States Army—the Command and General Staff School. But in addition to the school, two other important activities of the government were located there: the United States Disciplinary Barracks, where military prisoners were confined, and the United States Federal Penitentiary, an agency of the Department of Justice, where prisoners convicted by federal courts were confined. The Disciplinary Barracks was located within the post proper; the Federal Penitentiary, in the southern end of the reservation.

Entering the reservation through the main entrance at the northern edge of the city of Leavenworth, one followed Grant Avenue, a broad, tree-shaded avenue with bridle paths under the trees along each side, to the main part of the post, about two miles distant. To the right and the left were broad, open pastures, where teams of oxen and mules of the pioneers once gathered before setting forth on the immigrant trails and where now the horses of the school grazed during the summer seasons. A mile from the main gate, Highway 92 led off to the eastward toward the Missouri River and the bridge that crossed there into Missouri just under the river bluffs. Approaching the post, one passed between two small man-made lakes, Smith and Merrit, for fishing and winter sport in season.

Entering the post proper, Sedgwick Avenue led eastward past the Tenth Cavalry barracks to the stable area. Then Reynolds Avenue led eastward past the South Riding Hall. Then Meade, Augur, and Pope avenues led off eastward toward the river, all lined with two-story brick and stone officers' quarters on the tree-shaded streets. To the west was the Grant Avenue Polo Field, and then a dozen troop barracks which had been converted into the Pope and Doniphan apartments for student officers. Doniphan Avenue was an address only, for the apartments looked out over the polo field and golf course further to the south. Motor traffic used the alley at the rear of the buildings.

Pope Avenue was the first and principal cross street east and west through the post. North of it, single and double sets of brick and stone officers' quarters lined Scott, Grant, and McClellan avenues, as well as the northern and eastern sides of the Main Parade, Sumner Place. Kearney Avenue led westward from the Main Parade parallel to Pope Avenue. Engineer Hall, a huge three-story building which had once housed an entire regiment of engineers, faced south on Kearney, just off the Main Parade. This huge building had been remodeled into apartments, which had been given the name Bell Apartments in honor of the father of the modern school system in the army. Few who served at Fort Leavenworth will ever remember this building as other than "The Beehive," for so it was known throughout the army because of its teeming population!

North of the Main Parade and Sumner Place was the Disciplinary Barracks, loaned to the Department of Justice for a time during this period and used as an annex to the federal prison. To the west of the Main Parade and fronting on McClellan Avenue were troop barracks, the guardhouse, and, still further to the north, the veterinary hospital and quartermaster warehouses, which had once been cavalry and artillery stables, and the North Riding Hall. McClellan Avenue led on to "Bluntville," a collection of noncommissioned officers' quarters, and eastward to the flat in the river bend where Sherman Field, the aviation facility, was located.

Sheridan Drive followed the long wooded ridge along the western edge of the reservation, and bridle paths crossed and recrossed the ridge. Over on the western slope of this ridge was the Hunt Lodge, a stone clubhouse, which was the scene of many gay parties and hunt breakfasts. In the area south of the Pope and Doniphan apartments in the midst of the golf course was the golf club, where most formal receptions, dinner dances, and similar parties were held.

The Officers' Club, with some accommodations for transients, was located on McClellan Avenue between Pope and Kearney avenues. The post hospital and several sets of officers' quarters faced west on Thomas Avenue across the West End Parade, an open area used by the Disciplinary Barracks for rehabilitation drills and by riders and polo players for practice and exercise.

The post, even in its relatively restricted area, afforded ample space for drag hunts, polo, horse shows, racing, riding, tennis, golf, swimming, and every possible recreational activity for officers, men, and their families. Full use was made of all facilities.

Fort Leavenworth had long been associated with army schools. On May 7, 1881, in General Orders Number 42, War Department, Gen. W. T. Sherman, then commanding the United States Army, directed the establishment of a "school of application for infantry and cavalry" there. In a letter to Gen. Philip H. Sheridan, commanding the Division of the Missouri, with headquarters at Fort Leavenworth, General Sherman indicated his approval of General Sheridan's plans for the school, expressed his expectations that it would be most successful, and remarked, "I don't want to meddle with this new school or to have it the subject of legislation, because if that is done, like West Point, it will be made political and taken out of our control." The establishment of the school and the designation "School of Application of Infantry and Cavalry" was confirmed in General Orders Number 8, War Department, January 26, 1882.

The name must have occasioned some confusion in official correspondence, for on January 22, 1886, the War Department directed that "to secure uniformity in official communication addressed to or referring to it," the school would thereafter "be known and designated as the United States Infantry and Cavalry School." This name persisted until after the interruption occasioned by the Spanish-American War. Although there were changes in the curriculum during the years, the course remained primarily two years of basic training.

In 1901, after an interruption of four years, the school was enlarged and developed "along the lines of a post graduate college." The primarily basic instruction, which had formerly been given in the United States Infantry and Cavalry School, was now to be given in schools on other posts, which were to be "systematically organized and efficiently conducted" for the purpose. Officers who showed special merit in these post schools were to be given advanced instruction in the school at Fort Leavenworth, which was now to be designated the Command and General Staff School.

This seemed to have been a little too ambitious, though, for in 1905 the War Department again reviewed the course of instruction and returned to the designation of Infantry and Cavalry School. But once again the scope was broadened, and in 1907 the War Department once more changed the designation, this time to the Army School of the Line. So it remained until the border-troubles incident to the Mexican Revolution of 1910 and the World War, which followed in a few years, once again interrupted the regular courses. During the period of the World War, the facilities of the post were transformed into a very active training center which gave initial training to a host of newly appointed officers and to many units of special troops composed of men drafted for war service.

After the war, the National Defense Act of 1920 modernized the military policies of the United States and provided for a comprehensive reorganization of the armed services. The act provided for a great system of military education for the army, which would begin with West Point and would include the Reserve Officers' Training Corps (ROTC) in schools and colleges, with basic training in organizations of the Regular Army and the National Guard. Branch schools were established with basic and advanced courses of instruction. Then the school at Leavenworth was reorganized, and a course was established to provide the next step in the military education of the graduates of the branch advanced courses. The new Leavenworth organization was designated the General Service Schools.

The course of instruction in all of the schools, but particularly Leavenworth, was dominated by the experience of trench warfare of the World War, so fresh in the minds of military men. Students assigned to attend the courses at Leavenworth had graduated from their branch advanced courses. The designation of the school was changed again in 1922 and again called the Command and General Staff School. The course was intensely competitive. Class standings were posted regularly. Officers were made to feel that their entire future careers depended on their class standings. All of this during these early years, together with rather primitive living accommodations provided by the remodeling of barracks buildings into family housing of temporary flimsy construction, led to tensions. Some officers broke under the strain. There were even some suicides.

However, the leaven of change was working as the years passed. Money was found to remodel apartments into far-more-suitable living accommodations especially designed for facilitating study by mature officers who were heads of families and already well past the study habits of college years. The apartments on Pope and Doniphan avenues were remarkable examples of this efficient remodeling. The plans were designed to allow the intense concentration that the course required of student officers and at the same time allow family life involving teen-age children to continue normally without interrupting the student officer any more than necessary. Each apartment provided a master suite with bedroom, bath, and study, which could be isolated from the remainder of the apartment. Each apartment had a well-equipped kitchen, a dining room, an ample living room, and three bedrooms, with ample closets, baths, and hallways, all done in excellent taste with the best of available materials. These quarters were typical of the efforts that were being made to provide the best accommodations for student officers.

Then, in the year 1928, the school was again reorganized, this time as a two-year course for Regular Army officers. But it did continue a modified three-months' course for officers of the National Guard and the Organized Reserves. The location of the school itself remained the same on the post—at the end of Augur Avenue at its intersection with Scott Avenue, on the bluffs overlooking the Missouri River. It was housed in four connected buildings, two of them long associated with the history of Fort Leavenworth. Of the four buildings, three—Grant, Sherman, and Sheridan halls—were three-story and the principal academic buildings. The fourth, Wagner Hall, a two-story building at the east end, was the school library.

Sherman and Sheridan halls were both historic, having been part of the Ordnance Arsenal established there in 1859. Sherman Hall was successively headquarters for the Department of the Missouri and the home of the United States Infantry and Cavalry School and its successors. Sheridan Hall was used by the arsenal and then by the post quartermaster for storage before being taken over by the Infantry and Cavalry School in 1895. The buildings were joined by a central structure named Grant Hall in 1904. Needless to say, all of these buildings had undergone many changes and modifications during the years.

The school at Fort Leavenworth had begun as a two-year course, and nearly fifty years later it was again a two-year course. But what a difference! The original orders establishing the school prescribed:

> The school will habitually consist of three field officers of cavalry or infantry, with not less than four companies of infantry, four troops of cavalry, one light battery of artillery, and the officers attached for instruction as hereinafter described. These companies may be changed from time to time according to the exigencies of the service. The officers detailed for *instruction* will be *one* lieutenant of each regiment of cavalry and infantry, preferably such as have no families or who have not previously had the benefit of other instruction, who will be nominated by the commanding officers of the regiment and announced in general orders by the Adjutant General of the Army, by or before the 1st of July of each alternate year beginning with July 1881, for a term of two years. The officers so detailed will be attached to the companies composing the school, and will perform all duties of company officers in addition to those of instruction.

The officers "detailed for *instruction*" were students!

General Order Number 8, War Department, dated January 26, 1882, confirmed the establishment of the school and charged the commander

> with the practical instruction of every officer and soldier of his command in everything which pertains to army organization, tactics, discipline, equipment, drill, care of men, care of horses, public property accountability, etc., and generally of everything which is provided for in Army Regulations. These must be his first care and the second is "theoretical instruction," which ought to precede a commission, but is not always the case, *viz:* reading, writing, grammar, arithmetic, geography, algebra, geometry, and trigonometry sufficient for the measurement of the delineation of the ground, and such history as every young gentleman should be presumed to know: and third, the "science and practice of war," so far as they can be acquired from books.

The order went on to prescribe that the student officers on reporting were to be examined by the staff of the school and divided into two classes, the first only requiring the higher instruction, the second the whole course of two years. For the "First Class," those capable of higher instruction, the curriculum prescribed:

> Mahan's Outposts, Meyer's Signalling, Mahan's (Wheeler's) Field Fortifications, Ive's Military Law, Operations of War (Hamley), The lessons of War as taught by the great master, Colonel France J. Soady, Lectures by professors and essays prepared by the students from general reading, and Practical instruction in surveying and reconnoitering by itineraries and field notes, as prescribed for use of the Army.

It is also interesting to note that General Sherman's order establishing the school, General Orders Number 42, War Department, May 7, 1881, also prescribed:

> The senior field officer, present for duty, will command the school and the next five officers in rank will compose the staff of the school. All officers will purchase their own textbooks and stationary, but other expenses will be defrayed out of the post fund so far as existing Army Regulations permit, except blackboards, desks, tables, chairs, furniture, etc., which will be supplied by the Quartermaster's Department on requisition made by the commanding officer, approved by the department commander.

Fifty years later the basic educational qualifications for officers of the army had been established by graduation from the United States Military Academy or from other schools and colleges or by examination and testing. Officers who were selected for attending Fort Leavenworth now had received basic training in their respective branches and branch schools, where they had attended the basic or company officers' course and then graduated from the advanced course there before being considered for attendance at Fort Leavenworth.

Thus, officers who were detailed to attend the Command and General Staff School were considered ready for a thorough course of instruction in the modern concepts of command, leadership, and staff procedures. Two years was now considered none too much time to spend on these intensive studies, although the practice in some foreign schools no doubt had exercised influence in the determination of the length of the course. More important, however, was the diminishing influence that the experience of trench warfare in the World War had had on military concepts and thought. Technical developments in motor transport, aviation, armor, and mechanization were stimulating thought and indicating solutions to the stalemate of trench warfare. It was high time for this most important of military schools in the army to be brought up to date.

The school had come a long way in a half century. Subject matter now included such subjects as offensive operations, military intelligence, military history, historical research, military geography, defensive operations, marches, reconnaissance, security, counteroffensive, lines of communication, supply evacuation and logistics, mechanized units, motorization, tanks, methods of training, combat orders, solutions of problems, mobilization, legal principles, tactics, and techniques of the separate army. More than 950 hours were allotted to these subjects, and another 350 to terrain exercises, map problems, and equitation. It was by means of terrain exercises and map problems that the school tested the extent to which students had absorbed the principles and doctrines that were taught in the classrooms and also measured their ability to apply them in the solution of practical problems.

For the most part, textbooks were now prepared by the staff and faculty. Instruction was given by means of conferences, lectures, map maneuvers, map exercises, tactical rides, and command-post exercises, as well as in the terrain exercises and map problems mentioned above. The first year's course dealt primarily with the tactics and technique of the separate arms and the employment of the combined arms of the reinforced division. In the second year's course, the emphasis was upon tactical and strategical principles and the employment of the corps and army. Military history, military geography, historical research, and psychology and leadership were important subjects in both years.

Normally, nearly every Friday afternoon during the first year was devoted to the solution of a map problem. It was subsequently discussed with the class, and of course, students were graded on their solutions. During the second year, students normally solved one map problem each week but did the work at home, with twenty-four hours allowed for the purpose. These problems were also graded and discussed with the class. There was no restriction whatsoever as to the use of notes, textbooks, or other material in preparing solutions. Students found them to be intensely interesting and enormously valuable. No "approved solution" was issued, as was normally the case in the first year. But the "school solution" was usually made evident during the discussion.

Changing to the two-year course and easing the tense atmosphere in the school after the World War no doubt resulted from the effect the tensions had on some of the students. The standard of selecting students was far removed from that early day when "preferably such as have no children" was the prime criterion. Far from it. The emphasis now was to provide so much for the accommodation, education, recreation, entertainment, and amusement of the wives and children that the student officer was relieved of all interference with his studies. At least as far as that might be possible. School and post authorities did a magnificent job in this respect.

The commandant of the Command and General Staff School was also the commanding general of the post. Since there were no regular troop formations stationed on the post except for the school detachment or those who were otherwise associated with the school, the only purpose of the post organization was to support the school and conduct some summer training activities. The commandant had an administrative staff, headed by the post executive officer. They supervised the administration and maintenance of the post and directed the usual administrative service, such as medical, signal, engineer, quartermaster, and ordnance, as well as the "school troops," the Tenth Cavalry. This unit cared for the horses assigned to the school, provided janitorial service for the buildings, and fatigue details for necessary work on the post. The post staff also managed the clubs, post exchanges, and all recreational activities.

Under the commandant, the assistant commandant directed all academic activities of the school. His administrative assistant was the school secretary. His academic assistants were the director of instruction, the class directors, and the naval advisor. The Academic Division was organized into five sections, each headed by a chief and each one with primary responsibility for one category of instruction.

Section I, the first section, was responsible for instruction dealing with offensive operations, with the functioning of the commander and his staff, and with tactical and strategical principles; Section II, for instruction in military intelligence, military history, historical research, and some related subjects, as well as for special operations that did not pertain exclusively to Sections I and II; Section III, for instruction in defensive operations, marches, reconnaissance, security, counteroffensive, and lines of communication; Section IV, for supply, logistics and evacuation, and the functioning of the G-1 and G-4 Sections of the General Staff; and Section V, for certain miscellaneous subjects, such as the estimate of the situation, combat orders, solution of problems, psychology and leadership, legal problems, methods of training, and preparation of exercises. In 1934 this section also dealt with motorization, mechanized units, and tanks.

All instructors were assigned to one of these academic sections, and each was also assigned to his own branch subsection, thirteen in number, which were responsible for instruction in the tactics and techniques of each of the branches. However, the instruction was carried on under the direction of one of the five sections.

The offices of the commandant, the assistant commandant, the post executive officer, and the school secretary were all in Grant Hall. Here, too, were lecture and conference rooms, where school doctrines were expounded. These rooms were equipped with tables, chairs, screens for the display of motion pictures and slides, blackboards, and sliding panels of wallboard, upon which the instructor could display his maps, charts, and other instructional aids.

The directors, chiefs of sections, instructors, and most of the school shops and clerical staffs were located in Sheridan and Sherman halls. The top floor of each of these two halls was a huge room, provided with tables and chairs, and these rooms were used for map problems, tests, map maneuvers, and command-post exercises. Here students became familiar with the vagaries of "General A" and the various and sundry members of his staff and the elements of his command. And it was here that the school tested our progress, determined our class standings, and measured our individual knowledge of "what the school teaches."

The Book Department, where students obtained tackle boxes, crayons, map pins, grease pencils, and all of the various office supplies required by "General A and his staff," was located in the west end of Sheridan Hall. And on the ground level, near a sally port, Bob Baker, the barber who had been trimming hair for more years than most student officers had served in the army, had his barbershop. There the instructors and most students kept his appointment calendar filled for long hours six days a week.

School routine did not vary a great deal from day to day or from week to week. Only the subjects changed from time to time. Classes ran from 8:00 to noon and from 1:00 to 5:00 P.M. daily, Monday through Friday. There were usually several conferences or lectures daily, a total of some 175 during the first year course. Map exercises, illustrative of the tactical principles and doctrines expounded, would follow these lectures and conferences. Fifty or more such exercises, varying in length from two to eight hours or more, were conducted, along with a dozen or more tactical rides. In these exercises, the instructors and students discussed the application of principles in situations outlined on maps or on actual terrain.

There was a series of command-post exercises and map maneuvers in which students acted as commanders and staff officers on opposing sides, while instructors umpired the problems. Every night, student officers spent two or more hours of intensive study in preparation for their next day's assignment. Some students formed committees, which met once or twice a week, usually on weekends, to study texts and problems from previous years, as well as notes from previous years, passed on by former students. Many thought that this method helped them in the solutions of problems and thus in their class standings. Problems from previous years were readily available for reference, and the school authorities encouraged student officers to make use of whatever material they desired.

Friday afternoons were normally devoted to map problems, in which students solved specific requirements and upon which they were graded. There was always a discussion of these problems the following week, during which students found fault with the "school solution" unless they had happened to "hit it." Sometimes these discussions were most interesting. When the solution to the last requirement was turned in on Friday afternoon and students wended their way homeward, all looked forward to the forty-eight-hour period of relative freedom with pleasure and anticipation, particularly so when their solutions to the afternoon's problem had coincided with the "school solution." In any case, there was certain to be much discussion of the problem in the course of the many cocktail parties, dinner parties, and other social functions over the weekend.

Instruction at Fort Leavenworth, when it was the General Service School, had been dominated by the tactical principles and methods evolved from the experience of the trench warfare of the World War, particularly the warfare on the Western Front. Except for Allenby's cavalry campaign in Egypt and Palestine and some of the early actions on the Eastern Front, there had been little maneuver involved in combat during the war. There was almost none on the Western Front after the first few days. And except for some of the cavalry instruction, there was little maneuver involved in combat as taught in the General Service Schools. However, with the developments in aviation, motor transport, mechanization, and tanks, leaders in military thought came to believe that maneuver could be restored to the battlefield, bringing with it the opportunity for decisive victory and thus eliminating stalemates such as had occurred on the Western Front. With the reorganization of the school at Leavenworth, these views came to be reflected in the teaching of the school. The change in instruction in tactical methods is best reflected, perhaps, in what came to be known as the "wide envelopment."

During the years immediately preceding the reorganization, the school had taught that when a division attacked an enemy position, a part of the command would attack the enemy in front, to hold him in position, while the major part of the command moved right or left far enough to miss the enemy's organized position. Then it would attack in the direction of a terrain feature, the possession of which would render the enemy's position untenable, thus ensuring his defeat. This was called an envelopment, but the main and secondary attack forces were never separated very far, and the two directions of attack were relatively close together.

The "wide envelopment" envisaged moving the bulk of the command around one flank of the enemy position, as far as possible under cover of darkness, by marching, by motor, or by a combination of both, protected by a screen provided by the divisional cavalry squadron. Meanwhile, a portion of the squadron would screen the opposite flank for purposes of concealment. The main attack would then be made against an objective in the enemy rear, which he could not defend; and his position would thus become untenable and his defeat would be assured.

For officers who had undergone the indoctrination of "Leavenworth Teachings" during the years before their student year, and for those who had spent much time in the study of past textbooks and problems in preparation for the course, this was a revolutionary concept indeed, and it came hard to a great many officers. During these years, no hostess was ever able to keep the conversation among the male guests at her cocktail or dinner party from eventually turning to the "wide envelopment," and more particularly if there was an instructor or two among those present at the party. But aside from its value as a conversation piece, the "wide envelopment" was of the utmost value in stimulating thought among students and instructors alike.

There were some remarkable personalities who had an important part in directing the reorganization of the school and its teachings during this period. The following were among the most notable.

Brig. Gen. Edward L. King, commandant from July, 1925, to July, 1929, was charged with the initial stage of this reorganization. It was a task that he found much to his liking. This distinguished cavalryman had come to the Command and General Staff School from the Cavalry School at Fort Riley, where he had distinguished himself as an executive and school administrator. He was a man of distinguished appearance and bearing, a lover of active individual sports, an excellent horseman, and a fine tennis player. General King was a progressive and vigorous leader and a stern disciplinarian, a fact that did not render him overly popular with a few of his subordinates. All of these characteristics, together with his keen analytical mind, made him an ideal choice for initiating the reorganization of the school.

General King was followed very shortly as commandant by Maj. Gen. Stuart Heintzelman. This scion of a distinguished army family was the last of a line who had distinguished themselves in the service of the United States. He graduated from the United States Military Academy in 1899 and was commissioned a second lieutenant of cavalry. He saw service in the Philippines, China, and the Mexican border. He was a graduate of the Infantry and Cavalry School in 1905, the Staff College in 1906, the Army War College in 1920. He was outstanding as a military instructor, having served on the faculty at Leavenworth, at Princeton, and at the Army War College.

The *Cavalry Journal* of September–October, 1935, said of him:

> He spent the last six years of his life as Commandant of the Command and General Staff School where those who knew him and this work which was so vital to him realize what a powerful influence he exercised—and will continue to exercise—upon military doctrine underlying our plans and hopes for national defense.
>
> General Heintzelman was a profound student, especially of Military history, which he read with understanding, vision, and real analysis. He read it with eyes of reason, not with prejudice. Through these critical studies he became a scholar. To those who knew him—and to the nation which he honored by his devotion—he has bequeathed a definite and sound legacy for our national security—not "to wrest the scriptures (of history) to" our "own destruction" but to follow the example which he so clearly set forth throughout his life and which he so clearly attained to "study to show thyself approved . . . a workman that needeth not to be ashamed—RIGHTLY divining the word of truth.
>
> He laid down a fundamental truth for those who have pledged their lives to the cause of national defense when he said: "It is not sufficient to die bravely for your country—you must die intelligently."

He was a man of quiet, dignified, and distinguished bearing who charmed all with whom he came in contact. His broad experience, keen intellect, and positive approach rendered him an ideal selection for transforming the organization of the school and broadening the scope of the course. General Heintzelman guided the destiny of the school from July, 1929, to July, 1935, when his promotion to the rank of major general led to his assignment to a corps-area command.

Another change in the course at the school was coincidental with General Heintzelman's departure. It was the abandonment of the two-year course and the compression of the instruction once again into a single year. Increasing tensions in Europe, particularly in Spain, Italy, and Germany, again affected our military policies. There was increasing pressure for the modernization of weapons, motorization, mechanization, aviation, and organization in general. And the War Department decided that there was need in the army for more officers with Command and General Staff School training. Hence, the return of the one-year course in 1935. The first of these classes graduated in June, 1936, along with the last of the two-year classes.

Three notable officers directed the school during the last half of this decade of the thirties, and then the mobilization of 1940 brought forth another change. Brig. Gen. Herbert J. Brees, another distinguished cavalryman, followed General Heintzelman, remaining little more than a year until his promotion to major general and his assignment to a corps-area command. Brig. Gen. Charles M. Bundel, an artilleryman, followed General Brees and remained until his retirement for age in June, 1939. General Bundel was followed by another artilleryman, Brig. Gen. Lesley J. McNair, who was to become the commanding general of the Army Ground Forces, responsible for the training of the wartime army. The school was fortunate to have had these men serve as commandant during these days.

The commandants who served had the assistance of able men as their assistant commandants and directors of instruction, some of whom were outstanding in their influence on the direction of school policies. Two of them are characteristic of the several who served in these capacities.

Col. Wilson B. Burtt, infantry, was assistant commandant from May, 1933, to June, 1936. He was a graduate of the Military Academy, class of 1899, an honor graduate of the School of the Line in 1911, of the Army Staff College in 1912, and the Army War College in 1927, and had also served tours on the General Staff. Not unduly impressive in stature and actually on the stout side, this notable officer was most impressive in intellect and in his direction of the staff and faculty. He had broad experience in staff work during the war, which had only served to stimulate his thought along military lines. He was a military student whose contribution to the school was material.

He was ably assisted by his director of instruction, Col. Joseph A. ("Sandy") McAndrew, who was a 1904 graduate of West Point, of the Army Signal School in 1914, the School of the Line in 1922, the General Staff School in 1923, and the Army War College in 1924. A brilliant thinker, positive in thought and action, he merited the nickname "Sandy" not only for the coloring of his hair and complexion but also for the determination that he brought to the task of directing the instructors and the instructional matter of the school along approved lines.

There was a routine for families, as well as for the student officers and instructors. The officers of the post had children ranging in age from kindergarten to high school. So, when the officers departed for school, so did the children. Kindergarten and elementary-grade children who were too small to walk were gathered in a mule-drawn bus and taken to class. The other elementary grades walked to school on the post, and the high-school age rode a bus to Leavenworth, where they attended Leavenworth High School or the parochial Immaculata High School.

There were bridge clubs and book clubs for the ladies and dramatic clubs for both officers and ladies. Officers of the Tenth Cavalry conducted riding classes for the ladies, which were enormously popular. Riding classes for the children were continuous in the riding halls on Saturday and Sunday afternoons, and these, too, were immensely popular. There were swimming pools, tennis courts, baseball and football fields, and organized athletics of all sorts for women and children. Golf and riding were the most popular activities. Boy- and girl-scout troops were well organized and well conducted. There are few places where recreational activities were as well organized and well conducted as they were at Fort Leavenworth in those days. And this was a matter of policy, in order to permit the student officers to concentrate to the fullest extent possible on their professional studies with a minimum of interference from normal household activities.

Kansas remained "dry" after the repeal of prohibition, but not so Missouri. Kansas City was only thirty miles away. Liquor was plentiful there, but there were other sources of supply close by. "Austin's" opened as a small roadside café but gradually expanded by adding a small room for the sale of "bottled goods." Customers soon outgrew the small room, so that it was finally expanded into a full-fledged liquor store that catered to personnel on the post and that could supply any brand or type of liquor a person might want. Austin prospered mightily and numbered many officers of the post among his customers and friends.

Friday night, after the weekly map problem, was always a time for relaxation among the students, either to celebrate having approached the school solution or to drown their sorrow for having failed to do so. It was a common practice for friends in the same apartment building to gather for a cocktail party and let off steam about various activities of the week, and more particularly to rehash the map problem of the afternoon. Later on, there were other and larger cocktail parties and dinners and the weekly dance at the Officers' Club. A vast amount of talk was expended during all of these activities in the discussion of school doctrines, problems, and personalities. It might not always have been at the highest intellectual level, but nevertheless it sometimes served to ease troubled minds.

Saturdays, there was golf, tennis, riding, and polo for those who were interested, and nearly always there were cocktail parties and dinners for this evening as well. Traditional customs of the service still guided official and personal social lives. Official affairs were always conducted with a due measure of formality, and there was usually some formality in purely social affairs. All supper and dinner parties, and most cocktail parties as well, were with black tie or appropriate uniform. This phase of school life always began the year with an official reception, attended by all officers of the post. It substituted for the interchange of formal calls among the student officers. However, all student officers and new arrivals always called on the commandant, the assistant commandant, school instructors, and senior personnel on the post. Most student officers exchanged calls with personnel of their own branch and with personal friends. There was always much entertaining, both of personal and branch nature, formal dinners as well as more informal partying.

Orders that detailed officers to attend the school usually directed them to arrive on dates that were staggered, to facilitate the administrative arrangements of settling new arrivals into both their quarters and the post routine well before the start of the school year. Household goods were usually shipped by rail, for there was little or no moving by long-distance van at this time. They were delivered to quarters by the post quartermaster. Details from the Tenth Cavalry provided labor for delivering, uncrating, unpacking, and placing furniture and household goods in quarters. There were few posts where this necessary work was so well organized and handled with such efficiency.

Army social life is not without its entanglements, and Fort Leavenworth was no exception. One incident during this period received widespread notice in the press and resulted in no small amount of embarrassment to the individuals concerned, as well as to the school authorities. It even had repercussions in the War Department. Two army wives departed quietly in the spring for Arkansas, where they established residence under the six-weeks' residency law in effect there at the time. The two ladies lived together during the period and quietly obtained divorces from their husbands. The husbands then joined them, and they all immediately remarried, but to different spouses. Some enterprising reporter discovered this "wife-swapping" episode, and the wires of the press services soon spread it across the nation. There were investigations and a very great deal of comment. However, no laws had been violated, and the parties concerned were soon able to resume normal lives with their new spouses.

Most families who were in Fort Leavenworth during these years will remember Harris and his ponies. He was a colored soldier of considerable girth and great humor. He was a genius with horses and with children. Officers leaving the post in previous years had given him four or five Shetland ponies. Every evening when classes were over and a day's work was done, Harris would saddle his ponies with a nondescript collection of children's saddles, then, mounted on some refractory or spoiled animal that he had reclaimed, he would set off with the ponies on lead lines and head for Doniphan, Pope, and Kearney avenues—or some other street well populated by children of tender years. His cheerful voice and infectious laugh could be heard for a block or so, and both drew children like a magnet.

All along the curb, little children would be waiting. Harris would soon fill the saddles with little boys and girls and take them for a gentle ride of a half hour or so. When one of the youngsters, perhaps at the prodding of some mother, asked Harris what he charged for the ride, Harris would reply with a shout and laugh that could be heard all over the neighborhood, "Ole Harris don' charge y'all nuthin'. Jes tell Ethel (or whatever the maid's name might be) that ol' Harris jes wants some po'k chops and hot biscuits!" And again the lilting laugh. While he no doubt acquired many plates of "po'k chops and hot biscuits," mothers saw to it that the little hands had quarters and dimes for Harris, and the father always passed him a dollar or so on occasion. He was a fixture; he was a wonderful part of Fort Leavenworth.

Practically all of the noncommissioned officers in the Tenth Cavalry were men of long service, and all of them were married men with families. A great many of the other enlisted men of the regiment were also married, and those who could not have quarters on the post found accommodations in the city of Leavenworth. Many of the wives, daughters, and relatives of these men found employment on the post as cooks, maids, and laundresses. Competent catering service was always available for parties in the club or for private quarters at reasonable rates. The post orderly service provided janitorial service for maintaining public halls, attending furnaces, the outside police of public areas, and similar work. These janitors were also available for orderly service in officers' quarters for a period of about two hours each week and for special work on occasion. They were paid by the officers for this work at prescribed rates.

Fort Leavenworth was a pleasant place to live in those years. The care and attention given to the professional and personal lives of the officers and their families proved to be a most worthwhile investment for the United States Government. There were no nervous breakdowns or suicides during the period, and the war record of the officers who attended the school during those years speaks for itself.

Graduates of the school organized, commanded, staffed, and trained the army and the air corps of the United States in the Second World War. An examination of the records of the two-year classes of 1935 and 1936 and that of the first one-year class, which also graduated in 1936, is indicative of how well the school was performing its mission. It is also some measure of the value of the two-year course. The Army Register of 1946 indicates that of the 106 members of the two-year class of 1934 and 1935, 1 attained the rank of general; 2, lieutenant general; 22, major general; 39, brigadier general; and 36, the rank of colonel. Of the class, 6 were retired for physical disability or were lost in action during the war. The 109 members of the two-year class of 1935/36, produced 3 lieutenant generals, 14 major generals, 35 brigadier generals, 42 colonels, and had 15 officers retired for physical disability or lost in action. There were 109 officers in the one-year class which also graduated in 1936. Of these, 1 became a general; 1, lieutenant general; 10, major generals; 35, brigadier generals; 59, colonels; and 3 were retired for physical disability or lost in action. Each of these classes had several marine officers and officers of foreign armies among its members, and some others who are not indicated in the 1946 register. Other classes showed comparable records.

Horses, horses, horses! In many ways, Leavenworth was almost as much of a cavalry post as Riley. All officers had an hour of equitation each week.

Horses were used for tactical rides and terrain exercises. There was outdoor polo during the spring, summer, and fall for officers interested in the sport, and the games usually drew a good gallery of spectators. Interclub competition with the Cavalry School and the Kansas City Country Club was frequent, and the post was occasionally the scene of Circuit Championships. There was indoor polo several nights a week during the winter, a valuable form of exercise for the considerable number of officers who played.

And the post had the Fort Leavenworth Hunt, with the master and the hunt officials always in "hunting pink" and the rest of the field in appropriate riding costume. There was always a large field of both men and women, especially on Sundays, when student officers were able to attend. They were also held on Wednesday afternoons and Sundays. There was even a "midget hunt," on which an officer with two or three very young riders on lead lines followed the field from check to check, much to the amusement and delight of everyone.

Harris took care of the children who were too young for riding classes, which were continuous on Saturday and Sunday afternoons. Ladies' classes were held several times weekly. And riding for pleasure was available to all early in the morning or late in the afternoon, as well as on Saturdays and Sundays. Horse shows for novices were held frequently in the riding halls, and every spring there was a formal outdoor horse show and race meet, which was well attended by riders from Fort Riley, the Artillery School at Fort Sill, civilian riders from Kansas City, and others. So, even though the golf course was widely used by both officers and ladies alike, the horse was "king" at Fort Leavenworth in those years.

But the pressure was on! And the cavalry was definitely on the defensive. Many officers of the General Staff in Washington and in other branches believed that aviation, mechanization, and motorization could perform all cavalry missions. And there was a great deal of experimentation in the army in all of these fields. In the keen competition for the limited funds and manpower available in those depression days, the cavalry bore the brunt of budget cuts in both manpower and money.

Two cavalry regiments, the First and the Thirteenth, had already been transformed into mechanized cavalry regiments and formed into the Seventh Cavalry Brigade (Mechanized) during the early years of the decade. There was also much experimentation with divisional organization involving motorization. Many of the theoretical studies dealing with these subjects and much of the testing in war games were done by the faculty of the school, preparatory to the field tests which followed.

Unfortunately, the chief of cavalry was bitterly opposed to mechanization of the cavalry, even though the missions to be performed were still cavalry missions. Gen. John K. Herr believed in *horse* cavalry. He was fighting every form of mechanization at the expense of the horse cavalry at the time when all trends in military thought in all modern armies was toward mechanization and armor. He was preaching to all who would listen or read the doctrine that "cavalry (meaning horse cavalry) should be employed in large masses," but few military men and no military students could agree with him. It was unfortunate, for in the year 1940, most cavalry officers were seeking an opportunity for experience in the new field of armor, where such cavalry stalwarts as Chaffee, Patton, and Scott were already exercising such an important influence.

No one who left the Command and General Staff School in 1940 had any idea when and where the war would come, but few doubted that the United States would become entangled in the European struggle in due course. So it was that one left Leavenworth with a real regret. The old order was changing. What the future held was problematical, almost frightening—and challenging!

7. CAVALRY HORSES: IRON AND THOROUGHBRED IN THE BLUEGRASS

A man in armor is his armor's slave.
—*Browning,* Herakles

God forbid that I should go to any heaven in which there are no horses.
—*Robert Bentley Cunningham-Graham*

The National Defense Act of 1920 created the offices of the chiefs of branches for the line troops, infantry, cavalry, and artillery, corresponding to the chiefs of the service branches, such as the engineers, quartermaster, ordnance, and medical corps, which had long been in existence. In general, the chiefs of the branches were responsible for the control and management of personnel, the development of tactical doctrines, methods of training, and all research and development involving weapons, organization, and special equipment pertaining to the welfare and utilization of the branch. There had been no such chiefs of the combat branches since the Civil War, and it was thought that the line combat units would profit from having a "friend at court," just as the service branches had. All chiefs of branches constituted the special staff of the War Department, each of whom was to speak with authority on matters of interest to the branch.

The branch chiefs were all major generals, selected from the colonels of the branch and appointed for four years, at the end of which they could retire with the rank of major general. The chief of staff, of course, held a commission higher in rank. All major generals ranked according to date of that commission. Most War Department General Staff officers were majors, lieutenant colonels, and colonels. Some chiefs of sections were brigadier and major generals. All General Staff studies in the War Department concerning organization, personnel, and budgetary matters that pertained to the branches had to be coordinated with the chiefs of the branches. Naturally enough, every chief resisted all inroads on his branch for funds or personnel for the expansion that was then in progress in the fields of aviation, armor, mechanization, and motorization. And none resisted more bitterly than the chief of cavalry, for that branch was bearing the brunt of the demands.

Maj. Gen. John K. Herr became chief of cavalry in 1938. He was a graduate of West Point, class of 1902, the Mounted Service School in 1910, the Cavalry School Advanced Class of 1925, the Command and General Staff School in 1926, and the Army War College in 1927. He also had experience on the General Staff. Tall, lean, and rugged, he was the picture of a cavalryman. Active and energetic, he was a fine horseman and one of the army's best polo players. A magnetic and pleasing personality, he was greatly admired and respected on all sides. He was commanding the Seventh Cavalry when selected for appointment as chief of cavalry, an appointment that was warmly welcomed throughout the cavalry, for it was generally believed that his honesty, forthrightness, and outspoken dedication to the cavalry were the need of the hour in Washington. General Herr was attractive and possessed of great charm when he wished to exercise it, but unfortunately he was impatient with those who might hold contrary views, and he did not hesitate to make his opinions of such persons known on any and all occasions.

The general believed that the General Staff was intent upon destroying the cavalry because they did not like cavalrymen, because they considered the cavalry obsolete, and because they wished to profit at the expense of the cavalry. He would not recognize that armor would perform normal cavalry missions. It was a real sorrow to him that so many cavalry officers were seeking an opportunity for experience in the mechanized units and in the burgeoning armored force at Fort Knox. He was especially distressed that among these were many of the best horsemen and polo players in the cavalry.

Fort Knox, Kentucky, in 1940 had been the home of the Seventh Cavalry Brigade (Mechanized) for nearly ten years. During this period, a permanent brigade post had been constructed so that there were a number of permanent brick buildings for headquarters, officers' and noncommissioned officers' quarters, and troop barracks. However, there were not nearly enough for the accommodation of the Headquarters Armored Force and the First Armored Division, which were in the process of being organized there in the spring and summer of 1940. There were still some temporary buildings left over from the World War cantonment. They were still in use, and there was a vast amount of construction under way on the post.

U.S. Highway 60 and U.S. Highway 31 W follow the south bank of the Ohio River southwesterly for a distance of about twenty-five miles from Louisville. Highway 60 continues westward along the course of the Ohio River, and Highway 31 W turns southward. It is here that Fort Knox is located. In 1940, Highway 31 W led through the post, past the United States Gold Depository just southwest of the post, through Elizabethtown—or E-town as it was known to thousands—and on south to Nashville and Birmingham.

Most of the post was on the east side of Highway 31 W, the Dixie Highway. Approaching from the north, the direction of Louisville, one passed an airfield, Godman Field, on the right, then through the concurrent-training area, the scene of summer training activities. Avenues in the post proper ran east and west and were numbered successively from north to south, First to Eleventh avenues. North and south streets were designated by letters A to E eastward from Knox Street, which paralleled Highway 31 W and the Illinois Central Railroad.

The barracks of the Thirteenth Armored Regiment and the Sixty-eighth Field Artillery faced south on Third Avenue, looking out across the open parade ground. Officers quarters lined Fourth and Fifth avenues, and just to the south there was another parade ground, where the barracks of the First Armored Regiment faced north on Sixth Avenue. Centrally located between the parade ground and the highway were more officers' quarters, the Officers' Club, the Officers' Mess, and Post and Armored Headquarters.

In the southwestern part of the post were the ordnance's and quartermaster's warehouse areas. To the west of these and across the highway, amid the woods in an area enclosed by a high wire fence, was one of the most important buildings on the reservation—in the nation for that matter—the United States Gold Depository, where the government was storing gold from Europe and elsewhere as rapidly as it could be transported into the area.

The armored force had just come into being, without benefit of legislation but rather by War Department directive—in a manner reminiscent of the procedure by which General Sherman had established the school at Fort Leavenworth, and possibly for similar reasons. Quite appropriately, the first chief of the armored force was a distinguished cavalryman from a distinguished army family, who was widely known and greatly admired throughout the army, Adna R. Chaffee, now a major general, the same one whom we met in an earlier chapter when he was a major at Fort Bliss. Few officers ever had a more promising career in the army, and it was a great loss to the armored force, which he had been so instrumental in creating, and to the nation when he was taken from the scene by death almost on the eve of our entry into the Second World War.

Maj. Gen. Charles L. Scott, who had been busily engaged in organizing the Second Armored Division, then assumed command of the armored force. He had been chief of the remount service immediately after the World War. He had also been director of instruction at the Cavalry School, when Col. Bruce Palmer was assistant commandant, and had done yeoman service in assisting Colonel Palmer in making all cavalrymen cognizant of the capabilities of mechanization and armor in the further development of the cavalry.

The Seventh Cavalry Brigade (Mechanized) had formed the backbone of the armored force. The two regiments of this brigade, originally the First and Thirteenth Cavalry regiments, had also added the "Mechanized" to their designations. In the armored force, however, the designations were again changed, and they became the First and Thirteenth Armored regiments and, as such, formed the basis for the two combat commands "A" and "B" which constituted the First Armored Division. The division was stationed at Fort Knox with the Headquarters Armored Force. Maj. Gen. George S. Patton, Jr., had assumed command of the Second Armored Division when General Scott had assumed command of the armored force at Fort Knox.

So it was that during these months of 1940 and 1941, Fort Knox was a beehive of seething activity. People were coming and going in streams—officers and men for assignment; staff officers on inspections; important visitors from Washington and elsewhere; and dozens of the idly curious. There was a vast amount of construction under way in preparation for the planned expansion: roads, streets, bridges, buildings of all kinds. And the hundreds of workers employed on all these projects commuted from Louisville, Bardstown, Elizabethtown, and others of the surrounding communities. Roads and streets were filled with the incessant clanking and roar of tanks—combat cars they were called—the clatter of armored cars and half tracks, the clamor of motorcycles, and the accompanying clouds of dust and fumes of burning gasoline and oil, caused by troops in training or on the way to training areas. And twice every week the arrival of the "Gold Train" and the security measures connected with the transfer of the gold from the train to the depository imposed its own special activity, which disrupted the normal activities of the seething post.

Numbers of officers, especially field officers, far in excess of the immediate needs of the armored force, were being ordered to Fort Knox for indoctrination and training in anticipation of the planned expansion. These officers were attached to organizations of the First Armored Division for duty. The Thirteenth Armored Regiment, during the late summer and fall of 1940, had as many as thirteen field officers in excess of table-of-organization requirements. And this was typical of other elements of the division.

There were almost no transient accommodations in the Officers' Club at Fort Knox, and the nearest adequate hotel accommodations were in Louisville, nearly thirty miles away. To accommodate this flood of transient officers reporting to the armored force, the post erected two or three dozen pyramidal tents on floored frames adjacent to the Officers' Mess. The tents were arranged in streets, with gravel walks, each tent with water, but with a community bathhouse. Here, officers ranging in rank from colonel downward were billeted with their wives and children, awaiting assignment to elements of the command and the availability of quarters of a more permanent nature. Officers and their families had their meals at the Officers' Mess. Some remained in tents for many weeks, and some of the officers who were assigned to units stationed at Fort Knox lost hope of obtaining quarters on the post after two or three months and eventually sought apartments in Louisville or Elizabethtown as cold weather approached.

Immediately upon reporting to the armored force on their initial assignment, all officers were given a course of instruction in driving and first-echelon maintenance (that done by a vehicle's crew or driver) of every type vehicle used in the armored force and in the use of the weapons with which each vehicle was armed. Officers then joined units and participated in the drills and training exercises, which were almost continuous. There were section, platoon, and company drills and tests of communications. There were battalion, regimental, and division attack problems, day and night marches, and exercises in reconnaissance and security. Over and over. Day after day, and night after night. Constantly.

Roads in central Kentucky, where paved, were mostly blacktop, often with high crowns, and not so wide that a rolling tank did not occupy more than an undue proportion of its width. In this area of rolling Kentucky hills, an armored column thundering along a road at thirty or forty miles an hour was an awesome sight for motorists and presented many problems for anyone who sought to pass the column by weaving his way forward past the lumbering vehicles. This was so, even though usually the vehicles were well spaced and the tank commanders and drivers endeavored to aid with signals and to indicate when the road was clear ahead. Any motorist who met such a column was confronted with a frightening and dangerous prospect. In spite of the exercise of great care, accidents were frequent.

For that matter, accidents were frequent on all of the roads approaching Fort Knox, because of the heavy commuter and construction traffic, the narrow roads, and the limited visibility over the rolling hills. At one time the seventeen-mile stretch of road between Elizabethtown and Fort Knox was considered to be one of the most dangerous stretches of road in the entire country. Hardly a day passed without one or more serious accidents. While most of the road between Fort Knox and Louisville was a three-lane highway of recent construction, there was a narrow bridge over a deep stream bed where the road entered the reservation and where another bridge was under construction. This bottleneck caused serious traffic jams during the morning and evening rush hours, when construction workers, post employees, and military personnel were traveling to and from work. Officers who lived in Louisville and commuted to work found it necessary to start before the traffic flow began in the morning and to leave the post after the flow eased in the evening. Otherwise, they could not make the early hours for drill and training. So they saw little of their homes and families except during the hours of darkness.

One of the most important details that came to this large number of extra field officers during these months of intense activity was the investigation of accidents in which military vehicles and military personnel were involved. There were many of them, and most of them were of a serious nature, involving claims against the government or government personnel. One who investigated dozens of these claims could hardly help being impressed with the devil-may-care attitude of many young soldiers. Nor could one help being impressed by the willingness of the other party in accidents involving government vehicles or personnel to place blame on any soldier involved, even when he was clearly not at fault. Such claimants no doubt hoped to profit at government expense.

Social life at Fort Knox followed the general pattern of social life in the army during the period, with due allowance for crowded conditions, the sense of urgency that permeated the scene, and the feeling of uncertainty that influenced most individual lives. New arrivals called promptly on the chief of the armored force, the commanding general of the First Armored Division, their own regimental commander, and some other senior officials. There was the usual interchange of calls among friends and associates. There were the usual massive receptions for VIP's—Very Important Persons—who visited Fort Knox frequently. There was the usual attention to uniform and dress for occasions of a social nature and for official occasions also. But in these months, the feeling of stability that accompanied normal peacetime assignments—the feeling that one would remain on a post for a tour of three or four years—was missing. No one knew when a move would come, or where it would end. And these factors affected nearly all of the social activities on the post.

In 1940, the gold of Europe was fleeing the Nazi menace and also was purchasing the sinews of war with which to oppose that menace. Gold from elsewhere in the world was flowing into the United States, and the government, following the fiscal policies early established by the New Deal, was busily engaged in providing security for the gold by buying it and "burying" it at Fort Knox. "Burying" it is hardly the best descriptive term for the disposition that was being made of this gold, although it was a rather derisive term applied to the fiscal policy. Actually, the gold bullion, in the form of bricks of the approximate size of construction bricks but each weighing about fourteen pounds, was being placed in vaults. The steel vaults, about six by six by eight feet in size, with steel doors in which there was a small barred window, lined each side of an aisle way and reminded one of nothing so much as cells in a jail.

Such was the United States Gold Depository at Fort Knox. A modern building of attractive design and appearance, it had office space for the superintendent and his assistants and accommodations for the guards. Underneath were the vaults, where the gold was stored. Owing to the fact that the gold bricks had slight irregularities from the melting down and casting, treasury employees used small wooden pegs to ensure that the stacks from floor to ceiling and from rear to front were regular, smooth, and tight, as they worked from back to front of those cell-like vaults. When the vaults were packed tight with gold bricks, they were closed and locked. Meanwhile each brick had been carefully recorded by weight and measure of purity, and there were checks and double checks to ensure the highest possible measure of accuracy and security.

The depository was an agency of the United States Treasury Department, and the superintendent, his administrative staff, assistants, and all of the guards were civil-service employees of the department. The superintendent was responsible for safeguarding the gold once it was in the depository. Officials of the Treasury and Post Office departments were responsible for safeguarding the shipments during their transportation to Fort Knox. But the commanding general of the First Armored Division was responsible for safeguarding the shipments from the time they reached the Fort Knox reservation until they were delivered safely to the depository. This proved to be a unique and most unusual military duty.

The "Gold Train" arrived at Fort Knox every Wednesday and Saturday and was normally ready for unloading about seven o'clock in the morning. It consisted of five or six mail or baggage cars, with a dining car and a couple of sleeping cars for the train guard personnel. They consisted of a dozen or so treasury and postal guards and a small detachment of soldiers. The gold was carried in stout wooden boxes about the size of a packing case for ammunition or books, but each one weighed about five hundred pounds. Four of these cases were loaded on "gold skids" to facilitate loading and unloading by means of a dolly. Each of these skids carried about a ton of gold, and each railway car held about thirty tons of the precious metal. Owing to the concentrated weight of this load and the very small space it occupied, the floors of the railway cars were strongly reinforced.

The shipments were safeguarded by the posting of a guard detail from either the First or Thirteenth Armored regiment, each furnishing a detail on alternate shipments. In each regiment, the details were permanent, or as nearly so as exigencies of the service permitted. The guard consisted of a permanent commander, who was a field officer; two officers of the guard; eighteen noncommissioned officers and fifty-eight privates of the guard; seven scout cars; five combat cars (tanks); one command car; one motorcycle; and eight two-and-one-half ton trucks for hauling the gold.

One guard post, with an officer, two scout cars, and a light tank, inspected the bridge at the north edge of the reservation and remained on guard until the "Gold Train" had passed. The remainder of the guard was disposed in some thirteen posts, with a reserve. These posts surrounded the area of the railroad siding where the train was unloading, detoured all traffic around the area, and allowed no one to enter except authorized personnel with passes. The detail also provided a convoy to protect the gold from the train to the depository, a distance of something less than a mile. This convoy consisted of two scout cars, each with a driver, one noncommissioned officer in command, and two privates—all with a total armament consisting of four caliber .30 machine guns, two submachine guns, and four pistols.

The reserve consisted of one scout car, with a radio and a crew consisting of a driver, a noncommissioned officer, two privates, and a radio operator, armed with pistol, submachine gun and two caliber .30 machine guns; one light tank, with a crew of a noncommissioned officer, a driver, and two machine gunners, all armed with pistols, a submachine gun, and two machine guns; also a motorcycle messenger and one command car, with a driver, for the use of the officers of the guard, one of whom remained with the train during unloading, the other patrolling the area.

All weapons were loaded with ball ammunition, and the guard orders prescribed: "*Should it be necessary to use weapons, the guard will shoot to kill.*"

The unloading unit consisted of a pair of two-and-one-half ton trucks without bows or tops, which were protected during the movement to the depository by two scout cars, one at the head and the other at the tail of the columns. When the train stopped at the siding which was the unloading point, the two trucks backed up to the railway car, with the floors of the trucks on a level with the car doors. Postal employees wheeled the gold onto the trucks, loading four skids onto each truck, with the total of gold, skids, and boxes making a load of about five tons per truck. When the two trucks were loaded, the convoy would move out rapidly for the depository, and the next two trucks would back up to receive their loads.

At the depository, Treasury Department employees unloaded the gold by means of a special hoist, and loaded empty boxes from a previous shipment onto the truck. Meanwhile the security convoy had returned to the train to escort the next convoy to the depository. This process of unloading the train of more than half a billion dollars worth of gold and transporting it to the depository usually required several hours. The guard day therefore began with the initial inspection and verification of the guard in the regimental area at about three o'clock in the morning. It ended when all vehicles and personnel returned to the motor pool and barracks about noon.

The Gold Train stopped on a railroad siding almost in the center of the post. Highway traffic was interrupted on Highway 31 W during the unloading process, and a large area in the central part of the post was closed to all normal post activity. Only persons who had special passes were permitted to enter or transit the area. Thus, during two mornings each week, all post activity except that connected with the safeguarding of the gold shipments ceased in a large area of the post. It was an inconvenience to travelers, to post personnel, and to the many construction workers employed in the building activities then in progress. Considering the weight of the treasure and the mechanical problems that would have confronted any would-be train robbers, these security measures may have seemed out of proportion to the possible dangers. However, all of the inconvenience was accepted in good spirits on all sides, and there were few complaints. Most of the personnel assigned to this Gold Guard duty obtained a measure of satisfaction and even a thrill of sorts from participation in it.

During these months in the fall and winter of 1940/41, the army was undergoing a transformation. The Army War College class for the year had been canceled to make more staff officers available for the expanding army. A general headquarters for the army (GHQ) was in the process of organization and was occupying the buildings of the War College. Its organization was under the able direction of Gen. Lesley J. McNair, who had been called from the post as commandant of the Command and General Staff School for the purpose. New army headquarters were replacing the corps areas, and army corps were being established to assist in directing the training of the divisions. An intensive training program for all divisions was getting under way under the direction of GHQ. It was a period of the "phoney war" in Europe. No one could foresee American involvement in the European war, but the nation was preparing for all eventualities.

It was a period of change. Since staff officers were needed for the newly organized army and corps headquarters, as well as for the divisional and other units in the process of formation, it was not surprising that the excess of field officers in the armored force at Fort Knox was gradually thinned by assignment to units of the armored force and transfer to organizations in other areas. But even a few months of experience in the armored force brought knowledge of the capabilities and limitations of armor and some concept of the views regarding missions and methods of tactical employment. These months were therefore of the utmost professional value to the officers who had the experience.

Fort Knox was truly a cavalry station, even though the horses were "iron." It was probably not altogether through chance that the post was selected for the stationing of these organizations of armor. The bluegrass country of Kentucky is famous the world over as the home of thoroughbred horses. The Kentucky Derby, one of the most famous races in the world, is run each May in Louisville. The First and Thirteenth cavalry regiments, both steeped in cavalry tradition, had formed the nucleus of the armored force. The first chief of the force was General Chaffee, and other cavalrymen, such as Bruce Palmer, Charles L. Scott, and George S. Patton, had provided impetus, initiative, and leadership in the drive for bringing the organization into being. They and other cavalrymen had long recognized that aviation, motors, and armor would perform many of the missions that mounted men had performed in past wars, and would perform them effectively.

The spirit that all of these officers transmitted in such great measure to all personnel in the armored force during these early months was truly cavalry spirit, and it made this period of service all the more valuable to those who were fortunate enough to experience it. Many who looked forward to an opportunity to develop with the armored force received unrequested and unexpected assignments for duty with the General Staff with troops in other stations. They left the "iron horses in the bluegrass" with some measure of regret.

8. PRELUDE TO WAR

In peace, as a wise man, he should make suitable preparation for war.
—*Horace*

Who first invented work, and bound the free
And holiday rejoicing spirit down. . .
To the drudgery at the desk's dead wood?
—*Charles Lamb*

To one who has lived in the semiarid and desert regions of the Southwest, a first visit to the Pacific Northwest is a most notable experience. Even the tropical verdure of the Pacific islands or the travelogues in books and magazines do not prepare one for the immensity of the impact of the vegetation of the region. One does not envisage the enormous size and height of the towering trees nor the luxuriance of the dense forest growth beneath them. The mesas and bare rugged mountains of the Southwest have a beauty of their own which is truly inspiring. But the snow-clad mountains of the Northwest, with sunlight sparkling like untold millions of diamonds across their summits, are majestic in their grandeur.

One is struck by one point of similarity between the two regions—the rugged newness and closeness to nature of the countrysides. From an area of little or no moisture and the stunted growth of the arid desert regions, one is overwhelmed by the plenitude of water on all sides and by the frequency of rain, the evenness of temperature, the clouds, the fog, and the flower-bedecked landscape. Such was the impression of cavalry officers who were familiar with the Southwest and were ordered to duty in the Pacific Northwest for the first time in 1941.

The military reservation at Fort Lewis is a vast area of nearly one hundred thousand acres of flat, gravelly soil, heavily wooded, threaded with small streams, and with many small ponds and lakes hidden in the forest areas. It is located east of U.S. Highway 99 between the cities of Tacoma and Olympia, east of the southern reaches of Puget Sound. One turns east of the highway to enter Fort Lewis through the unique stone-and-log gate leading to the post. The Main Parade, a vast grass-covered, gravelly area, parallels the highway for perhaps a mile. At the southern end is the commanding general's quarters, and the post-exchange area and rows of troop barracks are along the western side. Just east of the southern half of the Parade is the area of officers' quarters, of brick and comparatively recent construction, and at the northern end of the Parade are the quartermaster, ordnance, and other service areas. Roads led eastward from the Main Parade to a regimental cantonment area and training areas on the reservation.

Tacoma is about eighteen and Seattle about fifty miles north of the post; both are on the eastern shores of Puget Sound. Bremerton, with its navy yard, lies just across a branch of the sound from Seattle. Between Puget Sound and the Pacific Ocean lies the Olympic Peninsula, almost a hundred miles on a side, dominated by Mount Olympus and the Olympic National Park. The area is almost primeval wilderness, an area of indescribable beauty. Olympia, at the southern end of the sound, is about ten miles from the post. McCord Field, one of the most important airfields of the army air corps, adjoined the reservation on the north.

The Cascade Range parallels the coast about fifty miles inland and overlooks the whole coastal area. About fifty miles to the southeast of Fort Lewis, snow-capped Mount Rainier, from its elevation of more than fourteen thousand feet, dominates the whole area south and east of Puget Sound. It is the highest peak in Washington, one of the most beautiful and accessible mountain peaks in the Cascade Range, and consequently a favorite recreation spot for lovers of mountains and winter sports.

Fort Lewis had been the home station of the Third Infantry Division since shortly after the World War, although elements were scattered in various other stations about the country. During the latter years of this period, however, permanent construction for a division had been completed, and all the elements of the division were now concentrated there. The division, incidentally, had been reorganized after the experimental trials of 1939 as a "triangular" division, that is, a division with three regiments capable of being formed into three regimental combat teams with their supporting artillery, engineers, and service troops.

When the National Guard was called into federal service for training during the expansion of 1939 and 1940, the Forty-first Infantry Division, composed primarily of troops from Washington and Oregon, was assembled at Fort Lewis and quartered in its cantonment area of temporary construction, typical of so many camps of the day. The division still retained the old "square" organization, that is, with two infantry brigades, each of which had two regiments, an artillery brigade, and all the usual service elements.

With the organization of General McNair's previously mentioned general headquarters, the old corps-area organization, which had been in effect since 1920, was replaced by an organization of four armies. Under these armies, corps were established as tactical and training commands. Administration was handled for the most part through a post administrative organization through the army channels. The Ninth Army Corps was the training and tactical command established at Fort Lewis under the Fourth Army headquarters at San Francisco. The Third and Forty-first Infantry divisions were the principal combat units of the command, and the 115th Cavalry (Wyoming National Guard) was the Corps Cavalry Regiment.

Maj. Gen. Kenyon A. Joyce, who had commanded the Third Cavalry at Fort Myer, Virginia, in the early thirties, had been promoted to brigadier general in 1936 and major general in 1939. He was designated to command the Ninth Army Corps, to supervise its organization, and to oversee its training. Some of the officers who were finishing tours at the Command and General Staff School, others who were made available by the cancellation of the Army War College Class of 1940, and some of the surplus officers in the armored force at Fort Knox found themselves assigned to duty with the General Staff with troops in all of these army and corps commands.

General Joyce, being an able and astute commander, felt the need for an able and competent chief of staff to assist in organizing his headquarters and carrying out the training mission. Being thoroughly familiar with the records and backgrounds of many of the graduates of the Command and General Staff School and the Army War College, he looked over the possibilities available to him. His eyes fell upon a lieutenant colonel who had been commanding a battalion in the Fifteenth Infantry of the Third Division for a short time. This officer was a distinguished graduate at the Command and General Staff School, a War College graduate, had much General Staff experience, and had recently been an assistant to General MacArthur in the Philippines. Lt. Col. Dwight D. Eisenhower was a natural choice, and he became the chief of staff, Ninth Army Corps, in the early spring of 1941. He was promoted to colonel on 6 March 1941.

General Joyce's selection of a chief of staff was a very fortunate one. Each one held the other in the highest esteem, and their mutual understanding and approach to common problems was complete. There was never a question about where the command responsibility rested. General Joyce dictated the policies and left the coordination and direction of the corps staff to Colonel Eisenhower, who kept the general completely informed of the problems confronting the corps during this organizational and training period and the progress being made toward their solution. When a command decision or approval of any proposal or contemplated action was required, Colonel Eisenhower—who was always thoroughly familiar with every step of the staff work involved in the complicated problems—invariably had the staff officer who was primarily concerned with the problem make the presentation. Then he stood by, ready with clarifying comments, assistance, or advice as required. The general conducted no staff conferences with the entire corps staff present, but rather, he dealt through the chief of staff. For that matter, Colonel Eisenhower conducted no staff conferences as chief of staff; he preferred to work with the individual staff officers concerned with the staff preparation on problems, and he was always readily accessible for consultation and advice to such officers.

In March, 1941, as the corps staff was assembled for duty, it was crowded into the post headquarters building as a temporary measure while a headquarters building of cantonment type was under construction at the southern end of the parade to the rear of the commanding general's quarters. The occupation of this building a month later greatly facilitated the organization of the staff and its preparations for completing the planning and for conducting the important training missions of the corps.

When the War Department established the army and corps organizations in 1940, a corps cavalry regiment was provided for each corps. In order to attain the strategic mobility necessary to operate with divisional and corps units that might be moving by truck, the cavalry branch had devised the Horse-Mechanized Cavalry Regiment for the corps. Two regular cavalry regiments had been transformed into such regiments and had been tested in maneuvers. Other corps cavalry regiments were to come from the National Guard.

The horse-mechanized regiments consisted of a headquarters and headquarters troop, a horse squadron portee' of three rifle troops, each of three rifle platoons and a light-machine-gun platoon, and a mechanized squadron consisting of two scout-car troops and a motorcycle troop. The regiment totaled 61 officers and 1,088 enlisted men. For the Ninth Army Corps, the 115th Cavalry (Wyoming National Guard) was called into active service and joined the corps in the spring of 1941, just as soon as the cantonment that was being built for them was ready. General Joyce took a great personal interest in the training of this organization and saw to it that members of the corps staff who were cavalry officers did the same. The regiment did exceptionally well during the year's training.

General Headquarters (GHQ) in Washington had directed a training program for all the divisions that were then in service. These exercises were to be prepared and conducted by these newly organized corps headquarters. However, GHQ would select one of the exercises in which inspection teams from GHQ would inspect the state of training of the division and, of course incidentally, the performance of the corps commander and his staff in carrying out the GHQ directives. GHQ had prescribed that there would be five of these exercises, and these were repeated for each division in the corps. In general, the exercises contemplated command-post exercises (CPX) involving command, staff, and communications personnel to afford training in command and staff procedures and communications. In addition there were twenty-four-hour field exercises (FE's), which were one-sided maneuvers in which umpires represented the location and action of the enemy and which involved the divisions in such operations as a night march and organization of a position, advance and attack in a meeting engagement, organization of a position, and others. The final division exercise was to be a free maneuver, with one division operating against another. And this was to be followed by a one-sided field exercise in which the divisions would use ball ammunition.

The War Department had recently acquired a large portion of the Hearst Ranch in California for use as a military reservation. It was decided that all of the exercises would be held on the Fort Lewis reservation except for the maneuver of division against division and the corps' field exercise. These two exercises would be held on the Hunter Liggett Military Reservation, as the new reservation was officially designated. This would afford the elements of the corps training in a strategic movement of several hundred miles, as well as the advantage of operating on unfamiliar terrain.

The preparation and conduct of all these exercises within a period of about four months required an enormous amount of staff work, much of which fell upon the shoulders of one staff officer in the G-3 (Operations and Training) Section of the corps staff. The necessary reconnaissance of the terrain for each of these exercises was made doubly difficult by the heavily forested nature of the reservation and the absence of any but woodland roads and trails. The actual problems for the different exercises had to be prepared, and then it was necessary to detail and train the umpires who would control the development of the exercises by representing the enemy. Since the two divisions of the corps were organized differently—one triangular and one square—two sets of problems for each of the exercises were necessary.

Not many of the officers and men who participated in the exercises will ever forget them. They were so realistic that only the shot and sound of battle were missing. Dense forest growth, utter darkness of moonless nights, frequent rain, and occasional fog—all contributed to the realistic nature of the exercises and increased the value of the training. The exercises also demonstrated the relatively high state of training of the officers and men and their readiness for whatever was to come their way.

A large "task force" of staff officers from GHQ came out from Washington to conduct the GHQ inspection of the First Division during one of the field exercises. This task force was led by Brig. Gen. Mark W. Clark, General McNair's deputy at GHQ. General Clark was one of two officers who had just recently been promoted from the rank of lieutenant colonel to brigadier general. Inspectors were assigned to practically every element of the division and followed them throughout the exercise.

There was a critique immediately following the exercise, held as soon as officers of the division, umpires, and members of the corps staff could be assembled. General Joyce arranged this early assembly so that members of the task force could attend without delaying their departure for Washington until the following day. In the critique, very little criticism of any kind was voiced by any of the inspectors from GHQ or the umpires. On the contrary, the staff officers of GHQ were loud in their praise of the realistic nature of the exercise and the manner in which it had been conducted. They were most complimentary concerning the conduct of the Forty-first Infantry Division and expressed gratification at the high state of the division's training.

General Joyce, the corps staff, and the officers of the division were all quite well pleased with themselves and congratulatory with each other over a job well done. Their satisfaction was short lived. For in the typical fashion of inspectors from time immemorial in the army, every member of the task force of inspectors had compiled a long list of critical comments on the elements of the division he had observed. When the task force returned to Washington, the comments were compiled in a thick document which criticized practically everyone connected with the exercise from General Joyce on down. All were considerably deflated but remembered that army inspections have ever been thus.

Considering the intense training activity at Fort Lewis during the year, social life was relatively normal. That is, it followed the usual army pattern of calls, receptions, teas, cocktail parties, and dinners. There were by no means sufficient quarters on the post to accommodate all the officers with families who were assigned to troops stationed at Fort Lewis at the time. In consequence, many officers lived off post. Many found accommodations in the communities surrounding American Lake, a very nice recreation and residential area that lay generally between the post and Puget Sound. Boating and fishing were important recreational pursuits for such time as the press of duties permitted during those days. Mount Rainier, the Olympic Peninsula, the Cascades, and British Columbia were inviting areas for weekend trips. Tacoma, with a population of perhaps twenty thousand, was favored by post personnel as a shopping center. Seattle had all of the advantages of a big city.

One always remembers Washington in the spring, when the salmon were running in the spawning grounds and fish of amazing size were thrusting into even small streamlets where there was hardly enough water to support them or for turning had that been their instinct. And one never forgets the great fields of yellow daffodils, to be followed by acres of tulips all in full bloom. With the overrunning of Holland by the Germans in 1940, bulb sources for American growers were greatly curtailed. Since this area was almost as ideally suited for the growing of bulbs as were the Low Countries, it was an enormously profitable commercial enterprise. Some of the growers were even then bemoaning the fact that they would be unable to grow daffodils and tulips on their fields because they were to be incorporated into the expanding military reservation. Even England, under the threat of invasion, sent orchids and other rare flowers to the Pacific Northwest for preservation. Timber and fishing were also important industries of the coastal regions, and ships of the world brought commerce of all nations to the ports of Puget Sound.

The Hunter Liggett Military Reservation was located about one hundred miles southeast of Monterey, California. It occupied the valley of the San Antonio River on the eastern side of the Santa Lucia Coastal Range almost due north of the main Hearst Ranch, San Simeon, on the Pacific side of the mountains. A lesser but extremely rugged mountain range bounded the area on the east, separating it from the Salinas River Valley.

The reservation was an ideal training ground for the final exercises of the corps' training program. There were no buildings of any kind in the semiarid area, but there were enough trees, grass, and other vegetation to make it an ideal refuge for wildlife, which it had been. Deer were plentiful, as were quail, doves, and other game. However, the game was soon driven to the higher ground when maneuvering troops disturbed their quiet refuge.

From the east, the area could be reached by only one mountain road of rather indifferent character, which was the main route of access into the southern part of the reservation. One or two roads followed deep valleys into the eastern range from the Salinas River side, but only trails crossed over the precipitous slopes into the valley where the reservation lay. In order to add realism to the proposed maneuver and to provide another access into the reservation, one of these trails was improved by the corps engineers to permit the passage of vehicles. The difficult nature of the terrain was emphasized by the fact that even with improvement by the engineers, artillery pieces had to be detached from the trucks that were towing them and lowered around one sharp, steep bend by hand. In the maneuver of division against division, the attacking division moved south from Fort Ord in daylight, with the vehicles moving individually at vastly increased distances between vehicles for protection against air observation and attack. They then crossed into the reservation by the two roads and assembled under cover of night to attack at daylight. A realistic and difficult problem.

After the maneuver of division against division, the training period terminated in the corps field exercise, with the corps, using live ammunition, attacking an enemy position represented by targets. There was the usual horde of visitors and observers from Washington, from Fourth Army headquarters, and from other commands to observe all of the exercises. This required the corps to provide a sizeable visitors camp to supplement the already overtaxed facilities of King City and other towns and communities in the Salinas Valley. It was a most successful training period and of enormous value to all of the officers and men who participated in it. Aside from the four months of intensive tactical training, the elements of the corps had experienced two strategic movements of several hundred miles.

The Ninth Army Corps suffered one very serious loss, however. Toward the end of the maneuver period at Hunter Liggett, General Joyce consented to the departure of Colonel Eisenhower to be chief of staff of the Third Army in San Antonio, under General Walter Krueger. The War

Department was planning the largest maneuvers ever held in our country in peace time. The maneuver area was to include most of the state of Louisiana as well as much of Arkansas. The maneuvers were to involve the Second and Third armies, the Second under General Ben Lear, with headquarters in Memphis, and the Third under General Krueger. It was a step up for Colonel Eisenhower and would lead to a promotion in the near future. However, General Joyce and all of the corps staff hated to see him leave.

Not long after the corps returned to Fort Lewis from Hunter Liggett, several of the corps staff officers were ordered to Camp Polk, Louisiana, to arrive "at such time as would enable them to report prior to 5:00 P.M. September 9, 1941 to the Director, Second vs Third Army Maneuvers for temporary duty in connection with the Second vs Third Army maneuvers" to be held during the period September 15–30, 1941. General McNair was the maneuver director, General Clark his deputy, and the director headquarters was staffed largely by officers from GHQ. Umpires were brought in from other army and corps headquarters. Umpiring these vast maneuvers proved to be a most valuable and interesting assignment for all of the officers called upon to perform this duty. The maneuvers themselves were of the utmost value to those who participated and were of value to the high command in sorting out some of the commanders who were engaged in it. The enormous value of the exercises would be demonstrated in little more than a year.

Those who went from Fort Lewis to the maneuvers had barely returned home when the command took to the field for more maneuvers, conducted by Fourth Army in the area of southwestern Washington and the Olympic Peninsula. They involved the corps from Fort Ord against the corps from Fort Lewis. The most memorable event occurred when the Fourth Army terminated the maneuver about noon on the tenth day and directed the troops to return to their stations. Both of the Ninth Corps divisions were entangled in the forest area of the southern part of the Olympic Peninsula, just west of the southern end of Puget Sound. The divisions from Fort Ord were in an area west of Olympia. The Fourth Army staff had not seen the necessity for planning the orderly return of the troops to their stations, nor had either of the corps staffs formulated such plans. The result was that the column of troops from Ord, endeavoring to move southward through Olympia, became entangled with the columns of troops endeavoring to move northward. There was actually only one road junction, and since they were all trying to use it and the limited road net around Olympia, there was a traffic jam of colossal proportions, which required many hours of untangling.

Officers who experienced the affair received an unforgettable lesson in the necessity for planning carefully the movements of large bodies of troops whenever road nets are limited.

The months from March to November were busy ones for the corps, but change was already in the air. And Pearl Harbor was but days in the future. Then our vast mobilization effort for war would truly begin and would test all that we had learned—and more.

9. FIDDLER'S GREEN

"Fiddler's Green" was inspired by a story told quite some time back by Captain "Sammy" Pearson at a campfire in the Medicine Bow Mountains of Wyoming.

> Having mentioned Fiddler's Green and found that no one appeared to have heard of it, Pearson indignantly asserted that every good cavalryman ought to know about Fiddler's Green and forthwith told the story.
>
> He said that about halfway down the trail to Hell, there was a broad meadow, dotted with trees and crossed by many streams (comparable, I suppose, to the Elysian Fields), and here all dead cavalrymen were camped, with their tents, horses, picket lines, and camp fires, around which latter the souls of the dead troopers gathered to exchange reminiscences and tell stories. There was also the old army canteen store (where liquor was sold), long since hounded from this mundane sphere by the zealous efforts of the WCTU.
>
> No other branches of the service might stop at Fiddler's Green, but must continue the march straight through to Hell. Though it was true that some troopers, feeling the call to eternal damnation, had packed their equipment, mounted and set out to continue their journey, none had ever reached the gates of Hell, but having finished up their liquor had returned to Fiddler's Green. "Fiddler's Green and other Cavalry Songs by J.H.S.," *Cavalry Journal*, April, 1923

Franklin Mountain, at the southern end of the San Andres Mountain Range, which lies chiefly in New Mexico, frowns down upon the city of El Paso, in the extreme western tip of the state of Texas, and upon Ciudad

Juarez, just across the Rio Grande in Mexico. The craggy mountain also dominates the United States Military Post of Fort Bliss, which overlooks El Paso from its location on the mesa along the northeastern edge of the city about five miles from the heart of the downtown business district. The military reservation in 1941 was only some six thousand acres in extent, but adjoining it were many thousands of acres of unfenced mesa where only cactus and the hillocks of drifting sand, caught in the clumps of greasewood, interfered with movement.

In November, 1941, the post of Fort Bliss was the home of the First Cavalry Division, and the entire division had been concentrated there for almost a year. The post had been the station of the division headquarters and all troops of the division except the First Cavalry Brigade since the reorganization of the army after the First World War. During that war, cavalry regiments along the border had been organized into the Ninth Cavalry Division, with headquarters at Fort Bliss. So, the post had long been a cavalry station, and it was well known to generations of American cavalrymen.

The *Cavalry Journal* of January, 1931, described the post in these terms:

> Let's picture the post:
>
> Winding out a modern highway from El Paso (its business section only five miles away) Fort Bliss looms up impressively on a rolling mesa. Approaching the south gate, the year-round splendidly turfed polo field is reflected in the sun.
>
> On through the gate one halts to decide which shadowed, tree-flanked road to follow—there are twelve miles of them. To the left and right runs Sheridan Road, its left course passing the long row of two storey sets of quarters of the Commanding General, his staff and ranking officers. Bordered with evergreen hedges, they rise out of a cluster of locust and mountain cottonwoods, while across the parade ground stretches gracefully an unbroken chain of Spanish type barracks.
>
> Setting off the parade ground is Howze stadium and the Olympic jumping ring, home of the El Paso–Fort Bliss Horseshow. With the horseshow over, it serves as a playground for children.
>
> Circling the parade ground, with its bandstand and flag pole in the center, one finds himself on Pershing Road. He passes the post theater—a modern talkie palace, advertising the latest from Hollywood. Thence down into the heart of the Seventh Cavalry area, the low

rambling bungalow officers' quarters facing Sheridan Road on the right and the cantonment buildings of the enlisted men to the left.

Back over Pershing Road, the modern brick bungalows for non-com's of the first three grades, past brigade and division headquarters, buildings forty-seven years old, and into the homeland of the 82d Field Artillery which resembles the Seventh Cavalry area.

Of the permanent officers' quarters there are forty: fifteen of the two-story type and twenty-five bungalows. There are fifty-one temporary sets of frame quarters.

For the hunter, Bliss is an ideal post. There is an abundance of duck, quail, and doves within a radius of twenty-five miles. Deer are found near Sierra Blanca, eighty miles to the east. The fishermen fish the Rio Grande, east of El Paso and at Elephant Butte Dam, west in New Mexico.

For the mounted sportsman El Paso is on an assured polo footing, and the First Cavalry Division's annual polo tournaments draw military and civilian teams from all the southwest. Also there's the El Paso–Fort Bliss Horse Show rapidly advancing and which is predicted soon will equal long established eastern shows. Those socially inclined find the officers' Club hops pleasant entertainment. There is an excellent mess at the club. Visiting officers are accommodated in modern quarters at the club's guest house. Adjoining the club is a swimming pool. Flyers landing at Bliss for the night go to Biggs Field where their ships are serviced.

The division maintains a vacation camp at Cloudcroft, New Mexico, in the Lincoln National Forest in the Sacramento Mountains 160 miles from Bliss. Nine thousand feet above sea level there are forty log cabins in the heart of a dense pine grove. Golf, tennis, and fishing provide diversion. Fort Bliss, high, mild, pleasant and healthful, is truly a great border post.

In November, 1941, ten years later, the face of the permanent post was little changed. Some officers' and noncommissioned officers' quarters had been added, and during the peacetime mobilization of 1940, a temporary cantonment-type brigade camp had been constructed, with troops housed in pyramidal tents on floored frames to permit the concentration of the entire division at Fort Bliss. South of the main parade, the edge of the mesa sweeps eastward, conforming to the valley of the Rio Grande, at right angles to the main parade of the post. It was along this part of the mesa that the brigade camp of the First Cavalry Brigade was located, with the stable area nearest the mesa's rim to the south. North of this brigade area was the huge drill field, where reviews of the entire cavalry division were often held. Between the drill field and the Second Cavalry Brigade's area in the main post was the area of ordnance, quartermaster, and service warehouses.

Following the reorganization and augmentation of 1940/41, the division consisted of division headquarters and headquarters troop, a weapons troop, a signal troop, an ordnance company (medium maintenance), the Eighth Engineer Squadron, the Ninety-first Reconnaissance Squadron, the First Quartermaster Squadron, the First Medical Squadron, the First and Second Cavalry Brigades, and the Eighty-second Field Artillery. The Reconnaissance Squadron had two scout-car troops, a motorcycle troop, and a combat car (light tank) troop. Each brigade had a headquarters troop, a weapons troop, a special-weapons troop, and two squadrons of three rifle troops each. The Fifth and Twelfth Cavalry regiments constituted the First Cavalry Brigade; the Seventh and Eighth, the Second Cavalry Brigade.

"Notes from the Chief of Cavalry" in the September–October, 1940, issue of the *Cavalry Journal* said:

> Armament for this new division is indicative of its combat power:

Light machine guns, caliber .30	299
Heavy machine guns, caliber .30	416
Caliber .50 machine guns	268
Caliber .45 Sub-machine Guns	649
37 mm. Antitank guns	36
81 mm. Mortars	28
60 mm. Mortars	28
Pistols	7020
Rifles	3160
Scout Cars	178
Mortar Carriers	12
Combat Cars	17
Motorcycles	420

> and a total of 187 motor trucks. It is believed that this new Cavalry Division represents the most formidable unit of its kind ever designed in any Army.

With more than seven thousand officers and men, nearly six thousand horses, and this formidable armament, the division was indeed a powerful combat unit, capable of operations in any kind of terrain.

The division was commanded by an eminent cavalryman of a distinguished army family, Maj. Gen. Innis P. Swift. This rugged soldier was a graduate of West Point, class of 1904, of the first- and second-year classes at the Mounted Service School in the years 1908 and 1909, the Advanced Course at the Cavalry School, 1922, the Command and General Staff School in 1923, the Army War College in 1930, and the Army Industrial College in 1931. An ardent horseman and a fine polo player, General Swift was held in the highest esteem by subordinates and superiors alike. Indefatigable in all that concerned the cavalry arm, he brought to every problem an unparalleled devotion to the branch and the division, but an even greater love and devotion to the army. Easily accessible to juniors of all ranks, he welcomed every idea and suggestion for improvement of cavalry organization and equipment and methods of tactical employment. A strict disciplinarian, his gruff "bark was usually worse than his bite," and he was always quick in the recognition of merit.

On a quiet Sunday morning in a border cavalry station, warm sunshine had dispelled the early morning chill. Officers, soldiers, and families pursued the activities normal for Sunday mornings in cavalry posts. Families were returning from Sunday School and church. Children were playing on the parade ground and among the lawns. Casual riders, on the "postman's holiday" usual in cavalry stations, were returning to the stables. The troop horses frisked about corrals, where they had been loosed after Sunday morning stables. In troop kitchens and those of private quarters, preparations for the midday meal were nearing completion. Off across the mesa, a flash of color, the sound of the huntsman's horn, the baying of hounds, and a trail of dust marked the course of the Sunday-morning drag hunt to its final check. On the parade ground a few soldiers rather idly tossed footballs back and forth. In day rooms of troop barracks, radios were blaring, and there were sounds of radios playing in quarters along the line of officers' quarters. Suddenly the music stopped. An excited announcer interrupts in a breathless voice charged with emotion: "The Japanese are attacking Pearl Harbor!"

No details. Only repetition. Unbelievable but true!

So it was that war came to Fort Bliss.

The first reaction to the dreadful news of Pearl Harbor was one of disbelief. Then shock. As the fragments of information sifted in to indicate something of the magnitude of the blow we had suffered, the feeling of shock gave way to one of bitter anger at the perfidy of a government that would launch such a dastardly blow under cover of serious diplomatic endeavors then in progress in Washington, seeking to resolve the differences. This feeling of anger persisted, curdled by our feeling of utter frustration and bitterness at our lack of preparation and our complete inability to strike back. It grew as the Japanese invasion of the Philippines got under way and progressed toward the inevitable conclusion on Bataan and Corregidor. This feeling was magnified many times over because there were so many of our cavalry comrades numbered among those fighting there to the death.

But there was positive action of a sort in the Cavalry Division. Border regions are always fruitful areas for the spread of rumors. Knowledge that many Japanese were resident on the western coast of Mexico, as well as the possibility of German agents in our sister republic, gave impetus to a flood of rumors. Then, too, there was a legitimate fear of sabotage along lines of transportation and communication. Transcontinental railways, highways, and communication lines passed through the "Pass of the North." Interruptions could interfere with and delay our industrial and military mobilization efforts. Almost immediately, detachments of troops were spread out along five hundred miles of border to guard bridges, tunnels, and other vital points against the possibility of sabotage and destruction.

It seemed to be little enough that we could do, but it provided some relief to the desperate desire for action in this hour of the nation's need. But as is ever the case when positive information is lacking, the flood of rumors continued. Someone might wonder if it could be possible that Japanese might be organizing in the mountains of Mexico. Soon such speculation became a rumor that such indeed was the case, and the rumors became more and more positive as they were passed along.

Training activities, already thorough, were intensified. There was the usual drill, mounted and dismounted, common in cavalry training. There was increased attention to tactical exercises for small units and to the training in leadership of officers responsible for such units. There were schools for all ranks. There were lectures, demonstrations, exhibitions. The division was making every effort to familiarize officers and men with every shred of information that came our way concerning the techniques and methods of war used by our enemies.

The War Department, Headquarters Army Ground Forces (which had replaced GHQ), and Third Army Headquarters were all intent that the American soldier should not only know "why he was fighting." He should also know as much as possible about the geography of possible theaters of operations, traditions, and habits; the nature of our enemies and their methods of combat; and of the objectives of our own country. To this end, a most comprehensive program of lectures and conferences was prescribed for presentation to all officers and men. The vast theater was the scene for the presentations. Here officers, especially selected from among those with experience as teachers and instructors, repeated carefully prepared lectures three times or more until every officer and man in the division had received every element of instruction. Such training by no means made men expert in areas or in enemy methods. But the training did make men aware of the immensity of the national problem and gave them some concept of the reasons why we were at war and the objectives the nation hoped to accomplish.

In addition to normal mounted training, American cavalry was always as thoroughly trained in the techniques of dismounted combat as were American infantrymen, for cavalry did most of its fighting dismounted. The two branches employed the same weapons and applied the same tactical principles and doctrines. Only one additional training feature was needed to permit cavalrymen to add full qualification as infantry to their qualifications as cavalrymen—*dismounted marching.*

This qualification General Walter Krueger, the army commander, and General Swift proceeded to attain, for they realized that an emergency might require the employment of this well-trained division, without its horses, as infantry. During the winter months of 1941/42, training in dismounted marching was directed and emphasized. Troops and squadrons made practice marches progressively of five, ten, and fifteen miles carrying full field equipment. The final test was a march, made by the entire regiment, of twenty miles, which all accomplished without difficulty and in which the minimum required rate of two and one-half miles an hour was exceeded by all elements. Every officer and man in the division, unless precluded by illness or accident, was required to qualify in these marches.

There were few complaints, although most men had selected the cavalry to avoid this "foot slogging." There were no more blisters and sore feet than any infantry command would experience. There was the usual good-natured griping among the troops, but the cavalrymen of the division entered into these tests in good spirit and with good will. When the tests were ended, the cavalrymen actually preened themselves a bit that they were now "foot cavalry" in the full and literal sense of the words.

The training was to stand them in good stead.

Almost immediately following the Axis declaration of war, War Department plans for mobilization of the army, which had been taking form, began to have their effect on the First Cavalry Division at Fort Bliss and in all regular army formations. New divisions could be organized only as camps for their reception were constructed and as cadres were formed to receive and train men assigned to such new units. The Cavalry Division was directed to constitute a cadre for the organization of the Ninety-first Infantry Division when the time came for the assembly of that organization. Each organization in the division was directed to constitute a cadre, which it would designate formally and list by name for dispatch when the time came for initiating the organization of the new division.

No old-line unit could be expected to place its very best men on such cadres, and oftentimes such units disliked to part with even their second best. Such calls for transfer from organizations had all too often provided an opportunity for first sergeants and even inexperienced company commanders to remove some of their less desirable personnel. They were naturally enough anxious to maintain the best in the unit in which they expected to serve and upon which their own records would depend. To overcome this natural reluctance, the Fifth Cavalry, for example, directed the submission of two cadres. One would be dispatched to form the new unit when the time came to dispatch it; the other would remain with the parent Fifth Cavalry. The cadre to be dispatched, however, was to be selected by the regimental commander by lot. It was an excellent method and proved to be a great morale builder.

After the initial shock of Pearl Harbor, life settled back to normal, modified only by the realization that we were at war, by the security measures that became necessary, by the intense training activity, and by the thirst for news from the war fronts which was felt by everyone. Family life continued its normal pattern. Children attended primary schools on the post and high schools in the city. School buses came and went. Deliverymen made their normal rounds. There were the usual weekly dinner dances or hops at the Officers' Club. There were the usual theaters and dances for enlisted personnel. There was even an increase in formal and official receptions, teas, and cocktail parties, for there was a vast increase in the flood of VIP's arriving at the post for inspections, conferences, or stopovers.

Officers, ladies, and children continued their riding for pleasure, as did many men. Everyone pursued and enjoyed his or her favorite sports. All polo fields were busy two or three times a week as usual, for polo in winter was one of the pleasures of the border climate. There was somewhat less hunting and fishing perhaps, but the officers and men who loved the sports found time for some. Football and basketball leagues continued as favorite sports among the troops and attracted the usual crowd of enthusiastic spectators. There were actually only two limiting factors on social life and activities. One, everyone knew we were at war; and two, the location of every officer and man had to be known at all times, a requirement that was somewhat restrictive in nature.

There was a great desire on the part of everyone to be of service. An evidence of this was the vast increase in registration for training in Red Cross courses, such as first aid, canteen management, nursing, and other services designed to support the war effort. Nearly every woman on the post registered and worked with one or more of this type of activity.

There was never a week without some parade, review, or inspection by regiment or brigade, but the truly thrilling spectacles were the mounted reviews and inspections of the entire division. These were held on occasions when General Krueger made an inspection and for other important dignitaries or visitors. General Swift was not at all backward in his desire to show off the division to these VIP's, for his pride in the Division and its state of training was boundless.

All parades and reviews of large units are impressive and thrilling sights, but the mounted review and inspection of the First Cavalry had a very special fascination; it was without doubt one of the most thrilling and inspiring of all large unit formations.

Picture the scene. The huge drill field on the mesa north of the area of the First Cavalry Brigade and east of the area of the Second Brigade. The hard-packed soil, calichelike in its consistency, cleared of all vegetation. Beyond the drill field, the mesa stretched for fifty miles, thinly covered with patches of greasewood and cactus. A beautiful clear winter morning, characteristic of the border area. The sun midway in the morning sky has burned off the morning chill but has not yet started the "dust devils"—the desert whirlwinds—scurrying across the landscape. Not a trace of a cloud in the whole, vast dome of the brilliant blue sky. A crystal-clear desert day.

The troops, with their red-and-white guidons fluttering, have come forth from their respective areas and are now assembled in line of masses, formed up, sabers drawn, in readiness for the ceremony, the center of the line opposite the reviewing stand, directly across the parade ground. The division band is facing the troops just to the left of the reviewing stand. The line of troops, with the two brigades from right to left, in order of the rank of their respective commanders, for this was traditional in the army. Then the massed Artillery Regiment, the Reconnaissance Squadron, other combat elements, and the division trains. Well to the front and centered on this mass formation between the troops and the reviewing stand, a small group stands—the commander of troops and his staff. Immediately in the rear a dozen yards, the line of the regimental commanders, with their small staffs and the standards of their units, the national and regimental standards showing flashes of color in the bright sunlight.

Then, along the line of massed horsemen and troops, the line of squadron commanders, and behind them, the line of troop commanders. Last-minute adjustments have been made; final words of caution have been passed back through the columns. There is a hum of voices as troopers are patiently waiting; bits and curb chains rattle; occasional sounds of caution or command. There is a tossing of horses' heads, the occasional testing of a bugle note. All is in readiness.

A caravan of automobiles, with general-officers' flags fluttering from the bumpers, escorted by military police mounted on motorcycles, approaches from the direction of the post and draws up just in rear of the reviewing stand. After a few moments the reviewing party has arranged itself in position on the reviewing stand, the guest of honor on the right, the division commander on his left. To their rear, in order of rank from right to left, stand the members of their respective staffs.

There is a stir as the commander of troops faces the massed troops and his bugler sounds "Attention!" followed by a single blast, which is the signal for execution for presenting the command. Four thousand sabers flash in the sunlight and point skyward in front of troopers' faces, standards, guidons; and all officers salute in unison. The commander of troops faces about and, with his staff, salutes. The drummers sound the "Ruffles" while the buglers sound the "Flourishes." The band sounds "General's March." Then the commander of troops faces about, and on command, the troops "Carry Saber."

The guest of honor indicates that he will inspect the command. Mounted on horseback, or in an open vehicle if not a horseman, accompanied by the division commander, he moves to the right of the line, passes along the front rank, circles the rear, and returns to his position. All the while the band plays.

Then the command "Pass in Review!" The commander of troops takes position in advance of the column of masses and passes in front of the reviewing stand, saluting as he passes. Then the march past, with sunlight gleaming on polished sabers, red-and-white guidons fluttering as they dip in salute, standards rustling as the bugles sound "Flourishes," the columns pass, wheel to the left, and wheel again, and sweep past the reviewing stand at the trot as the band plays. Around once more, this time at the gallop amid swirling clouds of dust. And as troops and trains pass the last time, they move off toward their respective areas. The mounted review of the Cavalry Division was indeed an inspiring spectacle.

So passed the early months of the war in Fort Bliss, the early months of 1942. There was a great lift in spirit among soldiers and civilians alike along the border when the news of the Doolittle Raid on the main islands of Japan flashed across the country. There was enormous pride that the nation had been able to strike back, and a great hope that this raid was just the beginning of a steadily increasing drive. That was not to be at the moment, and the feeling of pride soon turned to one of frustration that our efforts should be so feeble. Attention on the post was centered on the war in the Pacific, where so many comrades were engaged in the Philippines. We should have liked to have been more active.

But more change was in the air. Over the months there had been speculation among cavalrymen as to who would follow General Herr as chief of cavalry when his four-year term expired in March. There were rumors that the General Staff intended to do away with the cavalry; however, the garrison was busy enough with training activities that such rumors received scant attention among the rank and file. But change was in the air, and the organization of the army was still undergoing transformation.

General Headquarters had already become Headquarters Army Ground Forces to control the mobilization, equipment, and training of the ground forces of the mobilizing army. Headquarters Army Air Forces was established to perform the same functions for the air elements of our expanding forces. The Service of Supply was created to coordinate industrial mobilization and to produce supplies. The names of the respective commanding generals of these organizations were to become household words among Americans: General Lesley J. McNair, Army Ground Forces; General Henry H. ("Hap") Arnold, Army Air Forces; and General Brehon B. Somervell, Services of Supply. What a debt the nation was to owe these immediate subordinates of Gen. George C. Marshall, the chief of staff.

Army Ground Forces, under this reorganization, assumed responsibility for all matters pertaining to the combat arms—the infantry, the cavalry, the field artillery, and the coast artillery. The method that was adopted was to appoint no successors to the incumbent chiefs of branch when they retired and to absorb the officers and personnel in various special staff sections of headquarters Army Ground Force. Only the service branches retained chiefs who were general officers.

So it was that Maj. Gen. John K. Herr was to become the last chief of cavalry. There was great sadness in this ending of the career of a noble soldier and gallant cavalryman. After the war, he, with Edward S. Wallace, wrote *The Story of the U.S. Cavalry*, published by Little, Brown in 1953. That he was to see the worst of his fears for the horse cavalry fulfilled was to embitter his final years. To the end of his days he fought to reestablish the branch. It was General Herr's misfortune that he would not recognize that the missions of mechanized and armored elements were cavalry missions and that the office of the chief of cavalry should have been in the forefront of the organization and development of such units. His opposition to any change that would be made at the expense of horse cavalry and his advocacy of the doctrine that "cavalry should be employed in large units" was to bring him into conflict with the War Department General Staff. This conflict was long and bitter, and it was one to which there could be only one end.

There was some complaint among the rank and file of cavalrymen when it became apparent that no successor to the chief of cavalry was to be appointed, and there was some among the other branches as well. In the vicinity of Fort Bliss there was some criticism among civilians and especially among those who were interested in National Guard and Reserve activities of the cavalry branch. There was talk of political influence in opposition to this departure from the organization prescribed in the National Defense Act of 1920.

General Swift replied to such critics in an interview with the correspondents recorded in the *El Paso Herald Post* on Army Day, April 6, 1942:

> The recent reorganization of the Army leaves us for the present intact, as you can see by reading your own newspaper. The reorganization, in effect, simply placed all combatant branches under GHQ and called it by a different name. It is unquestionably a great forward step, in the general conduct of Army affairs, and will eliminate the branch consciousness which often in the past has had an adverse effect. The new organization does not contemplate any changes in the Cavalry as yet.

General Swift may have been a bit optimistic with regard to the elimination of branch consciousness, and he doubtless did foresee "changes in the Cavalry" for the future. But his statement is clearly indicative of the cavalry spirit of the day. The spirit is also indicated by two messages that he directed an officer who was reporting to Washington to relay to General McNair and others in authority. "We need more of those Doolittle raids," and "Tell General McNair that this division is undoubtedly the best trained division in the Army. If they need an outfit ready to fight, we are ready, even without our horses."

General Swift and the division were to wait almost a year for that call to come. The division's history, *The First Cavalry Division in World War II*, records it thus:

> In February 1943 came the welcome orders which alerted the division for overseas assignment as a dismounted unit. Immediately, horses and equipment were turned in; the 8th Engineer Squadron came back from the Desert Training Center to replace the recently activated 61st Engineer Squadron; and the 99th Field Artillery, a 75 mm. pack battalion was assigned to supplement artillery support. Transition to a dismounted status was completed well in advance of the scheduled movement date. The last elements of the division cleared Fort Bliss on 18 June 1943, staged through Camp Stoneman, California, departing from the United States on 3 July and closing at Strathpine in Queensland Australia, on 26 July 1943.
>
> To the men of the 1st Cavalry Division it had seemed to be a long hard battle just to get the privilege of fighting the enemy, but their opportunity came on the last day of February, 1944, and they were ready to make the most of it.

And make the most of they did. From the Admiralty Islands, through Leyte and Samar, on to Luzon and Manila, and to the occupation of Japan, this dismounted First Cavalry Division wrote a brilliant page in the annals of American military history—such a brilliant and glorious page that in the postwar reorganization of the division, although dismounted, it retained the designation First Cavalry Division. In the words of General of the Army MacArthur: "No greater record had emerged from the war than that of the First Cavalry Division—swift and sure in attack, tenacious and durable in defense, and loyal and cheerful under hardship. It has written its own noble history. My personal connection with it in many moments of crisis has especially endeared it to me."

No unit of American Horse Cavalry was to see service during the Second World War, although one provisional troop was improvised by the Third Infantry Division from captured horses and equipment in Sicily and saw service in Sicily and southern Italy. And the postwar reorganization of the army was to eliminate horses entirely from the United States Army.

So it is that the proud tradition of the cavalry lives on in this grand dismounted First Cavalry Division, in the regiments of armored cavalry that carry the standards of old cavalry regiments, and in the hearts of the men who were cavalrymen—whose horses await them in:

Fiddler's Green

Half way down the trail to Hell,
In a shady, meadow green,
Are the souls of all dead troopers camped,
Near a good, old-time canteen,
And this eternal resting place,

Marching past, straight through to Hell,
The Infantry are seen,
Accompanied by the Engineers,
Artillery and Marines,
For none but shades of Cavalrymen
Dismount at Fiddler's Green.

Though some go curving down the trail
To seek a warmer scene,
No trooper ever gets to Hell,
Ere he's emptied his canteen,
And so he rides back to drink again
With friends at Fiddler's Green.

And so when horse and man go down
Beneath a saber keen,
Or in a roaring charge or fierce melee'
You stop a bullet clean,
And the hostiles come to get your scalp,
Just empty your canteen,
And put your pistol to your head,
And go to Fiddler's Green.

—*J.H.S., Cavalry Journal, April, 1925*

INDEX